SEAL
OF HONOR

SEAL

OPERATION RED WINGS AND THE LIFE OF LT. MICHAEL P. MURPHY, USN

OF HONOR

GARY WILLIAMS

NAVAL INSTITUTE PRESS
Annapolis, Maryland

This book was brought to publication with the generous assistance
of Marguerite and Gerry Lenfest.

Naval Institute Press
291 Wood Road
Annapolis, MD 21402

First Naval Institute Press paperback edition published in 2011.
ISBN: 978-1-59114-965-1 (paperback)
ISBN: 978-1-61251-006-4 (eBook)

The Library of Congress has catalogued the hardcover edition as follows:
Williams, Gary.
  SEAL of honor : Operation Red Wings and the life of Lt. Michael P.
Murphy, USN / Gary Williams.
      p. cm.
  Includes bibliographical references and index.
  ISBN 978-1-59114-957-6 (alk. paper)
  1. Murphy, Michael Patrick, 1976-2005. 2. Murphy, Michael Patrick,
1976-2005—Military leadership. 3. Operation Red Wings, 2005. 4. United
States. Navy. SEALs—Officers—Biography. 5. Medal of Honor—Biography.
6. Heroes—United States—Biography. 7. Courage—Afghanistan—
Case studies. 8. Afghan War, 2001—Biography. 9. Afghan War,
2001—Casualties—United States. I. Title.
  DS371.4123.O66W55 2010
  958.104'7—dc22
  [B]
                        2010009801
⊚ Print editions meet the requirements of ANSI/NISO z39.48-1992
(Permanence of Paper).
Printed in the United States of America.

23 22 21 20 19 18 17 16 15 14   18 17 16 15 14 13 12 11

To my father, Richard A. Williams, a decorated Korean War veteran
who instilled in his children a near-reverent respect
for those who wear our nation's uniforms.
And to all those who went to war to defend our nation's freedom,
but never returned.

CONTENTS

ACRONYMS AND ABBREVIATIONS

ACLS	Advance cardiac life support
ACM	Anticoalition militia
AF	Assault force
AFB	Air Force Base
AOIC	Assistant officer in charge
AOR	Assistant operations officer
ASDS	Advance SEAL Delivery System
BATS	Bleeding, airway, tension pneumothorax, and shock
BUD/S	Basic Underwater Demolition/SEAL
CACO	Casualty Assistance Calls Officer
Candi-O	Candidate officer
CAO	Civil affairs operation
CENTCOM	Central Command
CERTEX	Certification training exercise
CFC-A	Combined Forces Coalition–Afghanistan
CIA	Central Intelligence Agency
CJSOTF-A	Combined Joint Special Operations Task Force–Afghanistan
CJTF	Combined Joint Task Force
CJTF-HOA	Combined Joint Task Force–Horn of Africa
CNO	Chief of naval operations
CP	Counterproliferation
CPO	Chief petty officer
CQD	Close Quarters Defense
CSAR	Combat search and rescue
CSC	Combat Swimmer Course
CSST	Combat Service Support Team
CT	Counterterrorism
CTF	Coalition Task Force
CTT	Combat Training Tank
DA	Direct action

DEVGRU	Naval Special Warfare Development Group
DI	Drill instructor
DMV	Department of Motor Vehicles
DOR	Drop on request
DUSTWUN	Duty Station Whereabouts Unknown
DZ	Drop zone
EOD	Explosive ordnance disposal
FDNY	New York City Fire Department
FID	Foreign internal defense
FLIR	Forward-looking infrared
FOB	Forward operating base
FRIES	Fast rope insertion/extraction system
FTX	Field training exercise
GPA	Grade point average
GWOT	Global War on Terror
HAHO	High-altitude, high-opening
HALO	High-altitude, low-opening
HLZ	Helicopter landing zone
HQ	Headquarters
IAD	Immediate-action drill
IBS	Inflatable boat, small
Indoc	Indoctrination Course
IO	Information operation
IRS	Internal Revenue Service
J-bad	Jalalabad, Afghanistan
JCET	Joint/Combined Exchange Training
JOTC	Junior Officer Training Course
LAR	Lung-activated rebreather
LDA	Lateral drift apparatus
LPO	Leading petty officer
LUP	Layup position
LZ	Landing zone
MAS	Military assault suit
MSC	Mission Support Center
MOPH	Military Order of the Purple Heart
MTT	Military training test
NAS	Naval air station
NATO	North Atlantic Treaty Organization
NATTC	Naval Air Technical Training Center

NAVCENT	Naval Forces Central Command
NAVSPECWARCOM	Naval Special Warfare Command
NOMI	Naval Operational Military Institute
NR	Naval Reserve
NROTC	Naval Reserve Officers Training Course
NSA	Naval Support Activity
NSC	National Security Council
NSW	Naval Special Warfare
NSWDG	Naval Special Warfare Development Group
NSWF	Naval Special Warfare Foundation
NSWG	Naval Special Warfare Group
NYU	New York University
O-course	Obstacle course
OCS	Officer Candidate School
OIC	Officer in charge
PACOM	Pacific Command
PC	Patrol Coastal
PCU	Protective combat unit
PEPSE	Personal environmental protection and survival equipment
PFA	Physical Fitness Assessment
PI	Personnel inspection
PJs	Pararescue jumpers
POW	Prisoner of war
PRK	Photorefractive keratectomy
PRODEV	Professional development
PRT	Physical Readiness Test
PSD	Personnel Support Detachment
PST	Pacific standard time; Physical Screening Test
PSU	Penn State University
PSYOPS	Psychological operations
PT	Physical training
QRF	Quick-reaction force
RDAC	Recruiting District Assistance Council
RIS	Rail interface system
RLI	Room and locker inspection
ROEs	Rules of engagement
RPG	Rocket-propelled grenade
RSO	Range safety officer

RTC	Recruit Training Command
SATCOM	Satellite communications
SBR	Special Boat Squadron
SBU	Special Boat Unit
SDV	SEAL Delivery Vehicle
SDVT	SEAL Delivery Vehicle Team
SEAL	Sea, air, land
SERE	Survival, evasion, resistance, escape
SETAF	Southern European Task Force
SF	Special Forces (Green Berets)
SFO(D)	Special Forces Operational Detachment-Delta
SIT	Squadron Integration Training
SLT	Swing landing trainer
SOAR	Special Operations Aviation Regiment
SOC	Special operations commander
SOCOM	*See* USSOCOM
SOF	Special operations forces
SOMPE-M	Special Operations Mission Planning Environment-Maritime
SOP	Standard operating procedure
SPIE	Special Purpose Insertion/Extraction
SPOTC	Senior Petty Officer Training Course
SQT	SEAL Qualification Training
SR	Special reconnaissance
SWCC	Special Warfare Combatant-craft Crewmen
TCCC	Tactical combat casualty care
TIC	Troops in contact (*or* combat)
UAE	United Arab Emirates
UBA	Underwater breathing apparatus
UDT	Underwater Demolition Team
ULT	Unit Level Training
UN	United Nations
USMMA	United States Merchant Marine Academy
USN	United States Navy
USO	United Service Organizations
USSOCOM	United States Special Operations Command
UW	Unconventional warfare
WMD	Weapons of mass destruction

FOREWORD

Of the four Navy SEALs who inserted into the Hindu Kush Mountains, Kunar Province, Afghanistan, on that terrible day in June 2005, I personally knew three: Matt Axelson, Marcus Luttrell, and Danny Dietz. The one SEAL I did not know was Michael Murphy. Now, thanks to Gary Williams' fine portrayal of Michael Murphy in *SEAL of Honor*, I know them all.

While I did not previously know Michael, my sense is that Gary's assessment of this SEAL leader rings true. He seems very much like Tom Norris and Bob Kerrey, SEAL officers I do know well and who share that singular distinction as Medal of Honor recipients. Both Norris and Kerrey are humble, understated, introspective, and physically average. Both struggled in SEAL training, and once in the SEAL teams, took their duties seriously. Both came from families and communities who raised these future heroes with a strong sense of personal accountability and responsibility. And Tom Norris and Bob Kerry are both humble in light of their battlefield accomplishments, almost to the point of embarrassment, and invariably seek to deflect praise from themselves to others who served with them. Had he lived, I think Michael Murphy would have been much the same.

Michael Murphy also shares that quality of selfless devotion to his duty and to his brother SEALs as did two other "Mikes" who were awarded the Medal of Honor. Mike Thornton and Mike Monsoor both risked all in deadly combat to go to the aid of their teammates. In the case of Mike Monsoor, he too gave his life so that others would have a chance to live.

In the words of William Holden in the closing scenes in of the movie *The Bridges of Toko-Ri*, "Where do we find such men?" The great American poet Carl Sandburg once said, "Valor is a gift. Those having it never know for sure whether they have it till the test comes. And those having it in one test never know for sure if they will have it when the next test comes."

Major Dick Winters, of *Band of Brothers* fame, when asked by his granddaughter if he was a hero, answered, "No, but I served in the company of heroes." I also feel that I have known some heroes from my generation who fought in Vietnam to the current generation of special warriors in the field today. They come from a variety of educational backgrounds and physical gifts; there is no prototype and no common trait save that of character. Like Robert Holden's character in *Bridges*, I've often wondered where, indeed, do we find such men. SEAL training, so ably documented in this work, may refine the character of a hero. However, they don't train men to be heroes, nor does SEAL training select men who are predisposed to heroic acts. It is my belief that those who perform such acts of valor are so inclined long before they enter military service or put on a uniform. With respect to Carl Sandberg, I believe this gift of valor is somehow imparted to our most gallant warriors by their families and their role models, and by the extended communities that help to raise them. Our military, and especially the Navy SEAL teams, have simply been blessed with young men who have been reared in an environment that stresses the Navy's core values of Honor, Courage, and Commitment.

A combat leader lives, and sometimes dies, by his ability to balance two often mutually exclusive duties: he must accomplish his mission *and* he must take care of his men. A great deal has been written about Operation Red Wings, and exactly what took place in those mountains on that fateful day we may never know. But we do know this: Mike Murphy did all in his power to accomplish his mission. When that became impossible, he did all in his power to take care of his men. In the face of impossible odds and mortally wounded, he fought and led until the moment he was killed. For those of us who have since learned of Michael Murphy's courage in those last terrible hours, we marvel at such gallantry. For the Murphy family and the small community of Patchogue, New York, their unimaginable grief aside, he was simply one of their own, doing his duty in a manner that was consistent with how he was raised.

—DICK COUCH
SEAL (BUD/S) Class 45
UDT 22/SEAL Team One

ACKNOWLEDGMENTS

A project of this magnitude cannot be accomplished by a single individual; while my name may appear on the cover, there are literally hundreds of individuals who made this effort possible. While many are named below, there are those critical individuals who provided firsthand accounts of much of the operational details whose names cannot be revealed due to the secretive or classified nature of their work. They know who they are. Anytime you begin to thank people, you run the risk of unintentionally omitting someone; therefore, I ask for their forgiveness.

First and foremost, I would like to thank my parents, Richard and Charlene Williams, who instilled the virtues of hard work, patience, and persistence, as well as a near-sacred respect for our military personnel and veterans. To my wife, Tracy, and my children, Aaron, Lisa, Bryan, David, Daniel, and Stephen, and grandchildren, Chantress and Caden, thank you for allowing me time and freedom to both research and write this story and, most important, for keeping me grounded. Your sacrifices are no less important or appreciated. I hope my efforts make you as proud of me as I am of each of you. A special thank you to my stepson Stephen, our resident computer expert, for easing my frequent frustrations with a few keystrokes or a click of the mouse.

The following individuals contributed in varying degrees to the success of this book. Whatever level of detail about and insight into the man Michael Murphy was that I may have brought to these pages would not have been possible without their contributions and support. They are the true authors.

Family of Lieutenant Michael Murphy: Father Dan, mother Maureen and brother John . . . it is very evident why and how Michael became the man he was. Thank you for your service, sacrifice, and willingness to share the most painful of life's events with me and the world.

Operation Red Wings: The families of Petty Officer Matthew Axelson, Petty Officer Danny Dietz, Petty Officer Marcus Luttrell, Senior Chief Dan Healy, Lieutenant Commander Erik Kristensen, Petty Officer James Suh, Petty Officer Shane Patton, Petty Officer Jeffrey Taylor, Petty Officer Jeffrey Lucas, Major Stephen

Reich, Lieutenant Michael McGreevy, Chief Warrant Officer 4 Chris Scherkenbach, Chief Warrant Officer 4 Cory Goodnature, Master Sergeant James W. "Tre" Ponder, Sergeant First Class Marcus Muralles, Staff Sergeant Shamus Goare, and Sergeant Kip Jacoby.

United States Navy: Vice Admiral Eric Olson, Rear Admiral Joseph D. Kernan, Rear Admiral Edward Kristensen (ret.) and Mrs. Suzanne Kristensen, Lieutenant Jeff Widenhofer, Lieutenant Commander Tamsen Reese, and Lieutenant Leslie Lykins.

Naval Special Warfare: Rear Admiral Edward Winters III, Rear Admiral Garry J. Bonelli, Captain Larry Lasky (ret.), Commander Gregory Geisen, Commander Todd DeGhetto, Commander Chad Muse, Lieutenant Commander Michael Martin (ret.), Lieutenant Andy Haffele (ret.), Lieutenant Nathan Potter, Ensign Chris Reed, and former Gunner's Mate First Class Luke Barker. To all those individuals who must remain anonymous as they continue to defend freedom around the world, thank you, gentlemen, and Godspeed.

United States Army, 160th Special Operations Aviation Regiment: Kimberly Tiscone, Major Myron Bradley, Chief Warrant Officer 4 Chad Easter, and those heroic individuals who must remain anonymous as they continue to defend freedom around the world. Again, thank you, and Godspeed.

Michael Murphy's closest friends: The O'Callaghan family—Owen, Jimmie, Kerri, and Sean—Jimmy Emmerich, and Jay Keenan. Everyone should have the honor of friends like you.

Other individuals were invaluable in this effort. They include Captain Andrew "Drew" Bisset (ret.), who was the first to sign on in this effort back on May 7, 2008, and served as an excellent mentor and technical expert working tirelessly to bring me up to speed on the Navy and the SEALs in very short order. I want to extend a very special thank you to Captain Kent Paro. His tireless efforts in reviewing this manuscript and his near-photographic recall of details contributed immensely to the clarity of this work. Most appreciated was his demonstrated patience of Job when it came to working with me, a nonmilitary individual who possessed only the utmost respect for those in uniform and the deep desire to learn. Thank you seems so inadequate.

Roger Froehlich, a staunch advocate for those who wear this nation's uniforms, was and remains willing to do anything to advance this project; his belief, encouragement, and facility in putting me in contact with the right people at the right time saved time and frustration. At a time when he is increasingly consumed with family concerns, he remains a source of encouragement and strength.

I would also like to thank former secretary of the navy Donald C. Winter, Vice Admiral Joseph Maguire, and Admiral Gary Roughead, Chief of Naval Operations, whose staff provided support and encouragement that was extremely helpful in keeping this entire project within the Navy family, as well as Rick Russell and the staff at the Naval Institute Press, who demonstrated great patience while ushering an unknown author through the sometimes intimidating waters of the publishing world. Finally, a special thank you to legendary Hollywood actor Jon Voight for his tireless advocacy of and undying respect for our nation's veterans and his words of encouragement and support.

INTRODUCTION

Why would a highly successful graduate from a prestigious university, having been accepted into law school, forgo a lucrative law career? What causes a twenty-two-year-old college graduate to work as a lifeguard and plumber's assistant while waiting on an opportunity that may never materialize? How does one decide to ignore the advice of loving parents and set a course so demanding that less than 1 percent succeed? Who volunteers to put oneself through months of physical and mental pain and abuse for a position that only a few achieve? What is the source of the internal strength and moral courage that says, "I would rather die than quit"? Why would one deliberately step into a hail of gunfire?

Although I never had the opportunity to meet Michael Patrick Murphy, it has been the privilege of a lifetime during the past months to get to know him through his parents, family, relatives, friends, teammates, and acquaintances, whose lives were made better for having known the young man known as "Murph" or "Mikey."

When this project started in March 2008, I believed then, and even more so today, that it is a compelling story of an all-American boy from a small town on New York's Long Island who rose from obscurity to become one of this nation's most revered heroes, whose actions are now memorialized for all time in our nation's Hall of Heroes. The world came to know twenty-nine-year-old Navy SEAL lieutenant Michael P. Murphy for his legendary actions in the Hindu Kush mountains of Afghanistan on June 28, 2005, which resulted in his receiving posthumously the Medal of Honor from President George W. Bush on October 22, 2007.

However, there is much more to his story. On those two dates, the world became aware of what family and friends had known for twenty-nine years: that Michael Patrick Murphy was an ordinary man with an extraordinary sense of duty, responsibility, and moral clarity. Such moral clarity and sense of duty had its roots in a God-fearing set of parents who sowed within him the seeds of greatness that granted him the wisdom and strength to answer a call that few will ever receive.

It was this call to service that drove him to study and work and prepare himself for that moment in time when character met circumstance in the eternal struggle of good versus evil in the world's most forbidding terrain. While some may say that Michael chose to walk a path that he could have avoided, I suggest that he could no more have avoided his chosen path than deny the source of his moral clarity and courage. History is replete with those rare individuals who when called upon to make the ultimate sacrifice do so willingly.

Inscribed in a Wheaton College classroom are the words "He is no fool who gives up what he cannot keep to gain what he cannot lose." Despite our modern culture's obsession with winning and the rhetoric of subversion, was Michael Murphy's young life wasted, or did he know and understand something that we haven't yet figured out? Herein lies the real story. It is my sincere hope that my efforts have done justice to a calling faithfully answered, a duty justly upheld, and a life, while all too short, very well lived. Michael Patrick Murphy clearly had it figured out. He voluntarily gave up an earthly life he could not keep in exchange for an eternal life he cannot lose—demonstrating the wisdom many never achieve.

CHAPTER ONE

The Knock on the Door

You can almost see the blood run out of their body and their heart hit the floor. It's not the blood as much as their soul. Something sinks. I've never seen that except when someone dies. And I've seen a lot of death.

—MAJOR STEVE BECK, Casualty Assistance Calls Officer (CACO), United States Marine Corps, quoted in Jim Sheeler, *Final Salute*

Tuesday, June 28, 2005, Kunar Province, Afghanistan

Phase one of Operation Red Wings was only hours old as midday approached. (Note: the operation has been referred to by others as Red Wing or Redwing, but the official military name is Red Wings.) High in the rugged Hindu Kush region in the Kunar province of Afghanistan, the twenty-nine-year-old team leader, Lieutenant Michael Murphy, USN, and three other members of SEAL Team Ten spent the morning taking turns maintaining a vigilant watch on the village complex situated just west of Asadabad, in the Korangal Valley—a hotbed of Taliban and al-Qaeda activity. It was also the known hideout of Mullah Ahmad Shah, a Taliban fighter who aspired for greater recognition and leader of a group of insurgents known as the Mountain Tigers. Under his direction, they were responsible for inflicting numerous casualties on American forces operating in the area. The latest intelligence reports confirmed that as many as two hundred militants were in the valley ready to fight under the direction of Shah. Murphy and his teammates, Petty Officer Second Class Matthew Axelson, Petty Officer Second Class Danny Dietz, and Petty Officer Second Class Marcus Luttrell, had clear orders: observe the settlement in an effort to confirm the location of Shah, then call in a surgical strike to eliminate him. Things, however, began to go wrong very quickly. Around noon, three goat herders stumbled upon the team's concealed location. They were quickly captured, but their presence resulted in a dilemma for Murphy and the others, whose options were limited. They could kill the goat herders and compromise the mission, or they could let them go and hope they did not give away their location. They chose to let them go, abandoned their original positions, and continued their mission.

An hour later, the crackle of AK-47s and the roar of rocket-propelled grenades (RPGs) erupted on the mountainside. The men of SEAL Team Ten were under attack.

Tuesday, June 28, 2005, Patchogue, New York

Half a world away, Michael's mother, Maureen Murphy, was asleep in her Long Island home when the battle was joined. She awoke on the morning of June 28 feeling ill, placed a call to the local title company where she worked as an account clerk, and took a sick day. Although she did not usually watch much television, she found it a welcome distraction from the heavy traffic noise outside on a hot and humid June day. By the afternoon, the first reports that American servicemen had come under intense, heavy fire on a remote mountain in Afghanistan began to trickle out through the media. Few specifics were known, but it was widely reported that a helicopter had been shot down during an effort to rescue beleaguered soldiers on the ground. Although the story grabbed Maureen's attention, she kept saying to herself, "Nah. Couldn't be," when she considered the possibility of her son being involved. It was understandable, since she did not know Michael was in Afghanistan. She was not alone. No one without an operational need to know knew where he was.

For Dan Murphy, Michael's father, it was just another day. After a mentally stressful workday, the fifty-eight-year-old decorated and partially disabled Vietnam veteran, attorney, and former Suffolk County prosecutor was looking forward to an evening with his fiancée, Karen, her daughter, Kristen, and John Murphy, Michael's eighteen-year-old brother. As they made their way to the Lunt-Fontanne Theatre on Broadway for the evening performance of *Beauty and the Beast*, he was not worried about the news that broke that day. Michael, he believed, was in Iraq.

Wednesday, June 29, 2005, Long Island, New York

After a day of rest, Maureen returned to work. Almost from the moment she arrived at the office around 8:00 AM, coworkers began to ask anxiously if she was aware of the news reports about American soldiers who had come under heavy fire in Afghanistan. Like them, however, she only knew what she had heard in the news the day before. Throughout the day, though, more and more details continued to emerge. News outlets confirmed that an unknown number of Navy SEALs had been killed and that a rescue helicopter attempting to reach them had been shot down, killing all sixteen on board. Maureen later admitted that with each passing report her concern for Michael grew, and around the office everyone focused on the news with each updated broadcast. As well-meaning and concerned friends and coworkers continued to bring her attention to the unfolding events in Afghanistan, she tried to stay focused on her duties, but increased calls and reports on the local and national news channels made her efforts nearly impossible.

Early that same afternoon, Dan was reviewing cases in his office, where he was the chief legal assistant to State Supreme Court justice Peter Fox Cohalan. Immersed in work and away from a television, he was unaware of the new details of the fight that began to emerge. Still, his thoughts repeatedly drifted to his oldest son, Michael. He adamantly believed that he was in Iraq, based on a picture he had received from Michael on Father's Day via e-mail. Michael and his team were wearing light-colored desert fatigues, each holding their weapons. Michael was wearing his characteristic Oakley sunglasses and his large digital chrome and black watch. "It must be Iraq," he told himself.

John was also unaware of the new details in this unfolding story. He spent the afternoon with Karen and her daughter, Kristen, at the Holtsville town pool. As he sat in the sun and looked around, he recalled seeing the lifeguards at their stations while a feeling of dread came over him as he thought about his older brother Michael and his safety. The feeling was intense for several minutes, and though it gradually subsided, it never completely went away. Having never experienced such a feeling, he remained uneasy for the rest of the day.

Like Maureen, Heather Duggan, Michael's fiancée, grew more and more concerned with each passing minute that afternoon and was glued to the news. When she heard the reports about an accident involving Navy SEALs in the mountains of Afghanistan, she called Naval Special Warfare Command (NAVSPECWARCOM) in Coronado, California. Michael had given her the number to call in case anything ever happened to him. After several calls and repeated requests, she was provided with no information because she was not listed as a next of kin or spouse. Frustrated and angry, Heather hung up. Had she been a member of the immediate family when she called, her worst fears may have been confirmed.

While Heather called seeking information regarding Michael, the Navy was already sorting through the outcome of the engagement and making preparation to contact family members of the fallen and missing SEALs. Around midafternoon and deep in thought while walking in downtown Manhattan, Lieutenant Jeff Widenhofer's cell phone rang. It was the Navy's Northeast Regional Casualty Assistance Calls Office at the Groton Naval Submarine Base in Groton, Connecticut, calling to inform him that he had been assigned a "casualty call." Widenhofer was informed that Lieutenant Michael P. Murphy and the members of SEAL Team Ten were missing after they had been ambushed while conducting a reconnaissance mission in the mountains of Afghanistan. On top of that, a rescue helicopter containing eight Army Night Stalkers and eight Navy SEALs had been shot down, and all aboard were presumed to have been killed.

Widenhofer, a U.S. Naval Academy graduate and a veteran of three Middle East deployments, had been assigned to the Office of Naval Science at the United States Merchant Marine Academy (USMMA) in Kings Point on the North Shore of Long Island in June 2005. He was selected because he was only forty-five miles away from Patchogue. Already a difficult assignment, this casualty call was even more so because this one was his first. After making several phone calls, he learned he would not be acting alone while carrying out this responsibility. Commander Robert Coyle, command chaplain at the USMMA, and Lieutenant Commander Chad Muse, from Naval Special Warfare in California, would be accompanying him to the Murphy home.

Wednesday, June 29, 2005, Naval Special Warfare Command (NAVSPECWARCOM), Coronado, California

While the Murphys each went about their day, the action outside of Asadabad made the routine at NSW in California anything but normal. At his office at 5:30 AM, Commander Todd DeGhetto received a telephone call on an unsecured line. A helicopter had gone down in Afghanistan, he was told. Three of his men may well have been on it. About an hour later he received a secured call from Captain Tom Carlson, commodore, NSW Group Three, confirming the helicopter crash, the identities of those killed, and that three of his men were missing on the ground. Meanwhile, word had reached Captain Larry Lasky, assistant chief of staff for operations and planning at NAVSPECWARCOM, that Operation Red Wings had gone into a rescue posture, "with troops in contact with a numerically superior force." He knew from early reports that the four-man SEAL unit had come under heavy attack with limited support, lost communications, and was possibly trying to escape or evade the enemy by rapidly descending sheer cliffs. A quick-reaction force (QRF) consisting of several helicopters had been mobilized in an effort to extract the team, but the Chinook 47E helicopter carrying the QRF had been destroyed by what appeared to be a rocket-propelled grenade (RPG) and the remaining helicopters were ordered to abort the mission. The reports were pieced together from videotape and digital photographs of the battle area and the helicopter crash site captured by an unmanned MQ-1 Predator.

It did not take a man with Lasky's years of experience to know things were not going well. Based on these early reports, Captain Lasky recommended that the Crisis Action Center begin continuous operations, in order to keep Rear Admiral Joseph Maguire informed of the situation. At the time, Maguire reported to General Bryan D. Brown, commander of the United States Special Operations Command (USSOCOM), which controls and coordinates all special operations forces (SOF) components from each branch of the military and is headquartered at MacDill Air Force Base near Tampa, Florida.

Word of the engagement spread quickly. At 8:00 AM Pacific standard time (PST) in the NAVSPECWARCOM Operations Center, Commander Ray Major, the operations officer, received word that all members of the SEAL unit and those on the rescue helicopter had been declared DUSTWUN (Duty Station Whereabouts Unknown). Also on duty was Lieutenant Commander Chad Muse, who was serving as the assistant operations officer after recently returning from a seven-month tour in Iraq. He immediately recognized the names of Lieutenant Murphy and Senior Chief Petty Officer Daniel R. Healy. Muse worked with Murphy when both were assigned to SEAL Delivery Vehicle Team One (SDVT-1) in Pearl City, Hawaii, and again when Michael served as his operations officer for the Middle Eastern training exercise Early Victor in 2002. Commander Major instructed Muse to stand by to travel with the Casualty Assistance Calls Officer (CACO).

Naval Special Warfare is an extremely tight and close-knit community. It is common practice to dispatch with all CACOs an officer who either knows the sailor or the family. For Lieutenant Commander Muse, this was his unwritten sworn and solemn obligation, because both he and Murphy were Navy SEAL team leaders, each a member of a brotherhood, a community of elite warriors to whom the word "team" is not just a word or slogan, but the very essence of who they are. When he saw Michael's name on the list, he knew he was going to New York and began to prepare for the most difficult assignment of his military career. With orders to connect with Lieutenant Widenhofer before going to the Murphy home, Muse was dispatched to provide the family with answers to nonclassified operational questions.

Long Island, New York

By 5:00 PM Maureen had already received telephone calls at home, including one from Heather, who was nearly hysterical. In a panic, she told Maureen about her attempts to obtain information through NAVSPECWARCOM in San Diego. She was upset because she was told that no information could be released to her because she and Michael were not married. "Heather, we don't know anything. Let's not jump to any conclusions. Just try and calm down. Michael has been deployed before and we've heard nothing from the Navy," Maureen said in an effort to comfort her. However, neither Heather nor Maureen was comforted by their conversation. In fact, Maureen later remarked that Heather's call only heightened her concern as she watched the news with John, who had returned home from the pool.

Following the workday, Dan prepared for a quiet evening at his home in the Long Island town of Medford. He and Maureen, who had been divorced since 1998, had not yet spoken to each other about the disturbing news reports. In the absence of anything specific to Michael, there was little to do but monitor the local and national news reports as information regarding the engagement in Afghanistan garnered increasing coverage. While certainly concerned, Dan was still clinging to his belief that Michael was in Iraq when Heather arrived at his door, still very upset by the news of the helicopter crash. Dan anxiously retrieved a photograph of Michael and his team and showed it to her. "See, they are wearing desert fatigues. Michael is in Iraq," he told her, perhaps as much to assure himself as to comfort her. But Heather was unconvinced and asked, "What about those mountains in the background?" She was not the first to question Dan's belief about the location of the photo—his friend Anthony Moncayo, an Army lieutenant colonel, had questioned Dan's belief two weeks earlier. Trying not to add to her anxiety, Dan replied in a deliberately calm voice, telling her that "there are mountains in Iraq, especially in northern Iraq near Mosul," but to no avail. Within moments Heather was off to Maureen's. Dan began to share her concern, particularly after he learned through news reports that those who died were Navy SEALs.

At Maureen's, Heather joined her and John as they anxiously watched the news. As his mother and Heather become more focused and distressed by the reports coming out of Afghanistan, John too became more concerned. When Heather left for home she gave Maureen the telephone number she had called earlier, hoping that she would have better luck obtaining information about Michael. Maureen called immediately. She was pleasantly greeted by a woman who answered the telephone. After Maureen identified herself, the lady stated, "Mrs. Murphy, I know your son and he is a really good man. I just wanted you to know that. I'll put you through now." But there was still no news from the Navy.

At 9:00 PM reports continued to be broadcast on several news channels, but Maureen had heard nothing back from Navy officials. By this time Lieutenant Commander Muse had arrived from San Diego. By 11:30 PM Maureen and John still had heard nothing. "We haven't heard anything, so this is good, right? See, no news is good news," Maureen said to John as they climbed the stairs to their bedrooms. John agreed and began working on his computer, but despite not hearing anything official from the Navy, he was concerned.

Approximately ten minutes later, Maureen, a devout Roman Catholic, had completed her evening prayers, changed her clothes, and was standing next to her bed when she heard a car enter the Astoria Federal Savings bank parking lot across the street. Through the open windows above the head of her bed she heard three doors open and close. In the dark silence of the heavy summer night the sound traveled quickly, echoing off of the surrounding houses, carried by the gentle breeze that stirred the window curtains. Sheer terror struck her as she became fro-zen by fear. John, having heard the car doors too, went downstairs, where he stood in the foyer. His mother stood motionless in her room, overcome by a cold sweat as her heart pounded in her chest and she struggled to breathe.

As the mother of a member of the U.S. military, she was well aware of the noti-fication procedure. Although able to stand, she could not move. Fear had immobi-lized her, and she was hoping that those getting out of the car were not coming to her door but perhaps only visiting neighboring households—or maybe they were the neighbors returning home. After what seemed like an eternity, the deafening sound of the doorbell pierced the silence; both John and Maureen were startled by the sound, shocked back to their senses. "John, don't answer the door," his mother said, but it was too late. He was already in the process of slowly opening it when he heard her plea. "Mom, there are three Navy officers here to see you," he said in a somber, nervous tone.

By this time Maureen had changed her clothes and descended the five stairs to the landing. Visibly shaking and now covered with perspiration, she saw the offi-cers in full dress uniform standing on the other side of the outer glass door, their uniform brass glistening under the porch lights. Lieutenant Commander Muse and Commander Coyle were in their dark uniforms and Lieutenant Widenhofer was in his summer whites. She instantly saw the SEAL Trident on Muse's uniform. Before the men had even spoken a word, she took a step back as her knees buckled and she yelled, "No!" John reacted quickly and braced his mother from falling.

Father Coyle immediately tried to comfort her by telling her "all we know right now is that Michael is missing. We don't know anything else. Michael is missing." Terrified, she looked first at Father Coyle for several seconds and then took a deep breath before apologizing for her actions and invited the men into her home. All three men removed their uniform caps as they stepped inside. It was Father Coyle who introduced himself, Muse, and Widenhofer. After directing everyone to the living room, Coyle turned his attention to Maureen, now visibly trembling, and assisted her into the room. There, he encouraged her to sit, but she was too ner-vous to sit and remained standing. Each of her visitors, all consummate gentlemen and professional military officers, remained standing until Maureen apologetically asked them to be seated. Each responded with a thank-you but remained stand-ing close to her, as did John. John shouted, "It's the helicopter, isn't it. It's about the helicopter." Father Coyle replied calmly, "No, Michael was not on the helicopter. He was on a ground mission and right now all we know is that he and his team are missing." Muse then briefly explained his professional relationship with Michael and in very general terms went over the mission that Michael was leading, and answered Maureen's questions. Again, Father Coyle attempted to get Maureen to sit down, and once again she declined politely. All remained standing while Father Coyle led everyone in prayer.

Following the prayer, Widenhofer more fully introduced himself and informed Maureen that he also needed to contact Michael's father. Maureen cleared her thoughts, reoriented herself to the present, and made the call to Dan, who was at his home, just a ten-minute drive away. In a deliberately slow and calm voice she said, "Danny, the Navy is here saying that Michael is missing in Afghanistan. Do you want me to send them over to your house?" Stunned, Dan could only exclaim, "What!" After repeating herself more slowly, Dan's thoughts were immediately taken back to the two earlier conversations with Heather. He asked Maureen to keep the three men there and told her he was on his way. It was just after midnight.

On his way, he called his sister Maureen and her husband, John Bogenshutz. He asked his sister if she had "heard about the helicopter that went down in Afghanistan." Maureen said yes, and became immediately more alarmed as she detected the strain in Dan's voice. "Michael is in Afghanistan . . . he was not on the helicopter, but he was on a mission and he is now missing. The Navy is over at Maureen's house and I am going there now," he told her. Maureen told her husband about the call. Both were deeply concerned. After several minutes of silence and staring at the ceiling, it was clear to her that she would be unable to sleep. Full of anxiety and frustration, she looked at her husband and said, "Well, this isn't going to work. I can't just lie here. I think we have to go over there." Within minutes they were in the car and on their way. As he drove to Maureen's, Dan replayed the day's conversations with Heather over and over in his head. He turned into the driveway, slammed on the brakes, and rammed the transmission into park while opening the car door, then jumped out and closed the door in a single motion. Hearing the car door close, all three Navy officers rose and looked at the front door just before Dan burst through it and came into the living room.

Lieutenant Commander Muse then went over the same information previously given to Maureen and John, and introduced Lieutenant Widenhofer and Commander Coyle. The Murphys drew some comfort and a glimmer of hope from their words. Without confirmation, there was always hope, they believed. As Widenhofer finished, John and Maureen Bogenshutz arrived, and Widenhofer again went over the information that was known.

Assembling the Support Network

Around 12:30 AM, Maureen telephoned Heather and her family. She then called her sister Eileen Hillicke in Wilmington, North Carolina. Eileen, who was Michael's godmother, booked the first available flight for later that morning. Maureen also called her neighbors and close personal friends Tony and April

Viggiano and neighbors Joe and Benilde DeCabo, who arrived within minutes, as well as her cousins John and Linda McElhone. Linda was Maureen's closest friend and confidante.

She also called her nieces Cathy, who was in college in Ohio, Colleen, who was at her home in New Hampshire, and Kelly, who lived in nearby Huntington on Long Island. The Murphys were particularly close to the girls as they had raised them after their father Billy Jones, Maureen's younger brother, died of cancer. Cathy and Colleen left immediately for Long Island, while Kelly arrived within the hour.

The three Navy officers and the family members remained with the Murphys for the next three hours, leaving them just after 3:30 AM. During that time Father Coyle led everyone in prayer on multiple occasions. Although not everyone in the room was Catholic, all were Christians, and prayed for His will to be done; they believed that His will included Michael's safe return to those who loved him. Muse gave the family his hotel address, room number, and the room's telephone as well as his personal cell numbers, and all three officers promised to return later that morning. Dan too left for home, but there was very little sleep for any member of the Murphy family on that night.

By the time everyone retired to their homes and hotels, Michael's status was still unknown, but one thing was clear: both the Murphy and Duggan families were blessed with an extensive support network—military and civilian—a support system that became both necessary and sustaining in the days that followed the initial news. After strong encouragement from those arriving, Maureen finally agreed to surrender her attempts to meet the emotional needs of those gathered around her and allow them to begin to meet her needs and those of Dan and John as well.

CHAPTER TWO

Vigil for the Valiant

They're falling—either literally or figuratively—and you have to catch them. In this business I can't save his life. All I can do is catch the family while they're falling.

—MAJOR STEVE BECK, Casualty Assistance Calls Officer (CACO), United States Marine Corps, quoted in Jim Sheeler, *Final Salute*

Thursday–Friday, June 30–July 1, 2005

Having only a few hours of sleep, Maureen called the O'Callaghans at around 8:00 AM. Jimmie and Owen O'Callaghan, who also lived in Patchogue, were lifeguards with Michael and were his best friends. She remembered that Michael had told her to call Owen and Jimmie if anything ever happened to him, that they would "take care of everything." They arrived within twenty minutes.

As promised, arriving at about 9:00 AM in their dress uniforms were Lieutenant Commander Muse and Lieutenant Widenhofer, who remained for the rest of the day. Muse made frequent telephone contact with NAVSPECWARCOM, although most of the calls were very short. With Muse tied up with NAVSPECWARCOM, Widenhofer answered questions in between television news and updates from the Murphys' many extended family members and friends. Desperate for information, any information, the Murphys relied on the public news media despite their tendency for reporting unverified information as truth. The Navy, on the other hand, would only provide information that was properly verified.

The Murphys followed the Navy's advice and directed all media inquiries to the Navy's Office of Public Information. Always attentive to the needs of others, Maureen insisted that both Muse and Widenhofer return tomorrow in comfortable street clothes; both agreed. After a midmorning telephone call to NAVSPEC-WARCOM, Muse related that at least two helicopters carrying Navy SEALs responded to Michael's call for help. One helicopter was hit by an RPG and the other was forced to abort the mission, and there had been no further contact with Michael's team.

Having just arrived at work, Beth Risotto received a call from Jimmie O'Callaghan telling her of Michael's status. Being a close friend of Heather's, she called her, but without having to ask, she knew that Heather was aware of the situation. Leaving work, she went to the Duggan home in Mount Sinai, located directly north across Long Island from Patchogue, where she stayed for the next week.

The next day the Murphy family had begun to mentally sort through the information they had received and also accept the fact that the worst possible news could be coming. The O'Callaghans assumed the duties of managing the overwhelming number of telephone calls and personal messages and donations; but despite their best efforts, there was no way to keep track of those who had called or sent contributions or dropped off food items. The dining room table was completely covered with fruit baskets and the living room full of flowers and planters. The kitchen table and counters were covered with food donated by caring individuals and businesses. As the national and international media intensified its coverage of the events in Afghanistan, local media had begun camping out at the Murphy home. In Mount Sinai, in between news broadcasts, Beth and Heather spent their time taking walks and telling "Murph" stories and returned to the Murphy home each evening.

Saturday, July 2, 2005

After speaking to NAVSPECWARCOM, Lieutenant Commander Muse explained to the Murphys that the Navy was tracking a single beacon moving down the mountain. Tentatively, Maureen asked, "So is this good news for the SEALs or for the Murphy family?" Cautiously, Muse responded, "The Murphy family." While both exhaled with some relief, they knew that the relief was only temporary. Maureen turned to Dan as they realized that there appeared to be only one survivor and stated, "It's not Mike. It's not Mike. There is no way he would be the only one out." Dan and Maureen realized that Michael's character and integrity would not allow him to be the sole survivor. They knew that he would sacrifice himself to allow someone else to be the sole survivor, but it was simply not in Michael to be the only one out.

Muse explained that Michael and his team had been involved in an ambush. As Dan and Maureen processed the information they had received, Dan recalled his military training in Vietnam and asked if Michael's team had been ambushed or if his team had executed the ambush. He knew that if Michael's team had executed the ambush that they would have set the stage and environment in their favor—at night, with proper positioning and other tactical advantages. If they had walked into an ambush, that would not be good. Dan and Maureen continued to pray for the best but began to prepare themselves for the worst as the gravity and reality of the situation became more and more clear.

Around noon, Captain Andrew Bisset, a thirty-seven-year Navy SEAL veteran and Michael's SEAL mentor, called to invite Michael to his upcoming retirement party in Groton, Connecticut. The family did not take his call; they believed it was another member of the media trying to get a family member on the telephone. Well acquainted with the family, Bisset was confused. He was aware of the situation in Afghanistan but did not know that Michael had been involved.

Sunday, July 3, 2005

Again having received very little sleep, the family attended morning Mass at Our Lady of Mount Carmel Catholic Church, led by Father Robert O'Connell. Special prayers were offered for Michael, his team, and the entire Murphy family. They were overwhelmed by the expression of support from the more than twelve hundred parishioners in attendance. Following Mass, Dan and Karen went to Heather's home. The Navy had previously dispatched Lieutenant Jim Quattromani to stay with the Duggan family. While they were there, Heather received a telephone call from Marcus Luttrell's younger brother Morgan, who stated, "Marcus is all shot up! Marcus is all shot up!" The news devastated Heather. Jim took the phone from Heather and continued the conversation with Morgan. Morgan provided no additional information about Michael or any other member of the team. This did not go unnoticed by Jim or Dan, who just looked at each other but said nothing. Dan resigned himself to the inevitable but remained mentally torn. As a prosecutor, he was used to looking at a set of facts, analyzing and organizing them together in a logical sequence, reaching a logical conclusion. A simple straightforward process he had done for many years. However, as a father, he could not bring himself to the logical conclusion the facts showed him. To do so was unthinkable.

Having returned to Maureen's home and the nearly one hundred family members and friends gathered there, Dan and Karen repeated the previous day's routine. Rosary prayer vigils were constantly held as family members and friends worked and prayed in shifts. Early in the afternoon it was announced that Marines had rescued Michael's teammate Marcus Luttrell, and the names of the Navy SEALs and Army Night Stalkers killed on the helicopter were released.

Captain Bisset called again, but this time Maureen took his call, and after several questions she was satisfied that he was the "real" Captain Bisset. She told him of Michael's status, and he took several seconds to regain his thoughts. He reassured her that Michael was well trained and that if anyone could make it, Michael could. Maureen agreed. Even though the family was mentally and physically exhausted, the prayers continued. At one point Dan's sister Maureen noticed him with a set of rosary beads, the same rosary used by their mother when Dan was seriously wounded in the jungles of Vietnam thirty years earlier.

Monday, July 4, 2005

At about 2:00 PM, the family turned the television to CBS, as word had been received that there were news reports that two dead Navy SEALs had been recovered in Afghanistan. The family questioned Muse, who made an immediate phone call to NAVSPECWARCOM. Muse was told that the information being reported was not confirmed and that the Navy believed "someone was jumping the gun." Dan and Maureen, now desperate for information and despite being warned by the Navy to the contrary, began paying increased attention to the news reports as it appeared that more information was available, despite the media's reputation for releasing unconfirmed and sensationalized information as fact.

However, after the initial reports, there were no rebroadcasts or any additional information regarding the two Navy SEALs. Maureen became upset, voicing her concern that Michael and the others "could be seriously injured and bleeding to death and there is no one to help them. I don't want Michael lying out there alone, bleeding and in pain. Someone needs to help those boys."

Dan began to wonder if this was indeed a case of unconfirmed information being released, but this did little to affect his increased pessimism. As he intensified his silent prayers for Michael, he also began praying for Maureen, who visibly showed both the mental and physical strain of the ordeal. Although their family and friends continued to be optimistic in their conversations, Dan and Maureen both had consciously begun to accept what they believed was the inevitable, this being the sixth day since Michael's team had come under fire. Beth and Heather returned to Mount Sinai, and Lieutenant Widenhofer returned to his apartment and wife in Queens.

The Inevitable

At about 11:00 PM, Muse made his usual late-evening call to NAVSPECWARCOM. This call was different. Dan knew that Muse's usual routine was to go outside in the front yard, make his call, and then return within three to five minutes and report that there was no new information. Tonight was different.

After just a minute or two into the conversation, Dan saw Muse walk to the end of the tree line and stand along the road as he engaged in an extended conversation. Dan walked out onto the front porch to observe as the conversation continued for another twenty minutes. Dan knew that it was not good news and tried mentally to prepare himself for the worst.

After completing the call to NAVSPECWARCOM, Muse immediately telephoned Widenhofer and explained the situation. Michael Murphy had been killed in action. As the CACO, Widenhofer asked Muse to wait until he arrived to inform the family. Seeing Dan standing on the front porch, Muse explained that Dan had been watching him and that he could not go back into the house and not tell them what he knew. Both agreed, then Muse hung up. After informing his wife of the news, Widenhofer changed into his uniform for a quick and emotional trip to the Murphy home.

Muse took several deep breaths and then, with a lot of "self-talk," walked back toward the house with his head down, desperately searching for the right words as he approached Dan. Dan yelled, "No, I'm not going to let you tell me what you have to tell me. No!"

"Mr. Murphy, I am so sorry."

Dan, mentally and physically exhausted, began to walk away, but after a couple of steps he turned to Muse and said, "You are going to have to tell Maureen. I can't do it; she has been through enough already." Muse nodded his head and entered the house. Dan began pacing around the front yard and crossed the street to the bank's parking lot, which was surrounded by a tall wooden fence. Muse found Maureen in the kitchen. She appeared mentally and physically exhausted. She looked up at him with her very tired blue eyes. His heart ached as he put his hand on her arm and said, "Mrs. Murphy, I am so sorry, but Michael didn't make it." Immediately her knees weakened as an unbearable stabbing pain deep inside her stomach took her breath away. She winced and fell back against the refrigerator. Muse braced her from collapsing. After about ten seconds she regained control and threw her hands up and said, "No. If Michael is not here, he is in a better place. He is not alone and he is no longer in pain and bleeding." There were no tears—yet.

The word of Michael's death immediately spread throughout the house. John heard the emotional cries and walked into the hallway just outside the kitchen. The crowd of people was so big that he was unable to see his mother or into the kitchen.

"What's going on?"

James and Thomas Allmer, John's cousins, embraced him and said, "I'm so sorry, man." John instantly realized his brother's fate. Stunned, he turned and walked slowly down the hallway and out the back door. James and Thomas followed him to the redwood table on the patio where he and Michael had spent many hours over the years hanging out and talking. He reminisced about the years that he idolized his brother and how he had always looked after and protected him, how he had included him in many activities, such as swimming, lifeguarding, and social events, and how he had taken him to Penn State for a week when Michael was a student there and used him as a "chick magnet."

Across the street in the parking lot, Dan yelled at the stars, "Life is so dammed unfair!" In anger and frustration as a constant stream of tears ran down his face, he punched the wooden fence over and over, alone with his thoughts.

Having brought John inside, Dan's sister Maureen began to look for Dan. His fiancée, Karen, went out the front door and saw Dan punching the fence and yelling. She crossed the street and heard him talking incoherently. He did not respond to her repeated attempts to gain his attention. She noticed blood dripping from his hands, as well as the rosary he was holding.

Dan's sister Maureen saw Karen leading Dan toward the house. She watched as he walked over to the trash can, lifted the lid, and threw something in, then walked toward the house. After Dan and Karen were inside, his sister went out and emptied the trash can onto the driveway, sorted through the loose trash, and retrieved the rosary beads.

After a hurried trip across Manhattan, Lieutenant Widenhofer arrived within forty-five minutes. After he entered the house he immediately expressed his condolences to Maureen and John, and sought out Dan, who was now on the back patio with several other family members. Hearing Widenhofer's voice, Dan said, "I don't want to talk to Jeff, I don't want to talk to Jeff!" Widenhofer overlooked the outburst and expressed his condolences, then gave Dan some time to continue the grieving process.

Within minutes after Muse had delivered the worst possible news, he telephoned the Duggan home. Dan Duggan, Heather's father, who served as the Mount Sinai police chief, took the call using the upstairs telephone away from Heather. Heather and Beth were busy in the kitchen downstairs, cleaning and getting ready to retire for yet another night of nerve-racking uncertainty. As her father came down the stairs, both Beth and Heather turned toward him. Seeing the redness of his face and the tears that streamed down his face, both knew. After Dan informed her of the news, Heather screamed and crumbled to the kitchen floor, sobbing uncontrollably.

Shortly after the Duggans learned the news, Michael's friends Jay Keenan, James Emmerich, and Jimmie, Owen, Sean, and Kerri O'Callaghan arrived. Beth went outside to meet them, while Heather remained in the arms of her parents on the kitchen floor, unable to talk to visitors. Beth could tell that everyone had been crying, and at that moment reality sunk in. She just sat down on the driveway and cried. As the group slowly approached, each knew that life had changed for every one of them and would never be the same.

After nearly an hour of crying and sharing memories of the many good times they'd had with Michael, Jay Keenan, Jimmy, Owen, Kerri, Beth, Heather's sister Brianne, and Jim Quattromani walked around to the Duggan's patio deck. There they spent the next several hours telling more stories about Michael and the "good old days." In the midst of their sorrow, they could still celebrate Michael's life.

One of them began to tell a story that Michael was not particularly fond of. Just then it began to rain and they all laughed. They believed it was Michael's way of getting them to stop telling the story. As soon as they stopped talking, the rain stopped. But soon the laughter subsided and the reality of Michael's passing began to sink in. Each knew they were better for having known Michael.

Tuesday, July 5, 2005, Dover Air Force Base, Delaware

Early the next morning, Muse and Widenhofer explained that Michael's and Danny Dietz's remains had been recovered, but Matt Axelson was still missing. Michael's and Danny's remains would be escorted by SEALs from Bagram Airfield in Afghanistan to Landstuhl Regional Medical Center, the U.S. military hospital in Landstuhl, Germany, and then brought to the United States under an Air Force honor guard escort. The plane was scheduled to land at Dover Air Force Base, Delaware, at about five o'clock that afternoon.

Believing that Michael would know that his family was with him, the Murphys asked to meet the plane at Dover. Although families usually did not attend arrivals, Muse and Widenhofer made the necessary arrangements. John and Maureen Bogenshutz realized that neither Dan, Maureen, nor John was in any physical or mental condition to make the nearly 250-mile drive themselves and insisted on driving them to Dover. The Murphys agreed. Early in the afternoon, Dan, Maureen, and John left for Dover in the Bogenshutzs' SUV, followed by Widenhofer and Muse. As it turned out, delays changed the plane's arrival time to between ten and eleven o'clock. They all met with the Dover Air Force Base commanding general and a chaplain, who explained the procedure after the plane arrived and that Michael's remains could not be returned to New York until all military matters, such as funeral arrangements and paperwork, were completed.

Back in Patchogue, the media had descended on Maureen's home, where Sharon McKenna, Justice Cohalan's secretary, and Karen handled the endless telephone inquiries. Dozens of media cameras, trucks, and personnel were set up in the front yard. Several members of the media went door-to-door and tried to get someone to make an on-camera comment. They got no takers, but neighbor Lance Marquis identified a yearbook picture of Michael. Lance called Dan and told him about the media onslaught, and Dan asked him to tell the media that the family would hold a media briefing at 10:00 AM the next day at Maureen's home.

At approximately 10:00 PM the family, along with the general and the chaplain, were driven in an Air Force bus to the tarmac and positioned about thirty feet from the plane that had just arrived. The side door of the plane opened and they could see the Air Force Honor Guard that surrounded the flag-draped coffin inside. A hi-lo machine was raised into position. The Air Force escort turned and saluted, then slowly lifted the coffin and placed it on the machine. They saluted again and went back inside the plane. As tears streamed down their faces, Dan turned to Maureen and said, "Maureen, there's our boy."

Peace Be with You . . . and Also with You

As Michael's remains reached the ground, Maureen mentally pictured Michael getting up in his white dress uniform and walking over to them, putting his arms around them, and saying, "I'm home." At the same time Maureen "saw" Michael approach, Dan was overcome by a sense of calmness and peace. He immediately turned to Maureen, who said, "Do you feel that?" Both acknowledged the sense of calm, as did John. Dan later described the moment: "It's was like Michael touched us, it was such a sense of calmness . . . and so unusual. It was something like I have never ever felt before . . . it was like this real emotional moment . . . there's this anticipation . . . this agitation . . . there's this anxiety, and then just when Michael came level to the ground, within seconds this overwhelming sense of calmness and peace enveloped us."

Maureen recalled, "It was such a calming experience, like I have never felt before. It was like I could picture when Michael's casket reached the ground, he got up and walked over to us and put his arms around us and said, 'It's OK, I'm home now.' I can't begin to tell you how comforting that moment was to me . . . to all of us."

Four Navy honor guard sailors marched toward Michael's coffin, saluted, and placed the coffin in the waiting ambulance truck, which drove slowly to the Charles C. Carson Center for Mortuary Affairs at the other end of the base. As described in his favorite book, *Gates of Fire*, by Steven Pressfield, Lieutenant Michael P. Murphy had returned home not carrying his shield, but on it, "because a warrior carries helmet and breastplate for his own protection, but his shield for the safety of the whole line. There is a force beyond fear. More powerful than self-preservation."

After the truck left, all reentered the Air Force bus, still feeling peaceful and calm. As they took their seats, the Air Force chaplain, having heard Dan and Maureen's comments, asked, "When did you feel this?" Dan and Maureen looked at each other and related their feelings, then the chaplain responded, "You know, it is not an uncommon occurrence. I can't explain it, but the few families who come here seem to get the same effect. Those who don't think spiritually find it difficult to explain." Dan and Maureen were comforted by the fact that other families had received the same healing they had just experienced.

Michael's Revenge

As they all sat in the bus, it refused to start. The general voiced his extreme displeasure to the unfortunate airman, who tried repeatedly to get the bus started.

The Murphy family laughed, because Michael had always been mechanically challenged when it came to cars. "This is not the airman's fault, it is Michael's revenge for making such a big deal of him coming home."

The family finally returned home, while Lieutenant Commander Muse and Lieutenant Widenhofer remained at Dover to coordinate funeral and transport arrangements with Maureen's uncle, Eddie McElhone, who owned and operated the Clayton Funeral Home in Kings Park, across Long Island on the North Shore.

Wednesday, July 6, 2005

After a few hours of needed rest, Dan, Maureen, and John met with the press. Six television stations and forty to fifty members of the broadcast and print media had packed the front yard. Dan, an attorney, was accustomed to dealing with the media and with crowds. He spoke for the family, as John and Maureen were somewhat intimidated by all of the bright lights, the microphones, and the shouting of questions. He explained that they had been at Dover AFB as their son's remains were brought back to the United States. After the briefing, several members of the media were invited into the home to photograph pictures of Michael. Generally, the members of the media were very sympathetic and supportive of the family. But the family did have one painful experience. A cameraman noticed a picture of Michael at his graduation from Officer Candidate School sitting on the large wooden shelf above the living room sofa. In order to properly get a picture without the glare of the glass, he placed the picture on the floor to shoot the picture at a straight angle. Maureen gasped and covered her mouth with her hand as tears streamed down her face.

Dan cried, "No, you can't do that. We do not want our son's picture on the floor."

The cameraman apologized and said he meant no disrespect, but it was necessary to get a good picture. He continued to attempt a picture and Dan quickly picked the picture up off the floor.

"I don't care; you are not putting our son's picture on the floor." He placed it back on the shelf, much to Maureen's comfort.

Dan informed Lieutenant Commander Muse that he wanted Michael brought to New York as soon as possible, as he did not want his son left alone in a mortuary. Later that afternoon, the Murphys met with Eddie McElhone. Compassionately, Eddie explained the service and burial arrangements. The family refused the Navy's offer for Michael to be buried in Arlington National Cemetery and decided to bury him in Calverton National Cemetery, about fifteen miles from Patchogue. They accepted the Navy's offer for full military honors.

Sunday, July 10, 2005

Early in the morning, a motorcade consisting of a hearse, a limousine that carried Dan, Maureen, and John, along with John and Linda McElhone, and a Westbury police cruiser driven by Dan Duggan and carrying his wife, Lynda, and Heather left for Dover. The motorcade arrived just before 9:00 AM at the Charles C. Carson Center for Mortuary Affairs. The combined military honor guard solemnly placed Michael's flag-draped gray steel casket into the hearse, and two cruisers from the Delaware State Patrol provided an escort to the New Jersey state line. Dan rode in the hearse and kept his hand on the casket throughout the trip and talked to Michael, telling him that he was on his way home and describing the scenery as they passed.

Honoring a Hero

At the state line, two New Jersey State Patrol cruisers assumed the escort and led the motorcade to the New York state line. In New York, authorities had closed the Belt Parkway to the Nassau County line, with a uniformed New York City motorcycle police officer positioned at each entrance to the parkway. As the hearse approached, each officer snapped to attention and saluted, holding the salute until the motorcade had passed. Dan and Maureen were unable to control their emotions. They were in awe of the fact that total strangers would have so much respect for their son. Dan tried to describe the scene to Michael, but was unable to do so through his tears. At the Nassau County line, six cruisers from the Nassau County Police Department escorted them to the Suffolk County line into Kings Park, where additional local police cruisers joined the escort. As they waited outside the funeral home, Eddie McElhone and a Navy honor guard from the Naval Operational Support Center in Plainville, Connecticut, heard the sirens even though the motorcade was still several miles away.

Clayton Funeral Home

After the hearse backed into position, Michael's casket, with three members of the honor guard at each end, was carried through the front doors and placed on a church truck. From there it was wheeled into Chapel C, and the double-wide white doors were closed. The casket was taken to the front of the chapel, where the honor guard centered it on the bier. Members of the honor guard then faced the casket, saluted, and retired. Eddie then quickly prepared the room by placing a red lighted votive candle at each end of the casket and next to each votive a taller lighted torchère. He then centered the brass Resurrection Cross behind the flag-draped casket and escorted the family in from a nearby room.

As the family approached the casket and knelt at the prayer rail, Eddie walked slowly to the back of the room. After several minutes, Dan and Maureen stepped back and sat in the center of the front row, along with John. They couldn't help feeling the unfairness of it all. Michael's death violated the natural order of life. Children bury their parents. Parents should not have to bury their children.

After about ten minutes, the Duggan family was escorted into the chapel. They also knelt and prayed. After several minutes at the prayer rail, they joined the Murphys in the front row. The chapel was quiet, except for the sound of soft cries and sobs of parents and family.

Afterward, Dan pulled Eddie aside and asked to view Michael's remains. Even though Dan was a longtime homicide prosecutor, Eddie was strongly against it. Maureen then asked that Michael's beard, grown for the Afghanistan mission, be shaved before viewing. Delicately, McElhone explained that because of the manner in which Michael died, coupled with the time it took to recover his remains, he could not be viewed. He further explained that Michael had been tightly shrouded and his uniform pinned to the shroud. Undeterred, Heather asked that the wedding ring she had bought for Michael be placed on his hand. Reluctantly, McElhone agreed, which renewed Dan's desire to view Michael, or at least hold his hand before he was buried. Eddie again explained that he was strongly against this, and Dan finally relented.

When the family left the funeral home, they were met by a large crowd of people waving flags in the parking lot. Several called out words of sympathy and support, many politely applauded, and some just stood in solemn reverence. Dan and Maureen nodded and acknowledged them while they walked toward the waiting limousine.

After the family left, the members of the honor guard took their positions at each end of the flag-draped casket, where they remained until the funeral.

CHAPTER THREE

Funeral for the Fallen

It's not an ending. It's not a period at the end of their lives. It's a semicolon. The story will continue to be told.

> —MAJOR STEVE BECK, Casualty Assistance Calls Officer (CACO), United States Marine Corps, quoted in Jim Sheeler, *Final Salute*

Long Island Newsday, **Monday, July 11, 2005: Michael Patrick Murphy**

MURPHY—Lt. Michael Patrick. U.S. Navy SEAL Delivery Vehicle Team One. Pearl Harbor, HI of Patchogue, NY on July 4, 2005 in Afghanistan. Devoted son of Maureen T. (née Jones) and Daniel J. Murphy. Dear brother of John. Loving Fiancé of Heather L. Duggan. Cherished grandson of Kathleen (née McElhone) and Frank Jones and the late James P. and Elinor Murphy. Reposing at Clayton Funeral Home, Inc. 25 Meadow Road (corner of Indian Head Rd.) Kings Park, NY. A Mass of Christian Burial will be offered at 11:00 AM Wednesday, at Our Lady of Mt. Carmel R.C. Church, 495 N. Ocean Avenue, Patchogue, NY. Interment to follow at Calverton National Cemetery, Calverton, NY. Visiting hours Monday and Tuesday, 2–5 and 7–9 PM. In lieu of flowers, donations to Michael P. Murphy Scholarship Fund, c/o Clayton Funeral Home.

Funeral Preparations

The Navy quickly arranged to bring in Michael's SDVT-1 from Pearl City, Hawaii. Dan agreed to a request from V. Anthony Maggipinto, a lawyer colleague and a retired petty officer second class, to assist in the celebration of the Mass. Maggipinto served as the judge advocate for the Long Island Navy League and as a deacon at the St. Philip and James Catholic Church in St. James, New York.

By now it had become clear that Michael's funeral had captured the attention of the Navy at the highest levels. The family had been informed that several flag officers (admirals) would be attending Michael's funeral, including Rear Admiral Joseph Maguire, the commander of Naval Special Warfare. Part of the funeral arrangements included the selection of the Navy officer who would present Maureen with Michael's burial flag. Lieutenant Jeff Widenhofer explained the usual protocol, but Maureen insisted that Captain Andrew Bisset present Michael's flag, and she also requested that Michael's fiancée, Heather, also receive a flag.

To ensure that her wishes were honored, Maureen called Bisset and asked him to present the flag. This task was not new to Bisset, as he had performed this function at an increasing number of funerals for World War II and Korean War veterans throughout the New England region. He was humbled by Maureen's call because he felt guilt-ridden, having trained and recommended Michael for the very service that ultimately cost him his life. He knew that this would be the most difficult assignment of his career.

Back at the funeral home, floral arrangements surrounded the base of the ivory bier as the U.S. Navy honor guard remained motionless at each end of the casket. A full-length tripod with a large picture of Michael greeted visitors as they entered the chapel. Although the family had requested memorials be made to the scholarship fund newly established in Michael's memory, dozens of floral displays were delivered during the day that extended the length of the room on both sides, while additional arrangements were set in the hallway as well as an adjacent room that had been set up for additional seating.*

Visitation: Monday, July 11, 2005

The first of four separate visitations was scheduled to begin at 2:00 PM, but the line of those who waited to pay their respects began forming outside the Clayton Funeral Home by midmorning. By the time the doors opened, the line had woven its way through the rows of parked cars in the parking lot, along the sidewalk, around the front of the parking lot, and nearly two blocks north. Local law enforcement officials assisted with traffic, while a group of forty to fifty veterans on motorcycles, known as the Patriot Guard, lined the parking lot with large U.S. flags.

Two separate receiving lines were established, the first for members of the general public and the second for members of the immediate family and the military. The large military contingent that arrived was made up of active-duty, reserve, and retired SEALs and sailors, along with both active-duty and retired members of each of the other service branches and the Merchant Marine Academy. Because Dan had been the Suffolk County prosecutor, a large number of court officers, judges, and attorneys arrived, as well as local, state, and national political leaders, to honor the life and sacrifice of Lieutenant Murphy. For three hours, the Murphys received a continuous line of mourners.

---

* The LT. Michael P. Murphy, USN, Memorial Scholarship Foundation was established by Michael's family to provide college scholarships to senior students at Patchogue-Medford High School. Administered by a seven-member board of directors, the foundation's principal funds are held at the Suffolk Federal Credit Union in certificate of deposits, with the scholarships funded from the interest earned. The foundation was designated as a public charity 501(c)(3) corporation by the Internal Revenue Service on May 4, 2006.

Arrival of the SEALs

When visitation resumed at 7:00 PM, many of Michael's fellow SDVT-1 teammates, led by Lieutenant Commander Mike Marshall, arrived from Pearl City, Hawaii. Among them was Lieutenant Andy Haffele, who gave Dan a heartfelt letter he had written. The SEALs brought with them Michael's uniforms, pictures, and other SEAL mementos, which were displayed near the front of the room on several linen-draped tables. A large SEAL contingent from the Naval Amphibious Base, Little Creek, Virginia, also arrived, as well as Rear Admiral Joseph Maguire, the commander of Naval Special Warfare, and Rear Admiral Joseph D. Kernan, the deputy commander of NSW. During Maguire's short conversation with Dan, he leaned over and said, "Mr. Murphy, I just wanted you to know that I don't think that your son and his men went down easy, because there were Taliban bodies strewn all over the place, eighty-some causalities, blood trails everywhere. This was a pitched battle and they did not go down easy." Although he did not immediately realize the importance of his words at the time, he was extremely proud that Michael had not given up the fight, taking it to the enemy with his last breath—warrior's death, a hero's death.

Representatives from the New York fire and police departments soon arrived, including Engine Co. 53, Ladder Co. 43. As an officer, Michael had chosen Ladder Co. 43, "El Barrio's Bravest," as the symbol of his team. Even though the visitation was scheduled to end at 9:00 PM, the family remained until 10:30 PM and received nearly two thousand mourners. Although exhausted, they were humbled and honored by the unexpected large crowd. After returning home, Dan removed his jacket and was reminded of the letter he had received from Lieutenant Haffele. Despite being both physically and emotionally exhausted, he sat down and began to read the letter. It contained the innermost thoughts of a SEAL who had been spared death and who credited Michael with saving his life. The letter brought Dan comfort.

Visitation: Tuesday, July 12, 2005

Again having arrived early for the 2:00 PM visitation, the Murphy and Duggan families remained near physical and emotional exhaustion. By the time the doors were closed at five that afternoon, the families had again received nearly a thousand mourners. As the family arrived for the final visitation at 7:00 PM, another line of mourners extended the length of the parking lot. Although McElhone closed the doors promptly at ten o'clock, the families remained until the very last visitor had been greeted. Neither Dan nor Maureen remembered even a small percentage of the nearly four thousand people they had received over the previous forty-eight hours, but they were grateful that each of them had thought enough of Michael and his sacrifice to take time out of their busy schedules and wait in line for several hours in the heat and humidity to honor their son.

Family Prayer Service, Wednesday, July 13, 2005

The next day, with every detail of the funeral arranged, the Murphys awoke from their short night of sleep to a torrential rain, which only added to the early summer humidity. Dan arrived early at Maureen's home, followed by the limousine from the Clayton Funeral Home that waited to take the family to yet another round of emotional turmoil that had begun more than two weeks before with events that occurred in the mountains of Afghanistan. Since then, the object of their sorrow had traveled from Landstuhl Regional Medical Center in Germany to Dover Air Base, Delaware, then to Kings Park, New York, and now home to Patchogue, and would soon journey to Calverton National Cemetery, Michael's final duty station and resting place.

After they arrived at the Clayton Funeral Home, a short private prayer service was conducted for the immediate family and the Navy personnel in attendance, and all said their final good-byes. Dan requested that Eddie place on Michael's uniform the Purple Heart medal he had earned in Vietnam; Maureen, a St. Michael/ Navy SEAL keychain along with a key to her home. After the family left for the waiting vehicles, the casket was locked, secured, and covered with an American flag; the blue field at the head over Michael's left shoulder. The Navy honor guard carried Michael slowly to the waiting hearse. As the casket was placed into the hearse, a loud roll of thunder was heard overhead, which lasted until the casket was completely inside. Dan and Maureen just looked at each other. With a police escort, the motorcade made its way across Long Island to Our Lady of Mount Carmel Catholic Church in Patchogue.

Mass of Christian Burial

With North Ocean Boulevard in Patchogue cordoned off, the motorcade arrived at the church, turned into the crescent drive, and stopped at the base of the concrete steps that led up to the massive portico with two oversized doors. Above the doors was a large full-color mosaic of Blessed Virgin and Child. Although the intense rain continued, the curb, the sidewalk, and the steps were lined with New York court services officers, members of the New York City Fire Department, veterans in uniform, and active-duty Navy SEALs who stood at attention. The honor guard removed Michael's flag-draped casket and carried it up the front steps of the church and placed it on the rolling church truck with the family close behind. Inside the gathering space stood a crowd of about three hundred that extended up the balcony stairs on both sides.

Placing of the Funeral Pall

The casket bearers solemnly removed and folded the American flag as the family placed the funeral pall, as well as a crucifix and the family rosary, over the casket. The funeral pall, a white cloth placed on a casket as a reminder of the garment given at baptism as a sign of the life in Christ that Michael had lived, covered the casket and extended almost to the floor.

The sanctuary was filled with a standing-room-only crowd that exceeded the permitted capacity of twelve hundred. Everyone stood silently as the casket was slowly escorted to the front of the church, followed by the family. As the casket passed, members of the military snapped to attention and saluted. The only sounds were the sniffles and quiet sobs throughout the cavernous church, the sounds of emotion broken by the synchronized and haunting crisp sound of the steel taps of the shoes of Navy casket bearers on the marble floor.

At the front of the church, the honor guard turned the casket horizontally and then assumed positions at each end as the crowd was seated by Father Robert O'Connell and Father Robert Coyle, cocelebrants of the Mass. Seated in the left front row were Dan, Maureen, and John, along with Maureen's parents, Frank and Kathleen Jones, and Dan's sister and brother-in-law, John and Maureen Bogenshutz. In the right front row were Michael's cousins Kelly, Colleen, and Cathy, along with Michael's SEAL teammates and Lieutenant Commander Chad Muse and Lieutenant Jeff Widenhofer. As requested, Deacon Maggipinto served as the altar server.

At a Catholic Mass there are three readings, the first from the Old Testament, the second from the New Testament, and the third from the Gospel. The First Reading, given by Lieutenant Commander Muse, was selected from the book of the prophet Daniel (12:1–3). Muse was followed by Lieutenant Widenhofer, who read from 1 John 3:14–16. The Gospel Reading was Luke 23:44–46, 50, 52–53 and 24:1–6a and was read by Father O'Connell. The first eulogy was provided by Robert Lichtenberger, national commander of the Military Order of the Purple Heart (MOPH). He was followed by Lieutenant John Waggoner, Michael's SEAL teammate, who recalled with emotion that he and Michael had made a promise to each other that if anything ever happened to one of them the other would speak at his funeral. He never thought that he would ever have to act on that promise. The final eulogy was given by Father Robert Stegman, who at age eighty-eight served as the national chaplain for the MOPH.

> Maureen, Daniel, John, Heather, Kathleen, Frank, Cathy, Colleen, Kelly, my dear friends in the Lord . . . When his father and mother named him Michael they invited into his life and purpose the mission of St. Michael the Archangel, who led the good angels to overcome the bad angels, led by those who thought they could match God Himself. . . . At times like this we must remember that Michael has not

disappeared—he has just gone ahead of us to prepare a place for us—that he would want us to smile through our tears—knowing that he is alive forever and loving us even more than when he was with us on earth. We can do this if we remember each and every day these three simple things: God loves us, God knows us, and God understands us.

God loves us: That same God who created this whole world with a simple word—that Lord who could turn this world back into nothing—that God loves you, He loved Michael and granted him, as He will welcome you when he calls you home, his eternal peace. He will because He will not stop loving you—no matter if you fail—because God is love.

God knows us: He knows all Michael has done—his love for you, God and country. Michael's love for Him and what he has offered to the Lord—knows what your needs are and will reach out to you in your loss and your love.

God understands us: If I were to ask each one of you how you felt—each one would have a different answer and could say "you don't understand"—but the Lord looks into your hearts and says "I understand." Finally I believe that if Michael would speak to you today he might say something like this,

"To Those I Love and Those Who Love Me,

"When I am gone, release me and let me go, I have so many things to see and do, you mustn't tie yourself to me with tears. Be happy that we had so many years. I gave you my love; you can only guess how much you gave me in happiness. I thank you for the love you each have shown. But, now it's time I traveled on alone. So, grieve a while for me, if grieve you must. Then, let your grief be comforted by trust. It's only for a while that we must be far away, for life goes on. So, if you need me, call and I will come. Though you can't see or touch me, I'll be near.

"And, if you listen with your heart you'll hear, all my love around you soft and clear. And, then, when you must come this way alone, I'll greet you with a smile and welcome you home. . . ."

Replacing the Flag

Following the Mass, Michael was slowly escorted back down the center aisle to the sounds of the recessional hymn, "On Eagle's Wings." The family followed close behind holding hands. Through his tears, Dan looked toward the entrance and saw that the heavy rain continued. After they reached the gathering space, the family removed and folded the funeral pall while the Navy casket bearers replaced the American flag over the casket and secured it into position. As the honor guard reached the top of the stairs, the rain stopped. The honor guard then proceeded and placed Michael's casket in the hearse for his final journey.

Funeral Procession

Having grown to 120 vehicles, the motorcade pulled out escorted by ten uniformed local law enforcement officers on motorcycles, and at the rear of the motorcade were four motorcycles carrying uniformed law enforcement officers from various jurisdictions. As the motorcade proceeded, neighbors as well as strangers with American flags lined both sides of the road. The motorcade stopped momentarily in front of the house on Old Medford Road that Michael had called home for twenty-seven years. On the Long Island Expressway local law enforcement blocked off each exit and provided escort and chase vehicles. On the causeway leading into Calverton, sixteen fire ladder trucks from various Long Island departments lined both sides of the road with their ladders fully extended, forming a protracted arch with a large, thirty- by fifty-foot American flag that hung from the center of each set of ladders. Uniformed personnel at attention saluted as Michael passed, while the gentle breeze moved the flags in a manner that appeared to usher the motorcade into the cemetery.

With a large crowd anticipated, parts of the service open to the public were scheduled in the largest of the public assembly areas near the front of the cemetery, while the small, private graveside service attended by family, close friends, and the U.S. Navy personnel followed the public service. Many members of the local, national, and international news media were present, some intent upon attaining a photo of a grief-stricken family member. In an effort to protect the family from this invasion of privacy, a large contingent of active-duty military surrounded the media pool and greatly limited their field of view.

Military Honors

As the funeral party arrived at the public assembly area, about thirty feet from the funeral coach were twelve of Michael's teammates from SDVT-1, six as honorary pallbearers and six as casket bearers. The seven-man firing party stood at attention in the distance but remained visible to the family. As the funeral coach came into view, the six pallbearers and six casket bearers held their salute until the coach had stopped. The driver opened the rear door and slowly pulled Michael's flag-draped casket partway out. As Father Coyle took his position on the curb at the head of the pallbearers, the Murphy and Duggan families exited their vehicles, while the officer in charge ordered the pallbearers into position at the rear of the funeral coach. As the pallbearers removed Michael's casket from the funeral coach, the firing detail was ordered to present arms.

Father Coyle, followed by the officer in charge, led the way to the assembly area. As the casket passed through the pallbearer ranks, each turned and followed.

Directly behind the pallbearers were the Murphy and Duggan families, who were escorted to their seats under two large green canopies.

As the casket bearers placed the casket on the bier, Father Coyle stood at the head of the casket. Captain Bisset stood to his right. After the casket was properly positioned, all uniformed military personnel dropped their salute as the firing detail was ordered to order arms, then to parade rest. The pallbearers stood directly to the left of the casket and faced the Murphy family, while the casket bearers, in unison, raised the flag from the casket, held it waist high and stretched taut over the casket, and remained motionless throughout the remainder of the service. At the conclusion of the invocation by Father Coyle, Rear Admiral Maguire and Captain Pete Van Hooser, a senior East Coast naval officer holding the honorary rank of commodore, presented the Murphy family with two medals that Michael had earned as a result of his service in Afghanistan. First came the Silver Star, with the following citation:

The President of the United States takes pride in presenting the SILVER STAR MEDAL   posthumously to
LIEUTENANT MICHAEL P. MURPHY
UNITED STATES NAVY
For service set forth in the following

CITATION:
For conspicuous gallantry and intrepidity in action against the enemy while serving as part of a Special Reconnaissance element with Naval Special Warfare Task Unit, Afghanistan, from 27 to 28 June 2005. In his role of Assistant Officer in Charge of Alfa Platoon and the Reconnaissance and Surveillance ground element commander for the mission, Lieutenant Murphy demonstrated extraordinary heroism in the face of grave danger in the vicinity of Asadabad, Kunar Province, Afghanistan. Operating in the middle of an enemy-controlled area, in extremely rugged terrain, his Special Reconnaissance element was tasked with locating a high-level Anti-Coalition Militia leader, in support of a follow-on direct action mission to capture or destroy the leader and disrupt enemy activity. On 28 June 2005, the element was spotted by Anti-Coalition Militia sympathizers, who immediately revealed their position to the militia fighters. As a result, the element directly encountered the enemy. Demonstrating exceptional resolve and fully understanding the situation, Lieutenant Murphy's element bravely engaged the militia, who held both a numerical and positional advantage. The ensuing firefight resulted in numerous enemy personnel killed, with several of the Navy members suffering causalities. Ignoring his injuries and demonstrating exceptional composure, Lieutenant Murphy continued to attack the enemy, eliminating additional militia fighters, until he was mortally wounded by enemy fire. A champion of freedom, Lieutenant Murphy will be remembered for his sacrifice in the continuing Global War on Terrorism. By his bold leadership, exceptional professionalism, and loyal devotion to duty, Lieutenant Murphy reflected great credit upon himself and upheld the highest traditions of the United States Naval Service.

The Silver Star is the third-highest military decoration that can be awarded to a member of any branch of the United States armed forces for valor in the face of the enemy awarded upon recommendation by a general or flag officer.

Next, the Purple Heart, with the following citation:

THE UNITED STATES OF AMERICA
TO ALL WHO SHALL SEE THESE PRESENTS, GREETINGS:
THIS IS TO CERTIFY THAT THE PRESIDENT OF
THE UNITED STATES OF AMERICA
HAS AWARDED THE
PURPLE HEART
(Posthumously)
ESTABLISHED BY GENERAL GEORGE WASHINGTON
AT NEWBURGH, NEW YORK,
AUGUST 7, 1782 TO
LIEUTENANT MICHAEL P. MURPHY
UNITED STATES NAVY
FOR WOUNDS RECEIVED IN ACTION
ON 28 JUNE 2005

The Purple Heart, this nation's oldest military award, is awarded to any member of the military who is wounded or killed by direct enemy action. Not requiring a recommendation, the wounded or deceased is entitled to it by his action in combat.

Following the presentations, Father Coyle read from Psalms 129–130, followed by St. John 11, and the invitation to the Lord's Prayer. As Father Coyle stepped back from the casket, the firing party was ordered to attention and all military personnel in uniform saluted. In perfect unison, the seven-man firing party fired three volleys in a twenty-one-gun salute. Although the loud crack of the rifle volleys startled those who had gathered, the military personnel at attention did not move. After the final volley, as the echo and the smoke faded, the firing party was ordered to present arms, while in the distance a single bugler began the haunting notes of "Taps."

The Meaning of a Folded Flag

At the conclusion of "Taps," the honor guard began folding Michael's burial flag. The lower striped section was folded over and the folded edge was folded over again to meet the open edge. A triangular fold was then started by bringing the striped corner of the folded edge to the open edge. The first triangular fold symbolized life. The outer point was turned inward so that it was parallel with the open edge, forming the second triangle, symbolic of our belief in eternal life. The third fold was made in honor of our veterans who gave their lives in the defense of our country. The fourth fold represented our weaker human nature. The fifth fold was a tribute to our country, while the sixth stood for where the people's hearts lie—it is with our hearts that we pledge our allegiance to the flag of the United States. The seventh fold was a tribute to our armed forces. The eighth fold symbolized the tribute to Christ, who entered into the valley of the shadow of death on our behalf, that we might have eternal life. Fold nine was a tribute to all women and mothers, for it was through their faith, love, and loyalty that the character of those who have made this country great has been shaped. The tenth fold was a tribute to our fathers, for they too have given their sons and daughters in defense of their country. The eleventh fold was symbolic of King David and King Solomon's seal, which glorified the God of Abraham. Fold twelve symbolized eternal life, glorifying in Christians' eyes the Trinity. The thirteenth and last fold, with the stars facing upward, was to remind us of our nation's motto, "In God We Trust."

After the flag was folded, Master Chief Petty Officer Gary Lee delivered three shell casings from the twenty-one-gun salute to the officer in charge, who placed them inside the flag and tucked the end inside the fold. The folded flag looked like a cocked hat, which reminds us of those who served under General George Washington, and under Captain John Paul Jones.

After the folding of the flag, the clouds parted and a bright ray of sunshine reflected off Michael's casket. Dan and Maureen looked at each other and managed a smile through their tears.

On Behalf of the President of the United States . . .

The honor guard team leader delivered the folded flag to Lee. He then turned and approached Captain Bisset, who stood with Father Coyle and Rear Admiral Maguire. Lee cradled the flag with left hand over right and with the stripes facing toward the sky. He then sharply flipped the flag, right hand over left, with the blue field facing toward the sky and remained motionless. Bisset stepped forward, slowly saluted, and accepted the flag, right hand over left. Lee stepped back, saluted, turned, and resumed his position. Bisset slowly walked over to the Murphy family.

Maureen stood with John to her left and Dan stood to her right under the large green canopy. Captain Bisset who shared an emotional closeness with the Murphy family, was relieved to see that Maureen wore dark glasses that eliminated direct eye contact.

"Maureen, on behalf of the president of the United States and the secretary of the navy, please accept this flag as a symbol of your son Michael's outstanding and faithful service to his country and the United States Navy." With a whisper-quiet response of "Thank you," she accepted the flag and clutched it to her breast, as a mother would hold her infant. Bisset saluted, turned sharply, and returned to his position.

Next, SEALs Jim Quattromani, Jerry Caldwell, and James Westin of SDVT-1 approached Heather, who was dressed in black, ashen-faced, and physically supported by her mother, Lynda, and her sister Brianne. With all three at full attention, Quattromani, who was in the center, held the flag and dropped to his right knee and looked into Heather's tear-filled eyes. "Heather, on behalf of the president of the United States and the secretary of the navy, please accept this flag as a symbol of your fiancé Michael's outstanding and faithful service to his country and the United States Navy."

Accepting the folded flag, Heather exploded in an agonizing cry that released a flood of tears from many of the mourners. As her tears flowed, they rolled down her face and onto the flag she clutched to her abdomen.

The SEALs then formed a line on each side of the casket and removed their Tridents, the golden insignia of a Navy SEAL. Then, one at a time, each man approached the casket, saluted, and laid his Trident on the top of the casket, again saluted, then stepped back into formation. As Lieutenant Haffele placed his Trident on Michael's casket, Dan remembered the words in Haffele's letter. This solemn ceremony proceeded for nearly twenty minutes. In all, thirty golden SEAL Tridents rested atop Michael's casket. Father Coyle then resumed his position at the head of the casket and delivered the Committal. and concluded the public service with the Benediction.

Home . . . Finally

At the conclusion of the public ceremony and after the crowd had dispersed, Michael's personal friends Jimmie and Owen O'Callaghan, James Emmerich, and Jay Keenan, along with Lieutenant Commander Muse and Lieutenant Widenhofer, returned Michael's casket to the waiting hearse for the short ride to his final resting place for an intimate graveside ceremony to celebrate an earthly life that had been all too short, but very well lived.

As the hearse disappeared behind the cover of a small grove of trees, Eddie McElhone asked the driver to stop. While the driver watched, Eddie unlocked and opened the casket and placed the SEAL tridents around Michael's torso before proceeding to the gravesite.

After the brief graveside ceremony, family, friends, and a "widowed" fiancée slowly walked away with heads bowed as tears flowed down their faces. Several turned back to look at Michael's casket several times before they reached their cars; each time the sun's bright light reflected off the casket.

In a memorable moment, as Widenhofer and his wife, Jennifer, walked back toward the car, both looked back at the gravesite and watched as Jim Quattromani, up until that moment a pillar of strength and courage for the Murphy and Duggan families, approached Michael's casket. Although not close enough to see his face, they saw Jim gently place both his hands on Michael's casket, then lower his head as his body trembled uncontrollably for several minutes. They both watched in silence at the depth of the unbreakable bond of the warrior culture.

After everyone had left the area, Eddie approached the casket. Having worked tirelessly over the past several days and unable to properly grieve for a family hero—a national hero—he now took his own personal moment.

A Final Message from Michael

As Dan, Maureen, Karen, and Kristen walked back to their car, Maureen heard her cell phone ring. Her first instinct was to ignore it until later, but something prompted her to take it from her purse. Her cell phone signaled she had received a text message. She pushed the button to retrieve the message, and the words "Momma, home safe and sound. Mike" appeared on the screen. In shock, she dropped the phone, gasped, and covered her mouth. Maureen then picked up the phone and just stared at the message screen for several seconds before handing the phone to Dan. They looked at each other and managed a smile through their tears.

It had become Michael's practice to call or text message his parents whenever he left New York to let them know that he had arrived safely at his destination. Both Dan and Maureen remembered that they had not received a message after Michael's arrival back in Hawaii the previous March for what had turned out to be his last deployment. Now, apparently, Maureen had received that message. These devout Catholic parents, who believe that everything happens for a reason, felt sure that this was Michael's way of telling them that he had arrived at his eternal home, safe and sound.

On Permanent Station

As Eddie concluded his prayers, he checked the casket for the final time and watched as he lowered it into the concrete vault below. United States Navy SEAL Lieutenant Michael P. Murphy was now at his earthly rest. A rest well earned and deserved, but as a Navy SEAL, he remains on permanent station "On point" in Section 67, Site 3710 in Calverton National Cemetery, along with 187,000 more of this nation's military heroes.

CHAPTER FOUR

Seeds of Greatness

There is no cure for birth and death, save to enjoy the interval.

—GEORGE SANTAYANA, quoted at QuotationsBook,
www.quotationsbook.com/quote/10038 (accessed July 14, 2008)

Daniel James Murphy, a successful young Suffolk County prosecuting attorney and decorated Vietnam War combat veteran, and Maureen Theresa Jones were married on April 12, 1975, in the Saint Francis DeSales Catholic Church in Patchogue. Located fifty-five miles east of Manhattan, on the South Shore of Long Island, New York, Patchogue is a predominately white, Catholic, blue-collar, working-class village of 12,000 descendants of primarily Italian, German, and—like Dan's and Maureen's parents—Irish immigrants.

Dan and Maureen's first child, described by the doctor as a "beautiful bald baby boy," was born on May 7, 1976, and named Michael Patrick, after the archangel Michael, one of the principal fifty angels and viewed as the field commander of the Army of God. Michael appears in the book of Daniel as one who comes to Gabriel's aid as the advocate of Israel and a "great prince who stands up for the children. . . ."

Dan and Maureen took Michael home to their two-bedroom, second-story apartment in Holtsville, New York, on Long Island, where Charlie, their very protective black, flat-coat retriever, awaited their arrival. Charlie became Michael's constant companion over the next several years and kept a watchful and protective eye on him.

It became very clear when he was a toddler that Michael loved the water. At a backyard cookout at Dan's parents' home, Maureen saw Michael, not even two years old, climbing the stairs of the four-foot-high swimming pool. She took off to grab him, but just as she reached the ladder, he jumped into the water. Frantic, Maureen climbed to the top and saw Michael underwater with a big smile on his face. She reached down and pulled him out. Trying not to scare him, she told him that he was not permitted in the water without his inflatable life jacket. As Maureen turned to retrieve the jacket, Michael jumped back into the pool, surfaced, and sloshed his way to the side with a big grin on his face.

In December 1978, two-year-old Michael and his family moved into their newly built house on Old Medford Avenue. On their first day in their new house, Maureen took Michael upstairs and showed him his room. That evening, when Maureen was putting Michael to bed, he pointed to his diapers and said, "Not these, Mommy, not these. I'm a big boy." Michael never wore diapers after that— and never had an "accident."

The following summer in June, while at the home of their next-door neighbors, Ralph and Kathie Belmonte, Michael bolted for the large in-ground swimming pool and jumped in before Dan could get to him. By the time Dan jumped in, Michael had surfaced and got to the other side of the pool using a rudimentary swimming motion. When Dan lifted him out of the pool, Michael turned around, raised his arms into the air, and flashed a large grin.

Maureen frequently took him to the nearby Holtsville public pool and allowed him to frolic around in the baby pool. Although initially satisfied, he soon turned his attention to the larger pool. With his life jacket in place, Maureen took Michael into the pool with her, much to his delight.

One day in the summer of 1979, Maureen and Michael were enjoying a walk in the park in Holtsville when they came upon the town's diving pool. Michael bolted and began climbing the twelve-foot ladder. The lifeguard on duty frantically blew his whistle and began yelling at Michael to get down.

Hurriedly, Maureen climbed the ladder and talked calmly to Michael, hoping to catch up to him before he fell. But Michael, who was very quick, reached the top of the ladder and, without the slightest evidence of fear, ran out onto the board before she could reach him. Ignoring his mother's warnings, Michael jumped off the diving board, which immediately sent the lifeguard into the water. As Michael surfaced he again began his own particular swimming motion to the side of the pool. Unassisted, he reached the side, where the lifeguard lifted him out of the water. Michael stood proudly with a big smile on his face. Frightened by the experience, Maureen took Michael home, telling him, "We won't be doing that anymore."

Michael was reared in a loving home by parents with a strong moral clarity and a directed sense of purpose. With a father who served as a local prosecuting attorney and extended family members who served as police officers, firefighters, and other public servants, Michael learned early the virtue of sacrifice and selfless service to others.

As a toddler, Michael's favorite book was Watty Piper's *The Little Engine That Could*, a children's story used to teach the value of optimism and hard work. Michael knew the story by heart, and would slowly stride from room to room acting like a train engine, saying, "I think I can, I think I can, I think I can." After making the rounds through every room, he began running as fast as he could, saying, "I thought I could, I thought I could, I thought I could." The lessons learned from this story carried Michael through some of the most challenging times in his life.

Despite their best efforts, the young parents were frequent visitors to their doctor's office and the local emergency room to have their active and fearless child treated for cuts and other accidental injuries. After several visits for stitches, Maureen asked, "Why is it always my kid?" Dan later related, "Thank God I was a prosecutor, because I am sure otherwise they would have thought this kid was being abused."

When Michael was age three, Dan's youngest brother Brian was in the back-yard chopping wood. Brian was the "black sheep" of Dan's family. He was gregar-ious, but lacked considered judgment when it came to mature decision making regarding employment, his wife, and his two children. Maureen asked Michael to go to the edge of the patio and tell his uncle that lunch was ready. Instead of stop-ping at the edge of the patio, Michael went up to Brian, who didn't notice him and accidently hit him with the butt of the ax and knocked him down, leaving a large, heavily bleeding gash above his right eye. Brian carried him into the house.

When Maureen saw the gaping wound, she panicked, and excused herself to regain her composure as her sister tended to Michael. Maureen said, "I never pan-icked when it is someone else's kid, but when it is mine, I just went to pieces." Michael saw his mother crying and began wiping the blood from his face, saying, "It's OK, Mommy, it's OK, it doesn't hurt. See, Mommy, it doesn't hurt." She was overcome with emotion at Michael's sensitivity. Because the large, gaping wound obviously needing sutures, they made yet another trip to the hospital in nearby Smithtown.

During the summer of 1982, Michael would sneak out of the house early on Sunday mornings while his parents slept. He and Charlie would walk next door to visit the Belmontes, who always had their Sunday breakfast on the back patio. As Michael approached the Belmontes, he would say, "My mommy and daddy won't feed me breakfast. Can I have one of your bagels?" As they laughed, they pulled out a chair for him and served him a toasted bagel with lots of butter and a glass of milk, Michael's favorite. This soon became a ritual for young Michael throughout the summer, and one that the Belmontes soon joyfully came to expect. After a cou-ple of weeks, the Belmontes told Dan and Maureen of Michael's Sunday morning ritual. Although embarrassed, his parents got a big laugh at the tale.

Canaan Elementary School

Excelling in all of his academic subjects, Michael was an outgoing and likable student. He was a voracious reader, and would often read the same book several times—a practice he never outgrew.

A natural athlete, Michael played soccer in the first and second grade. At age six, he began playing T-ball with Dan as his coach. Two years of "B" ball and three years of "A" ball followed. In the fifth grade, he earned the coveted white belt that signified his position as a member of the Safety Patrol.

Dan's friend Tony Viggiano, who was connected with the local Sachem Athletic Club, asked Dan about enrolling Michael to play football. When asked, Michael jumped at the opportunity. At Tony's insistence, Dan agreed to be the team's coach, although he readily admitted he knew nothing about coaching football. Tony insisted that all Dan needed to do was to design a few simple plays and things would be fine.

After a few practices and several scrimmages against other teams, Michael displayed genuine athletic ability, speed, and throwing accuracy, and became the starting quarterback for the Sachem Wolf Pack in the Sachem Youth Football Club, sponsored by the Suffolk County Police Athletic League. On the very first play from scrimmage of the first game, Michael dropped back to pass the ball and was grabbed by the face mask and thrown to the ground. Witnessing the play, Dan immediately ran onto the field. Dan saw the referee throw his flag and approached him, saying, "Good, you saw that!" The referee told Dan that the penalty was against him, because the coach was not permitted to run onto the field. Michael ran over to his father and said, "Dad, you're not supposed to be out on the field. I'm OK." Dan and Michael laughed as the referee walked off the fifteen-yard penalty.

Of course, this being New York, street hockey was another of Michael's favorite sports, frequently and spontaneously organized by his neighborhood friends in any empty driveway or parking lot, an activity that he would continue into his middle-school years.

One evening, when Dan believed Michael was asleep, he began working on a gruesome murder case that he was trying. He laid out some large and very graphic color photos of the case and was absorbed in reviewing them. Suddenly Dan heard Michael ask, "Hey, Dad, is that chicken?" Dan immediately tried to cover the pictures with a newspaper. However, after a few seconds, Michael realized what the pictures were, turned very pale, and immediately vomited all over the pictures. Feeling guilty, Dan apologized and tried to calm Michael by talking with him about why he had the pictures and telling him that he was trying to convict the "bad guys who did such a terrible thing to that poor man."

During the summer of 1983, when he was seven, Michael was out in the front yard playing with some friends when his mother heard the loud screeching of a car hitting its brakes. Terrified, Maureen ran outside and saw Michael lying in the road about five feet in front of the stopped car. As Maureen screamed and ran for the road, Michael slowly got up clutching a small dog, which had escaped without a scratch. The driver, visibly shaken, got out of the car, and as she and Maureen reached Michael, they saw that he was no worse for wear other than a few abrasions on his arms, legs, and forehead. Frantically they asked him what he was doing. "This little dog ran into the street and was about to get run over, so I ran out and grabbed him." Later that evening at the dinner table, Michael admitted, "It was pretty scary. All I could see was those big black tires coming right for my head."

Michael was nurtured in an extended family of dedicated public servants and also benefited by his mother's acute sense of compassion toward others. Even at a young age he began to take a keen interest in protecting and helping other people, especially those he viewed as weak or being taken advantage of.

Dan's brother Brian always seemed to be down on his luck and frequently called to ask Dan for money to help his wife and infant daughter. Although he frequently wasted the money on beer and cigarettes, Dan always provided him with $20 to $40. Michael was now old enough to understand his uncle's wayward habits and their consequences.

One day, after his uncle had left the Murphy home with yet another $40 of his father's hard-earned money, Michael asked Dan why he continued to give away money when he knew that Brian would probably "just blow it." Dan explained that while he would indeed probably just blow it, Brian was his brother, and he would never turn away someone who genuinely needed help, especially family.

Young Michael never forgot that conversation, and by the time he left Canaan, he had internalized the school motto: "With the courage of a lion, always do the right thing." This motto was a frequent motivator throughout his life.

Saxton Middle School

Michael continued to clearly demonstrate his academic excellence throughout his middle-school years. It was during that time that his parents also began to see the development of his natural-born leadership qualities, his maturity, and his sensitivity toward others. Maureen later recalled that when she arrived for her first parent-teacher conference with Michael's new sixth-grade teacher, Mr. Schwab, he said, "Michael Murphy, yes. A great young man. Listen, I've been teaching for nearly thirty-five years, and this kid is really something. Mark my words, he is going to make his mark someday."

During middle school, Michael continued to play football and organized baseball, having moved to the "major leagues" with the bases now ninety feet apart instead of the previous sixty feet. At first Maureen and Dan worried that Michael's running ability had markedly decreased until they learned that the distance between bases had been increased.

Michael began to internalize his father's frequent mantra that "adversity builds character." In fact, Maureen remembered that on one particular occasion when

Michael had suffered yet another injury that required medical treatment, he said, "Mom, I've had enough character building. I would like for things to go right for a change."

Through his father's career as a prosecuting attorney, Michael was able to see both the good and bad in people, and that even "bad" people can do good things while "good" people do bad things. One case that really affected young Michael involved a young man his father was prosecuting for a string of burglaries. Dan had a sense that this was indeed a case of a good person who got caught up in a bad situation, and that if given the opportunity, the young man would make amends and live a good, honest life.

Although the young man clearly could have received a jail sentence, Dan explained to Michael why he was going to recommend probation, community service, and restitution. Several years later the young man came to the Murphy home and thanked Dan for his understanding and leniency. He said that he had opened his own shoe-repair business in a nearby town and was a successful businessman, and offered to provide free shoe-repair service for the family. That episode stuck with Michael. He subsequently and inherently believed the best in people and always gave them the benefit of any doubt.

On occasion Michael accompanied his father to work, where he was able to observe criminal court proceedings firsthand. One particular day, he watched his father argue before the United States District Court for the Eastern District of New York. After the long day in court, Michael asked his father if he had won or lost. Dan responded, "Michael, it's not winning or losing so much as justice being served and the truth being decided." That answer stayed with Michael and later appeared on his law school applications.

In another instance, young Michael and his friend Paul received the results of a major examination. Young Paul was very proud of his score and told Maureen that he had received a 92. Maureen turned to Michael and asked how he had done. Michael answered, "Oh, I did OK." Later that evening at dinner, the topic of school was discussed, and Maureen again asked Michael his score on the test. Michael responded that he had received a 96. When Maureen asked him why he did not mention his score when she had asked earlier, Michael responded, "Mom, Paul was so excited about his 92, telling him my score would have just thrown cold water on him, so I didn't say anything. It was not that important." Dan and Maureen just looked at each other and realized that Michael was much more mature than either of them were when they were his age.

CHAPTER FIVE

"The Protector"

The only correct actions are those that demand no explanation and no apology.

—RED AUERBACH, quoted at Good Fortunes,
www.goodfortunes.com/v/quote/sorry.html
(accessed March 5, 2008)

A t age ten, Michael's protective instincts developed further with the birth of his younger brother, John. He was very excited when John was born, and he immediately took on the role of protective big brother.

Because his father was politically active, young Michael was frequently around adults in a variety of business, political, and social settings. When Michael was twelve, the Murphy family took a summer vacation to Hersheypark in Hershey, Pennsylvania. At that time, Michael was very close to his cousin Tara Reidy, the daughter of Dan's sister Gerri. Tara went along and stayed with them at the exclusive Hotel Hershey. Unaccustomed to large, expensive hotels, Tara was apprehensive. On their first day, the family went to dinner. All of the various forks, other silverware, and folded napkins made Tara quite anxious. She said she couldn't eat because she didn't know what to do with all the utensils. Michael leaned over and said, "Tara, don't worry about it. You're never going to see these people again; use whatever fork you want. It really doesn't matter." Tara looked anxiously at Michael, who just smiled and nodded his head. Tara returned the smile and became perfectly at ease. After that, Tara and Michael developed a close bond that remained for the rest of his life.

While in the eighth grade, Michael saw a group of boys taunting a special-education child and trying to push him into a locker. Michael interceded and got involved in a fight with several of the bullies. After teachers broke up the fight, the principal of the school called Maureen and said, "Mrs. Murphy, I'm calling not to get Michael into trouble, but I am required to call because the incident happened." He explained that Michael had been involved in a fight defending a special-education child. While Michael's parents did not condone fighting, both Dan and Maureen could not have been prouder of their son. After this incident, Michael garnered the nickname "the Protector." The following year, while taking a shortcut home through a small wooded area, Michael came upon a group of students tormenting a homeless man who had been collecting bottles and cans in a plastic bag. Michael yelled for the other kids to stop. One of them turned toward him and said, "Aw, Murphy, are you going to start?"

Michael replied, "No, I'm not going to start, but you're gonna stop."

The students left grumbling. Michael approached the man, who was cowering near a tree, and said, "It's OK. Here, let me help you." Michael picked up all of the cans and bottles the boys had thrown and put them back into the large plastic bag. As Michael started toward the man to give him the bag, he began shaking and covered himself. Sensing his fear, Michael stopped and set the bag down and said, "It's OK. No one is going to bother you. I'm leaving. Your bag is right here when you want it." When Michael was a safe distance away, the man slowly got up and picked up his bag. Michael turned around and just smiled at the man and waved.

Dan and Michael spent many hours together doing yard work and playing sports. Dan occasionally talked about his military service in Vietnam. He explained to Michael the misfortunes of the enlisted troops on the ground in Vietnam, many of whom were killed as the result of the actions of incompetent or overzealous officers with little or no combat experience. He was adamantly opposed to his son serving in the military—so much so that he repeatedly told Michael that he would disown him if he ever enlisted in the armed forces.

During a memorable game in his last season in the "major leagues," which was also his last year of middle school, Michael came to the plate with one runner on base and his team down by one run. On the second pitch, Michael hit a home run to win the game. As he rounded the bases and returned to the dugout, everyone patted him on the back and said that he won the game. Taught by his father that a leader is only as good as his team, Michael was quick to point out, "Not really, guys. I only scored one run, and the rest of you scored the others. That's what allowed us to win the game, not me."

Michael remembered this invaluable advice from his father: "When you are the leader, when you are out front, someone will always criticize and try and find fault. As the leader, it is your job to lead—your job to make decisions." As the starting quarterback and the team captain for the Sachem Wolf Pack for four years, Michael became the unquestioned leader of his team. While not always correct, he never hesitated to lead, never hesitated to make a decision, and never abdicated his role as the leader.

Patchogue-Medford High School

In 1991 Michael entered Patchogue-Medford High School as an honor student and took a full college preparatory course load. Among his small group of friends, Paul Viggiano, Pete Lopez, and Tim Scott were his best friends. With his reputation as the Protector preceding him, Michael was the target of the occasional snide comment, but no one challenged him.

A couple of traumatic incidents that involved friends and acquaintances had a major impact on Michael. First, Michael's girlfriend Adrienne's younger brother was killed while riding his bicycle in the neighborhood. Later, a young girl who frequently sat with Michael at the lunch table was hit by a car and killed one evening while crossing the highway.

During the summer of Michael's junior year, in 1993, his uncle Billy Jones, Maureen's younger brother, lost his battle with cancer and left his wife and three daughters. Their mother was incapable of caring for them, and the three girls, Cathy, Colleen, and Kelly, faced being placed in foster care. This was unacceptable to both Dan and Maureen, so the three girls came to live with the Murphys.

As Maureen tried to set up sleeping arrangements, Michael approached her and insisted, "Mom, I have the biggest room. Put their girls in my room and I'll move to the sewing room. It's no big deal." With that Michael moved to the sewing room, the smallest in the house, without complaint. Naturally, the addition of three additional children in the house created a stressful environment until everyone got used to living under the same roof and to each other's personalities.

During the summers of both his junior and senior years, Michael served as an intern in the Supreme Court of New York. Here he had the opportunity to research past cases for attorneys and the court, as well as draft preliminary decisions, and having his work reviewed and critiqued by both attorneys and the court. He learned the importance of accuracy and strict attention to detail. Throughout high school, Michael was regularly on the Honor Roll and selected for the National Honor Society his junior year. Michael spent his junior year taking advanced-placement classes that resulted in his taking only two courses his senior year. His cousin Kristen Bogenshutz was two years behind Michael in high school and described him as "always humble. He was talented in every sport he played, and was considered a 'team player,' was dedicated, motivated, and put his team interests before his own personal pursuits. Mike did what was best for all involved, rather than choose to put himself in the spotlight. He was brighter than anyone knew, more athletic than we considered, more driven than we could have imagined. He was funny, had a sharp wit, intelligent sense of humor, and was always ready for a prank, but fiercely loyal to those he loved."

He spent a lot of time on college applications to schools both in New York and neighboring states. Graduating with academic honors in 1994, and accepted at several colleges, Michael chose Penn State University for three specific reasons: it was away from home but within driving distance, it had an excellent academic reputation, and it was a public school with a lighter tuition cost for him and his parents.

Having graduated from high school, Michael's first "real" job was with the Brookhaven parks department picking up litter and doing general maintenance. He also acquired basic aquatic and lifeguarding skills and began working as a lifeguard at several area pools and beaches, including Lake Ronkonkoma. While he mastered his lifesaving skills, he frequently enlisted the help of his cousins Kelly, Colleen, and Cathy, dragging them across the pool while practicing his water-rescue skills. Here he met Jay Keenan, the O'Callaghan's, Jimmy Emmerich, and others with whom he became lifelong friends.

When Kelly turned sixteen and was just sitting around the house, Michael walked up to her, dropped a Department of Motor Vehicles (DMV) manual into her lap, and said, "Read this." The next day he took her to the DMV, where she passed her written test and received her temporary permit. Michael exhibited great patience and composure and made sure that she was proficient and obtained her license.

Penn State University

Michael entered Penn State University (PSU) in the fall of 1994 with advanced academic placement. He finished the first semester with a respectable 3.02 grade point average (GPA), and become involved with the intramural football and ice hockey teams.

His 1995 spring semester GPA of 3.69 resulted in his first appearance on the dean's list, a feat he accomplished five more times, including every semester his junior and senior years. At PSU he led both of his intramural teams to championships while serving as captain.

At some point between his sophomore and junior years, Michael decided to pursue a career in the military. During a family dinner at the Cull House restaurant in Sayville, New York, Michael told his father and brother that he was seriously considering a career in the Marines. John believed Michael was kidding and did not take him seriously, nor did his father, who believed Michael was just expressing his newfound freedom of being in college. On the five-hour drive between PSU and Patchogue, Dan and Michael had lengthy talks about life, school, career, and relationships that strengthened the bond between father and son. It was during the long drives in his junior year that Michael talked about his desire to join the military—only now interested in the Navy. The first time Michael brought the subject up, Dan was so startled that he nearly ran off the road.

In an attempt to get his son back to a "correct" way of thinking, he said, "Michael, I thought you wanted to go law school and be a lawyer." After some hesitation Michael admitted to his reluctance in becoming a lawyer. He argued that there was an overabundance of lawyers and, as a result, the standards of getting in to law school were exceedingly high.

Dan insisted, "Michael, I told you that I would disown you if you ever went into the military." Although concerned, Dan was comforted by the thought that Michael was only in his junior year and would probably change his mind and appreciate the potential of a law career. Knowing his father's concern, Michael avoided any further conversation regarding the Navy. While this curbed Michael's talk of a military career, it did not lessen his interest.

During Michael's senior year, he became open and insistent about his desire to become a Navy SEAL, and it became a frequent topic of conversation on the long trips to PSU. Dan, now having backed off his threat to disown Michael, tried to impress upon him that he did not need the service to complete his character. He emphasized that the SEALs were called upon to perform the most arduous and dangerous missions, many of them covert. Due to the nature of their missions, many times they were left to their own devices with little or no support. Dan did not want a military life for his son; he was adamant that Michael forget about a military career and follow in his footsteps and pursue a lucrative law career.

Dan believed that military service was important for young men who had lost their way and needed regimented guidance or a heavy dose of discipline to get them on the straight and narrow. Michael needed neither, and Dan believed that he was wasting his time and talents forgoing a law career and pursuing the military. While Michael agreed that his father made several good arguments, his mind was made up. He would pursue Officer Candidate School (OCS) and Basic Underwater Demolition/SEAL (BUD/S) training upon graduation. If those two avenues did not materialize, he could always go to law school.

In early 1998, during his senior year and after having done well on his LSAT examination, Michael applied to numerous prestigious law schools, including Columbia, St. John's, Fordham, New York University (NYU), the University of Tennessee, Boston University, and Cornell. In April and May letters of both acceptance and rejection came back. Accepted into St. John's, the University of Tennessee, and Fordham, Michael was both disappointed and pleased: disappointed at not being accepted into NYU, but pleased because the letters strengthened his resolve to join the SEALs as a Navy officer. He continued doing extensive research on the SEALs and the Navy's Officer Candidate School.

CHAPTER SIX

Prep Schools for SEALs

Unless a man has trained himself for his chance, the chance will only make him look ridiculous.

—WILLIAM MATTHEWS, quoted at Famous Quotes & Authors,
www.famousquotesandauthors.com/authors/william_matthews_
quotes.html (accessed December 21, 2009)

I n early November 1997, during his senior year at Penn State University, Michael began seriously researching the Navy SEALs, including admission requirements, training, and selection process. During his research he learned of a former SEAL captain who served as the senior Navy representative and facility instructor at the U.S. Army War College in Carlisle, Pennsylvania, just eighty miles from PSU. Ryan J. McCombie had more than twenty-six years of service, having previously served as the commanding officer of SEAL Team Two, perhaps the nation's most elite group of special warriors. McCombie had spent most of his naval career in special operations and was highly decorated. He had received more than two dozen significant medals and awards, including the Bronze Star Medal with V device, which was awarded for valor, a Legion of Merit, and two Defense Superior Service Medals, as well as awards from the French and Vietnamese governments.

With the SEALs, McCombie trained and served with commandos from all over the world. He was the first American to complete the training for French marine special operators and served a two-year tour with the elite Commando Hubert. He served as operations officer of the highly regarded Red Cell Team, a U.S. special operations team essentially comprised of Navy SEALs that was the subject of much media reporting for its innovative and highly effective counterterrorist and antiterrorist missions. Because of his knowledge of French and special operations, McCombie was selected to be the first military attaché to the U.S. embassy in Brazzaville, Congo. Following that billet, he commanded SEAL Team Two from 1985 to 1987, and then served in high-level positions at the Defense Intelligence Agency in Washington, D.C.

After several requests, Michael was granted an appointment to meet with Captain McCombie at his home. McCombie seldom saw students or anyone there. He had long ago tired of those who were simply curious about the SEALs, as opposed to those with the determination and work ethic to become one. When Michael arrived at the house, he was directed to the backyard, where he found McCombie chopping wood. He stopped a few feet away as McCombie split a log with a single swing of his ax. Without looking up, McCombie said, "So, you are interested in talking about the SEALs?"

Michael responded, "No sir, I want to be a Navy SEAL. There's a difference."

Saying nothing, Captain McCombie looked at Michael from head to toe for several seconds, then continued chopping wood.

"We can talk when I am finished."

As he looked around, Michael noticed several big stacks of wood and another ax leaning against one of the stacks. He took off his jacket and tossed it on top of one of the piles, picked up the ax, and began chopping beside McCombie. Over the next several hours, the two exchanged some casual conversation as they worked. By midafternoon the work was finished.

McCombie invited Michael onto his back porch, where they talked for the next two hours. Michael laid out his background and discussed his studies and activities. McCombie learned that Michael was not only serious about becoming a Navy SEAL, but also a Navy SEAL officer. Michael explained that following graduation, he would enlist with the condition that he was accepted into Officer Candidate School (OCS) and Basic Underwater Demolition/SEAL (BUD/S) training.

Having dealt with many wannabes over the years, McCombie was skeptical regarding Michael's ambitious agenda; however, by the time their conversation ended, he was impressed with every aspect of the young man. As Michael was getting ready to leave, McCombie told him to contact Captain Andrew Bisset, the Recruiting District Assistance Council (RDAC) district coordinator in Stamford, Connecticut, who coordinated a SEAL training and mentorship program each month at the United States Merchant Marine Academy (USMMA) in Kings Point, New York.

That night McCombie telephoned Bisset and hold him about his meeting with Michael, including his obvious work ethic, determination, attitude, and desire. Later McCombie said, "If Michael just had watched me work, I wouldn't have given him the time of day. The fact that he picked up the other ax I had sitting there and helped me complete the work told me a lot about him. It turns out, I was right."

Prep School for SEALs

Captain Andrew Bisset, a Navy SEAL with thirty-seven years of combined active and reserve Naval Special Warfare (NSW) experience, had served for five years active duty with SEAL Team One and Underwater Demolition Team Twenty-one (UDT-21). While in the Naval Reserve (NR), he commanded two NR Special Warfare Group Two detachments, as well as NR SEAL Team Two and NR Special Boat Squadron Two, and ultimately served as reserve commodore of NR Special Warfare Command, the senior SEAL reserve position.

Following through on McCombie's instruction, on Monday, November 9, 1997, Michael contacted Bisset, who invited him to attend the RDAC mentorship and training program beginning the following January. Bisset told him about the program's standards and how it operated. He explained that meeting the U.S. Navy SEAL requirements was not enough to successfully complete the program; all candidates recommended to the Naval Special Warfare Command must far exceed the minimum SEAL standards. Undaunted, Michael accepted the invitation.

History of the SEAL Recruiting District Assistance Council (RDAC)

In the 1970s, with the increased demand for SEALs, the Navy lowered its training standards to increase the success rate, which was 25 percent, meaning that 75 percent of all those who began BUD/S training did not successfully complete the program. This lowering of standards concerned Captain Bisset, who strongly believed that by starting with a better-prepared BUD/S candidate, there would be a corresponding increase in the success rate.

Bisset founded the council in 1994. Its membership is composed of SEAL Naval Reservists and retirees who mentor SEAL candidates and prepare them for BUD/S. Statistics show that the cost of transforming a man into a Navy SEAL is very expensive—about $500,000—so efforts to produce a better BUD/S candidate could greatly increase the effective use of tax dollars and provide the Navy with better-qualified applicants. In addition to the mentors, the council also includes other high-level civilians who network with various spheres of influence within the civilian community that benefits the RDAC. The SEAL RDAC focuses on helping recruiters find qualified SEAL and Special Warfare Combatant-craft Crewmen (SWCC) candidates and then mentors, evaluates, and prepares them for BUD/S. Through Physical Screening Tests (PSTs) and mentoring sessions, candidates are taught swim-stroke and other strength-training techniques and given individual encouragement to prepare them both physically and mentally for the boot camp at Naval Station Great Lakes and then for eventual success as a SEAL operator after completing their training at BUD/S in Coronado, California.

RDAC Standards

To help increase the success rate of those recommended and selected for BUD/S, RDAC standards are deliberately much higher than those established by BUD/S.

The RDAC PST measures the same five areas: a timed swim, push-ups, sit-ups, pull-ups, and a run. To successfully complete the RDAC PST, the candidate must complete a timed five-hundred-yard swim using the breast- and/or sidestroke in under twelve and a half minutes. Following a ten-minute rest, they must perform a minimum of forty-two push-ups in two minutes, followed by a two-minute rest. The test continues with a minimum of fifty sit-ups in two minutes, followed by another two-minute rest. The candidate must then perform a minimum of six pull-ups with no time limit. Following a ten-minute rest, the candidate, wearing boots and long pants, must complete a 1.5-mile run in under eleven and a half minutes.

Saturday, January 16, 1998

Michael reported to the USMMA in Kings Point, where he was introduced to the RDAC mentors, then given a brief overview of the program, program expectations, and his initial PST. Records show that he completed his five-hundred-yard swim in nine minutes flat; did ninety push-ups in two minutes, fifty-eight sit-ups, and eighteen pull-ups; and completed his run in 8:46. While this certainly got Bisset's and the other SEAL mentors' attention, they withheld judgment and their excitement. They did encourage him to work out on his own in between monthly sessions, and reminded him that his commitment would be evident by his improved marks each month. Michael committed to continuous improvement, and established a daily workout routine.

Saturday, February 20, 1998

Again reporting to the USMMA, Michael's PST results were mixed. His 8:02 swim was a fifty-eight-second improvement, but his push-ups dropped to eighty-six. His sit-ups increased to sixty, his pull-ups went down to sixteen, and his run was clocked at 9:22, over his initial time by thirty-six seconds. Although Michael was dissatisfied, his mentors continued to encourage him to work out on his own, and emphasized their satisfaction with his swim. He committed to redoubling his efforts for the next month.

However, Michael was unable to make the March session because of academic requirements. He telephoned Captain Bisset and reiterated his commitment to the program, promising to continue to work out on his own and to report for the April session. He continued his self-designed workout program, and it paid off.

Saturday, April 24, 1998

Michael was able to report to the USMMA for his April session. While his swim was timed at 8:13, up from February, his push-ups increased dramatically, from 86 to 107, as did his sit-ups, from 60 to 83. His pull-up numbers also jumped, from 16 to 21, and he decreased his run time to 8:54. The RDAC mentors realized they had themselves a highly motivated individual. They also began to see Michael's leadership skills. Being one of the top finishers in the swim, he constantly encouraged the slower swimmers and encouraged others during push-ups, sit-ups, and pull-ups. After he finished the run near the front, he ran back several times and ran with and encouraged the slower runners. Although Michael had caught the attention of Bisset and the other mentors, they did not establish any type of personal relationship with him. They had found it better not to do so with a candidate until a preliminary decision to recommend was made, allowing them to maintain their objectivity.

Spring of 1998

To reinforce among the SEAL candidates the value of a life of selfless service and sacrifice as well as to involve them in a vital community outreach, in the spring of 1998, Bisset partnered with a local outreach agency called Rebuilding Together. This program assisted low-income elderly veterans or widows of veterans who needed home maintenance and repairs. This being the first attempt at such a partnership, Bisset approached Michael to get involved with the project for two reasons. First, as a potential officer candidate, he would need to demonstrate organizational and leadership qualities; second, this would give the RDAC team an opportunity to further evaluate him.

Bisset explained that as the "House Captain," he would be responsible for assembling a team to assess the property for needed repairs, draft a budget, obtain individual and corporate sponsors to provide the materials, and draft a work schedule. He would also have to assemble a team of SEAL candidates to complete the work. Bisset reminded Michael that he and his team would be under scrutiny during each step of the project and have their work assessed and evaluated at the end of the project. When Bisset asked Michael if he was up to the task, the young man just grinned and responded, "Yes, sir. I'll take care of it, sir."

With no other assistance or guidance from the RDAC mentors, in less than three weeks, under Michael's leadership, the project and all repairs were completed. Following the success of the inaugural partnership, the Rebuilding Together initiative continued as an integral part of the RDAC mentorship program.

In early May 1998 Michael Patrick Murphy graduated from Pennsylvania State University with academic honors and with dual degrees in political science and psychology.

Saturday, May 16, 1998

Again demonstrating that determination, hard work, and individual training paid dividends, Michael continued to better his overall PST numbers. He lowered his swim time by fourteen seconds to 7:59, performed one hundred push-ups and eighty-four sit-ups, increased his pull-ups to twenty-three, and finished his run in 8:57. As in the previous month, after he completed each phase of the PST, he encouraged those who were still working out and running. Again, the mentors noted this with admiration.

Saturday, June 19, 1998

After graduation, Michael resumed his position as the supervising lifeguard at Lake Ronkonkoma and other area beaches and began working at Hartcorn Plumbing and Heating in Ronkonkoma as a plumber's assistant.

On the nineteenth, he reported to the USMMA. His swim time dropped another twelve seconds to 7:47; he did 102 push-ups, 84 sit-ups, and 22 pull-ups; and he lowered his run time to 8:55. He accomplished all this even as he continued to encourage his fellow classmates

After the PST, Bisset called Michael into his office. Following a truly enlightening and revealing interview, Bisset completed the required NAVCRUIT 1100/13 Interviewer's Appraisal Sheet. He was impressed with Michael's goal-oriented determination and obvious work ethic. He awarded Michael the highest marks in categories of appearance, communication, leadership potential, and willingness to serve in a command or commissioned role, and made the following remarks.

> Mike Murphy is an outstanding and well-rounded candidate who appeared before me confident, clean cut, articulate and above all, committed to become Naval Officer in the SEAL program. He demonstrated to me in his interview that he has researched and is extremely knowledgeable on the Navy SEAL Program and their mission. He has an intensity and focus that are extraordinary. This he has demonstrated notably in his superb answers to me in his interview but also in his drive to obtain only the most competitive PST SEAL scores possible. Furthermore, he has displayed strong leadership skills notably as a supervising lifeguard in Suffolk County, NY but also as co-CAPT of a Penn State intramural football team. A team which he led to a campus championship at Penn State in an extremely competitive environment his senior year. I would be most eager to have this individual serve in my wardroom. Select now.

In his final comments, Captain Bisset added the following: "This is an intensely motivated individual who has the focus, determination and perseverance to carry him through the rigors of Basic Underwater Demolition SEAL (BUD/S) Training."

On July 26, 1998, RDAC SEAL Mentor Lieutenant (junior grade) Barry McCabe sent the following letter to the U.S. Navy Officer Recruiting Station in New York.

For the past three years, I have been working closely with Drew Bisset, CAPT USNR, in testing, screening and evaluating potential Navy SEAL candidates. Over that period of time, I have had the opportunity to meet, see and talk to many young men who aspire to become SEALs. Recently, one of those men, Mike Murphy, has stood out from the others and I'll tell you why.

We all know that physical prowess in the SEAL disciplines is a given when considering a SEAL candidate. But what truly counts is the mental determination and commitment to become a SEAL. I have monitored Mike in several SEAL physical screen tests, and each time he has produced excellent scores. And when it came to his commitment, I asked him to put it on paper why he wants to be a Navy SEAL. Well, it came back with one of the strongest, most enthusiastic rationales that I have seen and am convinced he will do the job and then some. And, it's worth noting, that his father served in Vietnam and his grandfather in World War II, which to me is a real plus.

In talking with Mike, and getting to know him better, I've been impressed with his knowledge and his clean-cut straightforward manner, which are important for a Navy officer. He has the energy, intellect, physical ability and attitude to be an asset to the U.S. Navy, and I think I'm in a position to know.

As for my background, I volunteered for Underwater Demolition prior to receiving my commission as Ensign at Columbia University in October 1944. After training at Fort Pierce and Maui, I was assigned to UDT 21 and served in the Pacific during World War II. Our team was the first military unit to land on Japan before the surrender was signed. Currently, as a member of the Recruiting District Assistance Council (RDAC), I assist CAPT Bisset in his recruiting endeavors and demonstrate as well as helping him evaluate SEAL candidates.

Being a senior citizen, and having gone through a war as a Frogman, I think I know how to evaluate a SEAL candidate's character, capability and commitment, and believe Mike has the necessary attributes and qualifications. Should you wish to discuss this further, please feel free to call me, I'd like to do whatever I can to see that Mike Murphy is given serious consideration.

Waiting for Good News

With his OCS and BUD/S applications in the works, Michael continued to work as a lifeguard and a plumber's assistant for Hartcorn Plumbing while he maintained his rigorous physical training regimen.

Navy SEALs required 20/20 vision, something Michael did not have. He researched surgical corrective measures, including LASIK. However, LASIK left multiple tiny scars on the cornea of the eye that could cause serious problem at the depths SEALs are required to dive. LASIK corrective surgery was unacceptable, leaving only the photorefractive keratectomy (PRK) as viable option. In November

1998 Michael underwent his PRK, and for the next six weeks he endured the discomfort and physical restrictions that followed.

After recovering from his surgery, Michael continued to work as a plumber's assistant while he waited on his acceptance into both Officer Candidate School and SEAL training. He also continued to train with the RDAC throughout 1999.

As the weeks and months dragged on, Dan seriously doubted his son's career decision. He reminded Michael that he had been accepted by several prestigious law schools and had the potential for a lucrative career, and that continuing to work as a plumber's assistant on the hope of being granted admission to both OCS and BUD/S might not be the wisest of career choices. Michael was also offered a full-time plumber's apprenticeship, which he declined.

Additional months passed, and Dan became increasingly concerned, which led to several more serious father-and-son discussions. During their talks, Dan posed several questions: What if he was accepted into one but not the other? What if he was accepted into OCS but not BUD/S? Would he be satisfied being a fleet officer? Would he then reapply to BUD/S? What if he was not accepted into OCS? Would he enlist in the Navy and apply for BUD/s after basic training? Would he then reapply to OCS? What about obtaining his law degree first, which, if he was then still interested in the Navy, would certainly strengthen his OCS application? What if the law schools withdrew his acceptances and his Navy applications were denied?

Michael did not have answers for all of his father's questions, but one thing remained perfectly clear—his goal of becoming a Navy SEAL officer. Despite Dan's increased persistence, Michael, with faith in himself and his abilities, held his ground and continued working as a plumber's assistant.

Meanwhile, his best friend, Owen O'Callaghan, had applied for a job with the New York City Fire Department, which required the passing of a demanding physical-fitness test. Michael trained Owen using his RDAC regimen, working one-on-one with his friend. Soon Jimmie and Sean O'Callaghan, as well as Jay Keenan, began working out with Michael and Owen. The training paid off when Jimmie passed his physical with flying colors and entered the New York City Fire Academy.

In the early spring of 2000 Michael's persistence paid off. He received official notification that he had been accepted into Officer Candidate School (OCS), after which he would enter BUD/S training. He did not attend the two RDAC sessions following his acceptance, but he did notify Captain Bisset that he had been accepted into OCS and BUD/S and was scheduled to begin OCS in mid-September.

The Saturday before he left for OCS, on September 11, 2000, Michael attended his final RDAC session. His PST numbers remained consistent with a 7:49 swim, 103 push-ups, 80 sit-ups, 20 pull-ups, and a 9:10 run.

Success Breeds Success

In 2000 Captain Bisset extended his commission for five years, which allowed him to continue the highly successful mentoring program he had established. As of December 2009, 89 of the 126 candidates Bisset has mentored have completed BUD/S training, for a 70 percent success rate, compared to the normal 25 percent. In addition to Michael Murphy, recipient of the Medal of Honor, Bisset has mentored two United Service Organizations (USO) George Van Cleave Military Leadership Award recipients: Michael P. Murphy and Nathan Hardy.

Assigned to Naval Special Warfare Development Group (NSWDG), Senior Chief Petty Officer Nathan H. Hardy, twenty-nine, of Durham, New Hampshire, was killed in Iraq in February 2008 while on his fourth deployment in the Global War on Terror. Buried in Arlington National Cemetery with full military honors, Senior Chief Hardy left behind his wife, Mindi, and a seven-month-old son, Parker.

CHAPTER SEVEN

Officer Candidate School

Patience and perseverance have a magical effect before which difficulties disappear and obstacles vanish.

—JOHN QUINCY ADAMS, quoted at ThinkExist.com,
www.thinkexist.com/quotes/john_quincy_adams
(accessed December 8, 2009)

The Power of Persistence

Officer Candidate School (OCS) is one of three ways a civilian can become a naval officer. The first is by graduating from the U.S. Naval Academy in Annapolis and the second is by graduating from a Naval Reserve Officers Training Corps (NROTC) program. OCS is a twelve-week course designed to provide candidates with a working knowledge of the Navy both afloat and ashore, prepare them to assume the duties of a naval officer, and help them reach their fullest potential by intensive immersion in leadership, physical, and military training and academics.

As a member of Captain Bisset's RDAC program, Michael was invited to participate in the annual program/demonstration on the flight deck of the USS *Intrepid* (CVS-11), a decommissioned *Essex*-class aircraft carrier. *Intrepid* participated in the Pacific theater of operations during World War II and in the Vietnam War. Since 1982, *Intrepid* has been part of the Intrepid Sea, Air & Space Museum, located at New York City's Pier 86. In early June 2000, Michael arrived at the *Intrepid*. Following the program and demonstration, Rear Admiral Thomas Steffens, serving as the chief of staff at the U.S. Special Operations Command, located at MacDill Air Force Base in Tampa, Florida, administered the oath to the newly enlisted members of the U.S. Navy. As his SEAL mentor, Captain Bisset, watched as Michael Murphy raised his right hand and repeated his oath of enlistment, thereby making him a member of the Navy.

Over the next couple of months, Bisset helped prepare Michael for the rigors of OCS. In addition to maintaining his physical training regimen, Michael continued to work as lifeguard and as a plumber's assistant while he waited to begin his naval career.

Naval Air Station, Pensacola, Florida

Michael reported to the naval air station (NAS) in Pensacola, Florida, on a sunny September Saturday in 2000. It was the beginning of another step in his journey to become an elite warrior—a U.S. Navy SEAL.

Michael checked in with base security. OCS is a military training center. It is designed to make candidates consider and then reconsider their choices and then reconcile those choices with their goals. At OCS, if you believe that you want to be a naval officer, it will become more apparent with each passing day. If you don't, that will become equally obvious. Michael was well aware that his personal honor, courage, and commitment would be tested and challenged to live up to the highest standards. Having done his research, and having talked extensively with OCS graduates, he knew that the hardest thing to learn was that at OCS, everything is regimented. Everything he did would be dictated by a candidate officer, a drill instructor, or OCS regulations, which he was expected to know completely. Michael got his orders stamped and met with a candidate officer, who told him about the procedure for the next day.

Indoctrination Week

The next day, Michael reported as ordered, and was met by a different candidate officer. Life for Michael was about to change. He was given his room, which was called a "space," and a small notebook and pen for recording "gouge," or information he would be required to know. The four main initial pieces of gouge are the Code of Conduct, the General Orders of a Sentry, the chain of command, and the rank structure and insignia of the Navy and Marine Corps. This information must be memorized verbatim and is essential for the candidate to successful complete the fourth-week inspection. From the moment he checked in Michael was deliberately placed under stress, often by many people at the same time, and disciplined for failing to do things that were impossible to do. He did not take it personally, because he understood four important things.

1. Fear is used to teach. In only twelve weeks, a significant amount of material must be learned; the use of fear facilitates this.
2. Fear strengthens, both physically and mentally. Since fear comes from the unknown, after a few weeks at OCS, fear is replaced by routine. In most cases OCS will be the most strenuous part of the candidate's naval career. However, this will not be the case for Michael.

3. Individuals must be broken down before they can be built into a team. Everyone must be at the same level.
4. All candidates get their head shaved and wear the same clothes, and everyone is punished when one of them makes a mistake.

The first week of training is known as Indoctrination and has several objectives:

1. To prepare candidates for the next twelve weeks of training. Basic marching, facing movements, military bearing, and gouging are taught.
2. To prepare candidates for the first meeting with the class drill instructor. Candidate officers, known as Candi-Os, lead class members from check-in until the class in which drill instructor and chief petty officer are introduced.
3. To complete all preliminary administrative work, including the Naval Operational Medicine Institute (NOMI), Personnel Support Detachment (PSD), book bag issue, and Navy Exchange.
4. To introduce the candidates to their class officer.

Michael received his military haircut on Tuesday. The OCS barbers were extremely proficient in hairstyling—as long as the style was a shaved head. On Wednesday his class met its drill instructor, class chief petty officer, and class officer. Also on Wednesday and again on Thursday, class members were occupied with medical examinations, uniform issue, and their Indoctrination Physical Readiness Test. On Saturday the class began physical training (PT). Thursday, Friday, and Saturday of Indoctrination are the most brutal for those at OCS.

From the minute he arrived, Michael stood or sat at attention with the familiar "thousand-yard stare." When standing or sitting, his feet were always at a precise forty-five-degree angle with his head and eyes straight ahead. At the position of attention, his hands were clasped into tight fists with thumbs along the trouser seam. While walking in buildings, his right shoulder remained four inches from the wall, known as the "bulkhead," at all times. As he approached a candidate officer or class drill instructor he had to "brace the bulkhead," positioning himself with his back and heels four inches from the wall, and give the greeting of the day. His communications had to be precise and given "ballistically," which meant that he shouted them with authority and conviction. There were only five appropriate statements or responses. To speak, he first had to request and receive permission. To answer a question, he had to say either "Yes, sir." or "No, sir." To respond to a command or order, he had to say "Aye, sir." If asked a question to which he did not know the answer, he had to respond, "Sir, this Indoctrination candidate does not know but will find out." His every action was scrutinized and any shortcoming was immediately and rigorously corrected. He understood and respected the strict Code of Honor. OCS is more a mental rather than a physical environment. His biggest enemy was time, as there never seemed to be enough to accomplish all that was demanded.

During Indoctrination it was critical that Michael and his classmates remained focused and not allow the drill instructors to get to them—which clearly was their intent. Each day was another day closer to graduation. The most stressful time for Indoctrination officer candidates was during meals. There is a strict procedure for entering, sitting, eating, and departing. To prepare the candidates for drill and to learn strict attention to detail, Michael and his class were taught chow hall procedures.

After chow hall procedures, the biggest stressor was standing watch. Here the candidates had be attentive to everything that was occurring at their station and salute all officers.

Week Two

On Monday of week two the class experienced its first PT session, followed by a two-mile run. Academic classes followed, with courses in personnel administration and naval history. All classes were given extremely fast and required a significant amount of memorization and word recognition. Tests were multiple-choice, with the first one given on Wednesday, two days after classes had begun, and final exams on Friday.

During this period, the candidates also began to receive basic military instruction, with an emphasis on military customs and courtesies, uniform assembly and requirements, inspection procedures, and training requirements. Rifle drills, conducted every afternoon from the second through the seventh week, taught the class discipline and how to obey orders, and also bonded the class and the drill instructor.

As the class settled into a routine, Michael and the other candidates endured long runs in the early morning, followed by classes until afternoon rifle drill. Breakfast and lunch were at predetermined times. After the evening meal the class was given thirty minutes of free time before the mandatory two-hour study period, which was followed by job assignments. "Taps" was played exactly at 10:00 PM, after which the drill instructors inspected the barracks for thirty minutes.

On Tuesday of the second week, Michael was given his initial swim test, which consisted of swimming twenty-five yards across the pool while performing the backstroke, the sidestroke, the breaststroke, and the American crawl.

Week Three

At this point, the pace of the program increased. They were given an average of two examinations and there was a personnel inspection (PI) every Monday. The candidates also prepared for the military training tests (MTTs), which consisted of room and locker and personnel inspections that were coming up the following week. The candidates' academic workload included training in navigational techniques. They studied dead reckoning, coastal piloting, rules of the road, and electronic navigation, and were required to plot simulated movements and positions of a ship at sea.

Week 4

On Wednesday the first MTT was given, with a required score of 85. The MTT was a unique experience, one best explained in the following excerpt from an article that appeared in the May 30, 1994, issue of the *Navy Times* and was written by Patrick Pexton.

The 34 Candidates dressed in well-pressed summer whites—seven others have already dropped out—are a diverse lot. They are black, brown, yellow, white, male and female, nuke and aviation, surface and unrestricted line. But they share one thing in common today.

They are all hating life.

Young men and women graduates from Harvard, Penn and state universities around the country, who weeks earlier were living carefree lives of students, stayed up until 3:00 AM last night polishing brass belt buckles until they reflected like mirrors.

They slept on the hard linoleum floor so their bunks would be pristine and wrinkle-free for the morning inspection. Like alchemists, they experimented with novel ways to prevent ancient, rusting waste cans from flaking onto the floor when the Drill Instructors pound on them during inspection. They did the same with what looked to be about 40-year-old brown leather book bags, which are cracked and worn with age.

The DIs enter the four-bunk rooms to smooth beds, clean weapons, and orderly lockers. When they end the inspection for each room precisely eight minutes later, slamming the door behind them, they leave behind a tornado-like path of destruction.

Candidates are left standing at attention, but looking disheveled and demoralized. Their pants pockets are pulled inside out, their belts unceremoniously ripped from their waists and lying on the floor, their voices hoarse from shouting rapid-fire responses to the demanding DIs.

Towels that were folded with precision and freshly shined shoes that were placed in straight, ordered rows are strewn about the room. Carefully ironed uniforms are pulled off their hangers in piles. The bunks, so perfectly made, with the pillow an exact 12 inches from the foldover of the sheet, are a wreck.

And the gunnery sergeants are just warming up.

The only defense to such a strategy was confidence, a loud voice, and the clock.

Weeks 5–6

Rifle drill was the main focus during this period. On the Thursday of week five, the final swim test, known as the third class swim, was held. This consisted of jumping from the ten-meter platform, swimming the length of the pool and back, treading water for one minute, and survival floating for five minutes.

Academic classes and tests were given in naval warfare, military law, engineering, and damage control. The good study skills Michael learned at Penn State proved essential here. He understood that academics were designed for stress as well as knowledge. Individuality was not tolerated at OCS; teamwork was the essential key to success.

The military training at Officer Candidate School comprised four broad categories.

Physical training. There were three Physical Fitness Assessments (PFA) at OCS: the Indoctrination PFA, the Mid-PFA, and the Out-PFA. Passing requirements were Satisfactory-Medium for the IN-PFA, Satisfactory-High for the Mid-PFA, and Good-Low for the Out-PFA.

Room and locker inspection (RLI). A candidate's room was subject to inspection at any time. To ensure cleanliness and to maintain standards, room inspections occurred at regular intervals in lieu of zone inspections. Rooms were to be maintained in accordance with the daily room standards. Racks were to be made between 5:00 AM and 10:00 PM.

Personnel inspection (PI). Each candidate was inspected for proper uniform, haircut, shave, hygiene, and general military appearance.

Drill. Approximately forty hours were spent learning and practicing drill. The candidates also marched to and from every evolution.

Graduation

On December 13, 2000, with his parents and brother in attendance, Ensign Michael P. Murphy graduated with Honor Class 07-01 and was commissioned as an officer in the U.S. Navy. After OCS, he returned to Patchogue, where he remained until mid-January. He then departed for San Diego and his next duty assignment—BUD/S.

CHAPTER EIGHT

BUD/S: The Price of Admission

The Only Easy Day Was Yesterday!

—BUD/S motto, Naval Special Warfare, www.sealchallenge.navy.mil/
seal/default/aspx (accessed December 9, 2009)

To begin to appreciate the level of skills and training possessed by Michael Murphy and his teammates, we'll need to take a look at his SEAL training.* The newly commissioned Ensign Michael Murphy reported to Naval Special Warfare Command, located at the Naval Amphibious Base in Coronado, California, and began thirty months of the most brutal training of any military unit in the world. Having arrived safely, he called his mother. He knew that 75 to 80 percent of those beginning BUD/S training do not finish. He also knew that the training was not designed to build a superior physically trained individual, but rather a member of a warrior culture with relentless drive to fight and win as a team—someone who would rather die than quit.

Despite the brutal training, Michael soon realized that almost anyone could meet the physical requirements of the SEALs, but the unending challenge from day one would be the mental toughness, that never-ending inner drive that pushes you forward when every nerve and muscle fiber in your body tells you to stop—to quit. That warrior mind-set—the mental toughness—is what separates a Navy SEAL from any other airman, seaman, soldier, or Marine, regardless of their level of training.

Michael Murphy had prepared for two years to get there. As a commissioned Navy officer, he completed his training alongside his fellow officers and enlisted men, although as an officer he was held to a higher standard. The men trained and suffered together in a ritual that built both a warrior and a warrior bond that united enlisted, junior, senior, and flag officers into a close, very tight-knit community

---

* For a detailed description of SEAL training, there is no better source than Dick Couch's book, *The Warrior Elite: The Forging of SEAL Class 228* (New York: Three Rivers Press, 2003).

that most people never realize exists or understand. The complete mental rewiring that takes place makes you understand that your teammates are more important than you.

Michael Murphy, and all of his classmates, were volunteers and could quit at any time. If a trainee quit, he had to return to the fleet for a minimum of eighteen months before he could return to BUD/S—but only if he had demonstrated potential and had been recommended for a second attempt.

Indoctrination Course (Indoc)

On day one, at 4:30 AM, Ensign Murphy joined the rest of his BUD/S teammates in Class 235 at the swimming pool, known officially as the Combat Training Tank (CTT), located along Guadalcanal Road. The class arrived to roll and put away the pool covers and string the lane markers. At 5:00 AM, he stood on the cool concrete that surrounded the CTT in nothing but his canvas Underwater Demolition Team (UDT) swim trunks. Soaking wet from a cold shower, he and his classmates sat in rows in bobsled fashion, chests to backs, to conserve body heat. Their military duffel bags, containing the few items they were permitted to bring, were beside them and separated each row of students.

As the instructor arrived, the class leader yelled, "Feet!" and all immediately sprang to attention, shivering in the cold. Each row of students made up a boat crew of seven trainees.

"Drop!" commanded the instructor, and all scrambled for a piece of the concrete in fully extended push-up position. "Push 'em out!" The class counted out twenty push-ups and returned to the fully extended position.

"Push 'em out!" The class again counted out twenty push-ups before hearing the same command for yet another twenty push-ups. After sixty push-ups the class instructor left them in the fully extended position as they all tried to shift their position to relieve the intense burning in their arms.

"Seats!" All sat on the cool concrete.

BUD/S training is separated into three phases, each phase designed to build on the skills of the previous one. First Phase is the conditioning phase. It is followed by Second Phase, diving, and Third Phase, weapons and tactics. However, before Ensign Murphy and his classmates reached First Phase, they had to complete the five-week Indoctrination Course, during which they learned the rules and protocols of BUD/S training—how to conduct themselves at the pool, how to perform at the obstacle course, and how to handle their small inflatable boats in the rough Pacific surf. They learned SEAL culture and began to internalize the ethos of the warrior. Every training evolution, whether PT or academic, was evaluated in some manner and every student's performance closely monitored by the Academic/

Performance Review Board, a committee of three BUD/S instructors. Failure to live up to the standards resulted in the student being held back, called a rollback, to the next class, or even a quick trip back to the fleet or his previous assignment.

Although every man present successfully completed the BUD/S Physical Screening Test (PST) prior to his arrival, each had to pass it again. The PST consisted of:

1. A five-hundred-yard swim using the breaststroke or sidestroke in 12:30
2. A minimum of forty-two push-ups in two minutes
3. A minimum of fifty sit-ups in two minutes
4. A minimum of six dead-hang pull-ups
5. A mile-and-a-half run in 11:30 wearing combat boots and long pants

After successfully completing the PST, only two things could remove a student from Indoctrination, or Indoc: a request to quit, known as drop on request (DOR); or failing the comprehensive psychological examination. After completing the PST, all successful students ran two miles to the chow hall. After breakfast, they ran two miles back and continued their training.

During Indoc, students underwent a physical training regimen designed to build solid, well-trained bodies, especially the upper body. The upper-body exercises of choice were pull-ups and push-ups with varying degrees of difficulty. Special emphasis was placed on the abdominal muscles. Here, the exercises of choice were sit-ups, crunches, log sit-ups, and flutter kicks. The students learned early that it paid to be a winner. Those who were not winners were losers and gained the unwanted attention of the instructors in the form of more cold water (ocean), sand, push-ups, pull-ups, sit-ups, and obstacle course (O-course) runs.

While in Indoc, the trainees lived in small, often-cramped barracks. Just as each BUD/S training phase was built on the previous one, each day in Indoc was more intense than the previous one. Each day began at 5:00 AM at the CTT. After a two-hour pool evolution, the trainees were ordered into their fatigue pants and shoes. Fully dressed, they were ordered back into the pool. Though they were cold and wet, they ran the two miles to chow and then back again to continue their day's training.

The Indoc trainees ran twelve miles a day just to eat and return. They lived on the run and were always cold and wet. At the training center they were ordered into the cold Pacific surf several times a day, then ordered to roll in the sand. Cold, wet, and sandy—that was everyday life for a BUD/S trainee. While the instructors may have seemed cruel and insensitive and at times even brutal, they knew that building spirit and character, both individually and as a class, was essential to the success of the SEAL trainees.

At the CTT the trainees learned that the water is what separates the SEALs from all other special operations forces. For most special operators, the water is an obstacle; for the SEALs, it is their sanctuary. The trainees learned buoyancy control and how to swim more like a fish than a human. They mastered breathing techniques and how to use their arms to make themselves longer in the water, which added balance.

The men in Michael's class completed their training in very modest surroundings. The classroom was a single large concrete-block room with pale yellow paint, a concrete floor, long, narrow wooden tables with unpadded chairs, and a large retractable projection screen centered on the front wall behind a slightly elevated platform and podium. Many times during classroom instruction, the students were ordered into the surf and sand and then sent back to the classroom for the remainder of the training evolution. Calisthenics and other physical training are conducted on the "grinder," a thick square area of asphalt just outside the classroom door. On the asphalt about three feet apart the numbers one through fifty were painted in yellow, designating a position for each student. During multiple twenty-repetition calisthenics, the students again were ordered into the surf and sand and then returned to the grinder to complete their evolutions. With PT completed, the class set out on a four-mile conditioning run in the soft sand, during which they were directed back into the surf several times. None of the training evolutions was designed to punish the trainees; instead, each was designed to teach a specific skill that will be needed when the men became Navy SEALs.

During the second week of Indoc, the class began inflatable boat, small (IBS) training. Here they learned to work together as a boat crew. The IBS was a 13-foot, 170-pound inflatable rubber boat. Poorly designed and too bulky for operational use, it was perfect for teaching BUD/S trainees to work together as a team in the surf.

On the final day of Indoc, each trainee's performance was reviewed by the Academic/Performance Review Board, which decided who would continue on to First Phase. The board could not remove a student from BUD/S, but rather only decided who continued on to the next phase of instruction. In addition, each student had the opportunity to evaluate each of his instructors and the training in writing. The review board determined that Michael Murphy had successfully completed Indoc and was given the rite of passage to the first phase of BUD/S training.

First Phase

Eight weeks long, First Phase was much like Indoc, only the intensity and expectations were elevated several levels. Running, swimming, and physical training grew harder as the weeks passed. Students continued weekly four-mile runs in combat boots and long pants in the soft beach sand, and were expected to decrease their obstacle-course times, swim distances of up to two miles wearing fins, and continue to learn small-boat seamanship and the importance of teamwork.

Drown Proofing

Drown proofing was an important part of basic conditioning. During this training evolution, the students learned to swim with their hands and feet bound, more of a psychological test than a physical one. It originated in the Vietnam era, when an American POW was hog-tied, then tossed into the Mekong River to drown. That POW proved that a man could swim with his hands and feet tied if he put his mind to it.

In order to pass drown proofing, the trainees had to enter a nine-foot-deep pool with their hands and feet tied, and (1) bob from the surface to the base of the pool for five minutes, (2) float on the surface for five minutes, (3) swim one hundred meters, (4) bob for two minutes, (5) complete forward and backward flips, (6) swim to the bottom of the pool and retrieve an object with their teeth, and (7) return to the surface and bob five more times.

Knot Tying

The students learned to tie knots underwater—not an easy task. The knots—bowline, sheet bend, clove hitch, and right angle—are important because they are used to secure underwater demolition charges.

Cold-Water Conditioning—"Surf Torture"

In the waters of the Pacific just off Coronado, the water temperature usually hovers around 65°, in the summer, never going above 68°. In the winter the water temperature never gets above 58°. The students were ordered to wade into the water up to their waists with their arms linked to prevent a student from being swept out to sea, and then sit while being pounded by the cold saltwater waves breaking over their heads. Another variation was to have the trainees lie with their arms linked and their heads toward the water's edge to allow the crashing surf to wash over them. On the very brink of hypothermia, they were ordered out of the surf and onto the beach for calisthenics to warm up, and then back into the surf in a training evolution that lasted for about one hour.

Unfortunately, cold-water conditioning was not a onetime experience; it was repeated frequently during BUD/S. Its purpose was to teach the prospective SEALs to mentally fend off the effects of hypothermia—which more than likely could save their lives in the future.

Log PT

This relatively simple but brutal training evolution required that a boat team carry an eight-foot, 150-pound log that was twelve inches in diameter over the men's heads while running in the soft beach sand wearing long pants and combat boots. During these timed beach runs, the trainees did hundreds of gut-busting sit-ups while holding the log on their stomachs; they also performed calisthenics such as jumping jacks and overhead tosses.

Rock Portage

In these evolutions the seven-man boat crew in their unwieldy IBS attempted to navigate the large piles of sharp rocks in the surf in front of the Hotel del Coronado. A five-star luxury hotel, Hotel del Coronado is located on the Silver Strand between Naval Amphibious Base, Coronado and Naval Air Station North Island. Extremely risky, these evolutions were conducted both day and night.

Obstacle Course (O-course)

Not to be confused with a confidence course, this intimidating true obstacle course must be seen to be believed. Requiring a twenty-yard sprint between obstacles, it demanded a combination of balance, coordination, upper-body strength, technique, endurance, and, most of all, a positive mental attitude. All obstacles were designed to teach, develop, and reinforce a specific skill that would be needed when Michael and the other trainees reached the SEAL teams.

- *Parallel bars.* Using only their arms, the trainees had to either "hop" or "walk" through a set of parallel bars approximately fifty feet in length with an initial 45-degree climbing angle.
- *Pilings.* This obstacle consisted of eight log pilings of varying heights and distances. The prospective SEALs were required to leap from one piling to the next to access the next obstacle.
- *Tires.* In a controlled, balanced sprint, the trainees had to pass through six rows of four tires without falling.
- *Low wall.* To navigate this obstacle, consisting of a wooden wall about fifteen feet high, the trainees took two hops and jumped up, keeping their bodies low while sliding over the top.
- *High wall.* The students had to grab a rope and "walk" up a wooden wall about thirty feet high. Staying low, they slid over the top and grabbed the rope on the other side, then walked down.
- *Barbed wire.* Keeping their heads down, the trainees had to crawl through a trench in the sand approximately thirty feet long and covered with logs and barbed wire.
- *Cargo net.* To pass over a fifty-foot vertical rope cargo net, the trainees had to climb close to the edge, where the net is tighter and easier to negotiate, while keeping three points of contact, with their hands on the vertical ropes and their feet on the horizontal ropes. They had to climb at a steady pace, stay low while going over the top, and come down in a controlled fall.

- *Balance logs.* The students had to run along the top of a forty-foot log, across a ten-foot section, and straight down another forty-foot section. If anyone fell off, he had to start over.
- *Hooyah logs.* With their hands clasped over their heads, the trainees ran up one side of six logs stacked in a pyramid and down the other.
- *Transfer rope.* Two twenty-foot ropes and a steel ring suspended from a wooden beam formed this obstacle. The trainees had to climb the rope, reach over and grab the steel ring, transfer to the other rope, and then descend.
- *"Dirty name."* To pass over this set of uneven log parallel bars, the trainees first had to climb on the step log, then jump and push themselves up. Maintaining their balance, they stood up and jumped up to the other log, then pushed themselves up and over the top.
- *Hooyah logs.* With their hands clasped over their heads, the trainees ran up one side and down the other of another pyramid, this one consisting of nine logs.
- *Weaver.* This low-level, ladder-shaped obstacle constructed of wide logs required the students to pass under the first bar and use their momentum to swing and weave themselves up to the next bar. They had to do this for a total of eight bars up and eight bars down the other side.
- *Burma Bridge.* This obstacle consisted of an elevated rope bridge accessed by a hanging rope. The trainees had to climb up the rope at one end, cross the bridge, and climb down the end rope.
- *Slide for Life.* The trainees surmounted a thirty-foot-high, four-level platform tower by jumping up onto the first level, then flipping up the next three levels to the top. There, they laid on top of the rope with one leg on the rope and the other hanging down for balance. Then using their forearms, they pulled themselves across a seventy-five-foot rope and down a 40-degree angle to the other side. They then got off the rope and descended another rope at the other end.
- *Rope swing.* The trainees had to swing over to a log beam, run down the beam to a set of monkey bars, using their arms to "walk" their way through the ten rungs to the balance beam, and then run the length of another log.
- *Tires:.* In a controlled balanced sprint, the trainees had to pass through six rows of four tires without falling.
- *Incline Wall.* To surmount this 45-degree-angle wooden wall, the trainees had to jump over the high end and slide down.

- *Spider Wall.* This obstacle consisted of a wooden wall with alternating flush-mounted two-by-fours. The trainees had to climb to the top on one side and descend the other.
- *Vaults.* The trainees had to cross over each of an elevated series of five logs using only their hands.

The student with the slowest O-course time had to wear a pink T-shirt that read "Always a Lady" until the next course run.

As if the O-course was not challenging enough, each boat crew was frequently charged with the task of carrying their IBS on their heads as they went through the course as a team.

Physical Testing

Prior to Hell Week, which is the most intense period of training during First Phase, Michael and his classmates faced an extremely challenging physical training evolution. The trainees had to complete a twelve-hundred-meter pool swim with fins in forty-five minutes, a one-mile bay swim with fins in fifty minutes, a one-mile ocean swim with fins in ninety-five minutes, a one-and-a-half-mile ocean swim with fins in seventy minutes, a two-mile ocean swim with fins in ninety-five minutes, the O-course in fifteen minutes, and a four-mile beach run in thirty-two minutes.

Additional Motivation

In the days leading up to Hell Week, the mental strain was apparent on the faces of many in Michael's class. Most were convinced that they could deal with the physical requirements of the week, but many were worried about the mental toughness they hoped they possessed and would need to muster to survive the upcoming ordeal.

Michael remembered his father telling him about the extensive leg injuries he suffered in Vietnam after being hit by an exploding grenade, and the weeks of agonizing surgeries and treatment he endured during his several months of hospitalization. He also remembered his father showing him a picture of him lying in a hospital bed in Vietnam receiving a Purple Heart from his commanding officer. He telephoned his father and asked him for a copy of the picture so he could look at it when he needed to reinforce his mental toughness the following week. Dan sent the picture out the following day. It arrived on Friday, and Michael looked at it frequently over the weekend. He believed that if his dad could endure being wounded by a grenade, multiple surgeries, weeks of hospitalization, and months of physical therapy to learn how to walk again, he could certainly handle whatever Hell Week dished out.

Hell Week

The first four weeks of First Phase were designed to prepare Michael and his class-mates for the fifth week, known as Hell Week, the most notorious part of BUD/S. By this time approximately 30 percent of the class had quit. Hell Week was the real gut check of First Phase and would be the defining moment in both the lives and careers of most of those who would go on to become SEALs.

During Hell Week, the students participated in five and a half days of contin-uous physical training, with a maximum of four hours' sleep for the entire week, with never more than two hours at one time. Deliberately designed as the ultimate test of physical and mental motivation, Hell Week proved to those who succeeded that the human body can do ten times the amount of work and exercise than they previously thought possible. The Academic/Performance Review Board reviewed each student's academic and physical training scores and decided who would go through Hell Week. Michael was cleared to proceed.

Anticipation

On Sunday, just after their noon meal, Michael's entire class was sequestered in the classroom. Along the back wall were brown paper bags, labeled with their last names, that contained a change of socks and underwear. Some of the men tried to sleep, some read, and some even halfheartedly attempted to watch a video on the screen.

Meanwhile, the instructors put the final touches on the initial "breakout" expe-rience, which was set to start at a predesignated time. Inside the classroom, all knew it was coming; they just didn't know when or how. They had heard stories about Hell Week from the previous class, but no two Hell Weeks begin the same. Several of the boat crews met to encourage each other, and some even engaged in bravado about being able to take "whatever they decide to put us through." As an officer, Michael personally talked with each member of his boat crew and offered words of encouragement. He knew that the six men he began Hell Week with might not be the same ones he would finish with. Despite his words, the looks on their faces and in their eyes revealed their real feelings. As they looked around the room, they were aware of the 30 percent that had already dropped out and that the statistics said they would lose another 20 percent in the next twenty-four hours and an addi-tional 20 percent before the end of the week. They couldn't help wondering if they had what it takes. Yes, they all knew it was coming, but they just didn't know when or how.

As the minutes and hours passed, the anxiety reached heightened levels, and many of the trainees began expressing their desire to "get this thing going." By midafternoon their frustration was becoming obvious. Some wondered aloud if the wait and anticipation was just as bad as what they were about to experience. Several students acted as lookouts, sitting next to the doors and watching for approaching instructors, and some sat alone with their thoughts. At 5:00 PM the movies were being repeated for the third time, but no one was really paying attention. The students, visibly apprehensive, began to walk around the room, and conversations among teammates were hushed and infrequent. While a few had relaxed and began playing games of cards, others sat quietly staring blankly into the distance. Certainly, something had to happen soon.

When All Hell Broke Loose
At 5:45 PM an instructor quietly crawled to the door near the front of the classroom and secured the lock. A few seconds later, several instructors flanked the rear door on each side. Armed with smoke grenades, Simunitions (simulated ballistic charges designed to provide realistic training) canisters, and semiautomatic weapons loaded with blank rounds, they moved into position. Outside, on the grinder, several more instructors armed with high-pressure fire hoses took up positions on both sides of the door. Numerous obstacles and barricades had been erected, as well as empty fifty-five-gallon barrels loaded with low-intensity percussion grenades.

Quietly and slowly an instructor turned the doorknob and opened the door just enough to get his hand in and shut off the lights. As the lights went off the instructors, rushed in, screaming through bullhorns, firing their semiautomatic weapons over the heads of the students, who had hit the floor and covered their heads and ears. As the instructors ran through the room trying not to step on anyone, hot spent shell casings hit the floor. Students started yelling, coughing, and hacking. After several minutes of total chaos and confusion, the instructors ordered the students outside, yelling through their amplified bullhorns. Several ran for the front door, but finding it locked, they immediately turned and ran for the back door. The doorway backed up with students, who fell over each other in total confusion. As a group of students cleared the doorway and reached the grinder, they tripped over several of the obstacles that were not there when they entered the classroom several hours earlier. High-pressure fire hoses knocked several to the ground, blinded by smoke and water.

Totally disoriented, some students crawled in every direction trying to escape, while others ran into one obstacle after another as well as into each other. The noise produced by the amplified music, bullhorns, gunfire, and fire hoses was deafening. Some students, totally confused and disorientated, resorted to crawling on the asphalt with their ears covered. Some tried to escape to the beach but were blocked and knocked backward by more instructors with fire hoses. The breakout had been designed to create chaos and confusion. It worked.

After about twenty minutes of mayhem and chaos, the hoses were shut off and the last echoes of semiautomatic weapons faded into the evening air. Bewildered, soaked, confused, and in total shock, the students were ordered to the beach for a roll in the sand then back to the grinder. Many were still coughing and hacking, several with their eyes still closed tightly from the irritation of the cordite, water, and smoke. There were numerous bleeding abrasions on knees, elbows, and ankles from crawling on the rough asphalt.

"Drop!" came the order over the bullhorn. Instinctively, each trainee assumed the fully extended position for push-ups.

"Push 'em out!"

In unison the class began its first of what would be twenty-five sets of twenty push-ups, alternated with ten sets of twenty sit-ups and hurried trips to the pull-up bars for additional repetitions, then back to the grinder for multiple sets of flutter kicks. During the push-ups, several vomited as they extended up from the asphalt. The instructors continued to issue the same order: "Push 'em out!"

Following their warm-up of five hundred push-ups and two hundred gut-busting sit-ups and multiple sets of pull-ups and flutter kicks, the trainees mustered for a run through the O-course. Several more vomited as they ran between obstacles but kept moving. Several students quit and returned to the grinder and their rooms. They had had enough.

Michael was well aware that there were two critical mental elements to surviving Hell Week: taking the punishment handed out by the instructors; and trying not to think about what was to come, because more often than not it was the anticipation that destroyed the will to go on, rather than the punishment itself. He also had a clear vision of where he wanted to go in life. Having this vision made him less likely to fall prey to the mental and physical torture of BUD/S.

Those who remained headed to the beach for another roll in the sand before they assembled in a line, linked arms, and entered the cold surf for another round of surf torture. Each realized that this was just the beginning of what was in store for the next five days: hundreds more push-ups and sit-ups, dozens of more miles to run, another dozen or more runs through the O-course, more surf torture, and more sand. Several more quit. After surf torture it was off for a two-mile run to warm up.

At about 11:00 PM the boat crews paddled their rubber boats fifteen miles around the waters off Coronado, after which they were ordered to place their craft above their heads and run the two miles for their breakfast. During Hell Week, the importance of teamwork was seared into both their conscious and subconscious minds. They ran everywhere they went, carried their 170-pound inflatable boat above their heads, and spent a significant amount of time in the 65° waters of the Pacific. Students endured the effects of deliberate and repeated hypothermia and exposure while highly trained medical teams constantly observed all training evolutions. Under the watchful eyes of the instructors and medical personnel, cases of hypothermia were immediately treated with warm intravenous fluids until the core body temperature rose to a safe level, then the student rejoined his classmates back in the water or in the next training evolution.

An unbreakable bond of community is developed among those who complete BUD/S. Great risk is involved in the training of the world's most elite warriors, and nowhere is that risk greater than in Hell Week. Stress fractures of the legs are common due to the constant running, as well as moderate to severe cases of cellulitis, an infection of the skin that can cause redness, swelling, cracking, bleeding, and seepage of fluids, from the extended submersion in cold, polluted saltwater. These and other injuries can result in hospitalization for a candidate and his being rolled back to the next BUD/S class. During meals it is not uncommon for students to fall asleep in their food, and many remain in a constant state of disorientation and confusion. The result is a class greatly diminished in size by the end of Hell Week.

Michael developed bilateral stress fractures and a severe case of cellulitis in both of his feet and lower legs. Somehow he was able to continue running and hide the swelling, redness, and bleeding from his teammates, the instructors, and the medical teams. Severe cases of cellulitis can compromise circulation to the affected areas and are considered extreme medical emergencies.

Tragedy in Training

After their Wednesday evening meal and following their routine examination by the medical staff, the fifty-two students in Michael's class entered the CTT for a training evolution known as the caterpillar swim. This team-building exercise required students wearing their fatigues and boots to float on their backs while interlocking their legs around the next man's torso, and using their arms to swim around the pool. At some point during the exercise, the senior student officer in the class, Lieutenant John Anthony Skop, began to have trouble staying afloat and was removed from the water by medics. Found to be without a pulse and respiration, medics began cardiopulmonary resuscitation and transferred him to the Sharp Coronado Hospital, where he was pronounced dead soon after arrival. After Skop's transfer from the CTT by medics, the NSW commanders canceled the remaining thirty-six hours of Hell Week. While all the students were stunned by Skop's death, nowhere was the loss felt more than among the officers. Unfortunately, this would not be the only training incident to deeply affect Ensign Michael Murphy.

Michael made his way back to his room and fell into a chair. His feet and lower legs were so severely red and swollen that he was unable to remove his boots or move his toes. After sitting for a few minutes, he was unable to move his legs and had no feeling below his knees, and he could not bend down to reach his boots. His roommate called for medical assistance. When the medical team arrived, they were unable to remove his boots and had to cut them off, along with his socks, as well as his pant legs to the groin. Both legs were very hot to the touch, with red streaks that extended above the knee to the groin. There was blackened dead and decayed skin between his toes and on the bottoms of both feet, along with massive swelling and several large cracks in the skin on both lower legs that drained a blood-tinged fluid. Several of his toenails were found in his socks.

Now barely conscious, Michael was transferred to the base hospital, where intensive intravenous fluids and powerful antibiotics were started in both arms. Following the surgical removal of the blackened dead skin, an aggressive wound management program was started that included antibiotic creams and painful sterile-dressing changes several times each day. He was confined to his bed with his lower legs elevated to assist in decreasing the swelling. After about forty-eight hours, Michael was conscious and more alert. When commanders and doctors told him that he could not continue BUD/S training with his class, he immediately tried to get out of bed and return to his boat crew. Only after BUD/S instructors told him that he would be rolled back and permitted to continue with a future class did he finally relent.

The Slow Process of Healing

While Michael remained confined to his hospital bed, he frequently thought about his father, who had been in the same position in Vietnam decades before. He drew both physical and mental strength from his thoughts. He spent his hours in bed reading books such as Bill O'Reilly's *Who's Looking Out for You?* and *The No Spin Zone: Confrontations with the Powerful and Famous in America*. Despite the aggressive therapy of the medical staff, the dead blackened areas of skin between his toes and the bottoms of his feet continued to grow and required additional surgical removal. The medical staff became very concerned about the circulation to both of his feet: if the condition worsened, he could well lose one or both of his feet.

With Michael's permission, the doctors notified Maureen and Dan, who arrived at Coronado the following day and met with Michael and his medical team. After another three days of aggressive treatment, Michael's circulation had improved, and the areas where the decayed skin had been surgically removed were showing signs of improvement. While this was certainly good news, his condition was still serious. After another week of continued improvement, doctors began an aggressive physical therapy program to restore full range of motion to Michael's toes, ankles and lower legs. Michael's parents flew back to Long Island, but remained in contact twice each day with Michael and his medical team. After three weeks of extensive treatment and therapy, Michael was discharged. As an outpatient, he continued on oral antibiotics and followed a highly structured and aggressive physical therapy and dressing-change program twice per day. His job was to follow medical instructions, heal, and prepare himself to return to BUD/S training. His dream of becoming a Navy SEAL had been delayed, but he would not be denied. Having been rolled back to the following class, Michael spent the next nine weeks healing both the stress fractures and his wounds. He also spent considerable time doing pull-ups and sit-ups and other upper-body-strengthening calisthenics that did not interfere with his healing.

Finally cleared to return to training, he joined Class 236 on the Monday following its Hell Week. The week was spent entirely in the classroom studying hydrographic reconnaissance, surveys, and charting, and gave Michael and his new classmates healing time for their abused bodies. On the following Monday, it was back to First Phase conditioning at pre–Hell Week levels.

Post–Hell Week Testing

Following Hell Week and the week of hydrographic reconnaissance training and mission planning, Michael and his new classmates were required to complete a two-thousand-meter swim and a one-and-a-half-mile night bay swim. In addition, the two-mile ocean swim with fins had to be completed in ninety-five minutes, a four-mile run in thirty-two minutes, and the O-course in thirteen minutes.

While a significant amount of time was spent on the physical requirements, an equal amount of time was spent in the classroom. The academic requirements to successfully complete BUD/S exceed graduate-level requirements at the most prestigious universities in the United States. Enlisted men must achieve a minimum of 70 percent on all their academics, while officers are held to the higher standard—80 percent. Michael would have it no other way. Academic subjects included dive physiology, Navy dive tables, weapons, hydrographic charts and reconnaissance, ground tactics, weapons nomenclature, leadership and communications, psychology, mission planning, and munitions.

Ben Sauers, one of Michael's new classmates, related the following story about him.

> During one of our frequent boat crew evolutions, the instructors had repeatedly told us not to use our knives while working around the IBSs. Michael was serving as our boat crew leader and we were determined to be the winning boat crew on this evolution. Something happened that resulted in several of the ropes on the IBS getting tangled in a knot and we were unable to get the IBS free. Michael took out his knife and began working on the ropes. Sure enough, he punctured the IBS. There was no way to cover this. The loud hissing sound attracted the instructor's attention immediately. As the instructors approached, they began shouting. Michael snapped to attention and immediately accepted responsibility and insisted that he should be the only person punished. Although certainly appreciated, we all knew that is not how BUD/S operates. We all completed a hundred push-ups with our feet on another IBS and our hands deep in the sand, which put our faces in the sand during the down phase of the push-ups. After our push-ups and another lecture from the instructors, we ran to get another IBS.
>
> Later that evening after the last evolution, Michael was walking with us back to our rooms when he turned to us and with a big grin on his face said, "Well, I won't do that again, but it went rather well, don't you think?" He then took off running as each of us chased him.

Monster Mash

On Thursday of the last week of First Phase, the final physical training evolution was a race called the Monster Mash, which proved, as always, that "it pays to be a winner." The students assembled behind the buildings surrounding the grinder dressed in T-shirts, fatigue pants, and boots, then headed down to the beach, where they all lined up. Start times were separated by thirty-second intervals. To start, everyone had to eat a jalapeño pepper. Officers were also required to take a big drink of jalapeño juice. Then each man took off down the beach to complete the first half of the O-course. After doing this, the student ran back to a section known as Gator Beach. Here he stripped down to his canvas swim trunks, threw his clothes in a truck, and ran up the beach, where instructors were waiting for him. The student grabbed his gear from another vehicle and then went into the water. He headed out to a huge pile of rocks about a hundred yards from shore, then returned to shore for a change back into his shirt, fatigues, and boots, and then ran back to finish the O-course. At the top of the Slide for Life obstacle tower there was a bucket of eggs and a bucket sitting at the bottom. If a student could drop his egg in the bucket, he was rewarded by having two minutes subtracted from his time. At the end of the O-course he ran back up the beach, did four sets of thirty push-ups, ran into the surf, then went into the sand, and was finished. The student with the slowest time overall got the honor of drinking the remainder of the jalapeño juice and wearing the pink T-shirt.

On Friday, the students evaluated their training and their instructors. The Academic/Performance Review Board again diligently reviewed the academic and physical-training performance of each student to determine who would proceed to Second Phase. The board reviewed with each student where he excelled and where he could use improvement. Michael earned the right to proceed to the next phase of BUD/S.

Second Phase

During Second Phase, also known as the dive phase, Michael and his fellow classmates would be expected to decrease their O-course times, do PT every day, and lower their beach run and ocean swim times and begin learning the process of becoming combat swimmers. The first three weeks were spent in the classroom learning diving physics and diving physiology. They learned about the Navy dive and treatment tables. They successfully completed extensive, rigorous examinations before entering the water and were subjected to the recompression chamber to monitor their ability to breathe pure oxygen under pressure. The equipment used was similar to that used by recreational or open-water divers. During what was called Pool Week, they learned the three different life-support systems: open-circuit compressed air; closed-circuit, 100 percent oxygen LAR V Draeger under-water breathing apparatus (UBA); and (3) closed-circuit mixed-gas MK 15 UBA.

Michael and the others were required to be completely familiar with their equipment so that they could prevent or remedy any malfunction underwater without panic. Surfacing from deep water was simply not an option. Also included in the dive phase were the basics of underwater navigation and long-distance underwater swimming. The trainees also learned how to work with limpet mines, underwater explosives that feature a time-delay exploder and are attached to the hull of a ship or submarine with a strap or a powerful magnet. The students made nearly fifty dives during this phase of training.

After eight weeks, all were considered expert divers by commercial standards, although it would take about three years of mission experience for them to be con-sidered competent combat swimmers. It is the dive component of SEAL train-ing—making SEALs as comfortable in the water as on land—that separates them from all other special operations forces. These diving skills would become essential in later training. After mastering these skills, the trainees were given a competency test. Here, they went one-on-one with an instructor who "attacked" them under-water, removing their regulators from their mouths, turning off their air supply, tying their hoses in knots, pulling off their masks and fins, then tumbling and turning them around. In response, they had to reestablish their equipment and air supply and repair their equipment underwater. Only as a last resort could they sur-face without their equipment.

After gaining competency and confidence in the CTT, they headed for the waters of the Pacific and San Diego Bay, learned underwater navigation and pace count, and began mastering the skills necessary to become competent combat swimmers, in both daylight and nighttime. Their last dive evolution was a five-and-a-half-mile swim from the NSW Center to Imperial Beach.

Dive Tower

After learning how to tie knots on land, it was time for the trainees to practice their skills underwater. This was done at the dive tower, a fifty-foot vertical steel cylinder filled with clear, heated freshwater. In the first evolution, the students dived to a depth of thirty feet and tied three separate knots on a post. The second evolution, a real confidence booster, involved tying a single knot during a fifty-foot dive. Instructors were in the water monitoring every student during the sec-ond evolution.

Physical-Skills Evolutions

First Phase scores were no longer good enough. The timed and graded evolu-tions now required a two-mile ocean swim with fins in eighty minutes; a four-mile run in long pants and boots in thirty-one minutes; completion of the O-course in 10:30; and successful completion of three-and-a-half-mile and five-and-a-half-mile ocean swims. As in First Phase, on Friday of the last day in Second Phase, the students evaluated their training evolutions and their instructors. The Academic/Performance Review Board again reviewed the academic and physical training performance of each student to determine who proceeded on to Third Phase. The board reviewed with each student where they excelled and where they could use improvement. Michael earned the right to proceed to the next phase of BUD/S.

Third Phase

Third Phase, also known as the Land-Warfare Phase, introduced the prospective SEALs to demolitions and tactics. This nine-week program was where the class learned the elements of land warfare as practiced by Navy commandos. As in the previous phases, this required specialized equipment used by the U.S. Army, including H-gear, weight-bearing harnesses, canteens, ammunition pouches, sleeping bags, and rucksacks. During Third Phase, sailors learned the basics of being a soldier.

H-Gear

H-gear was a canvas utility belt used to carry a light load of personal infantry gear. It was supported by a padded pair of nylon suspenders, and had to be set up in a prescribed manner: four ammunition pouches in front, two on either side of the front-buckle catch; a canteen hung just behind each hip; and a personal first-aid kit in the small of the back. The only piece of equipment with optional placement was the combat knife, which was usually placed opposite the rappelling line. All buckles and metal surfaces were painted flat black or covered with olive-colored tape to prevent them from making noise or reflecting light.

Timed Evolutions

The timed PT evolutions of Second Phase were no longer good enough and again lowered. Almost all of the conditioning runs in Third Phase were done with full rucksacks and H-gear. A fully loaded rucksack might weigh forty pounds, not including other equipment on the H-gear. The O-course time was lowered to an even ten minutes; the four-mile beach run in long pants and boots to thirty minutes. In addition, the trainees had to complete a two-mile ocean swim with fins in seventy-five minutes, and successfully complete a fourteen-mile run with a fully loaded rucksack.

Weapons Training

Week one of Third Phase consisted of learning the basics of using a compass, reading a map, and walking a line of bearing using a pace count to measure distance.

Week one also introduced field weapons, beginning with weapons safety and becoming familiar with the SEAL arsenal.

Monday of week two sent the students to NSW's Mountain Warfare Training Facility at La Posta, California. At an elevation of three thousand feet, this training center, located on thirteen hundred acres, includes a five-thousand-meter mountain-endurance training course for a timed land-navigation checkout evolution. The facility continues today to play a vital role in the training of NSW forces because the terrain closely resembles the environments found in Korea, Iraq, and Afghanistan.

During their field training, Michael and the other students were introduced to the SEAL's primary weapon, the M4 rifle, weapons training, and shooting qualifications. The training facility has a state-of-the-art shooting range that includes metal silhouettes at distances of fifty to one hundred meters. The trainees learned that smooth is fast. Speed comes from learning a correct, smooth technique. Firing two shots in rapid succession at each target, they were graded on both time and accuracy. NSW and all U.S. Special Forces use a modified M4, specifically the M4A1, a fully automatic variation of the basic M4 carbine. The M4A1 is a gas-operated, air-cooled, magazine-fed, selective fire, shoulder-fired weapon with a telescoping stock that provides greater maneuverability in close quarters and combat-extended range with lethal capability. It has an effective range of about five hundred to six hundred meters. The USSOCOM modification is a SOPMOD Block I Kit that features a rail interface system (RIS), a special hand guard, a shortened quick-detachable M203 grenade launcher, a leaf sight, a sound suppressor, a backup rear sight and a visible laser-infrared designator, reflex sights, and a night-vision sight.

"Gentlemen, This Changes Everything"

At about 5:45 Pacific time on the morning of September 11, 2001, Ensign Michael Murphy and his BUD/S classmates were conducting a morning PT session before continuing their reconnaissance training. One of the instructors suddenly called them into the classroom. There, two large television screens suspended in the corners at the front of the room displayed the carnage and devastation occurring on the other side of their country. For the next ninety minutes the men all sat in disbelief as both towers of the World Trade Center collapsed, the Pentagon was attacked, and a fourth plane was reported down in Somerset County, Pennsylvania.

As Ensign Murphy watched the events unfold so close to his home, he was concerned for his best friends, Jimmie and Owen O'Callaghan, both now serving as New York City policemen. He knew that they would be at the World Trade Center, along with their uncle, who was a member of the New York City Fire Department. As his thoughts of home moved like a video screen through his mind, he stared at the television. The images of the towers collapsing and the resulting deaths of thousands of his fellow New Yorkers was seared into every neuron of his brain.

Newly commissioned Ensign Michael P. Murphy receiving his first salute upon graduating from Officer Candidate School on December 13, 2000. *(Courtesy of the Murphy family)*

Graduation picture of BUD/S Class 236. Ensign Michael Murphy is on the far left in the top row. *(U.S. Navy)*

Left: When Michael's best friend became a member of the New York City Fire Department, Michael wore the station's patch as a symbol of solidarity while in Afghanistan. *(Courtesy of the Murphy family)*

Michael Murphy studies a land-navigation chart in Afghanistan. This photo was taken on the early morning of May 20, 2005. *(Courtesy of Ben Sauers)*

This is where the fight took place. The image also shows where Murphy, Dietz, and Axelson fell along with Lutrell's route of escape. *(Photo courtesy of Ensign Christopher Reed)*

Taken on June 18, 2005, as he prepares for yet another mission, this is one of the best-known pictures of Lieutenant Michael Murphy. *(Courtesy of the Murphy family)*

The ramp ceremony at Bagram Airfield, Afghanistan, on July 5, 2005. The flag-draped military cases are carrying the remains of Lieutenant Michael P. Murphy (front) and Petty Officer Third Class Danny Dietz (rear). *(Courtesy of Ben Sauers)*

Sixteen fire trucks from various Long Island fire departments formed an arch that suspended eight 30' x 30' flags as Michael's funeral procession entered Calverton National Cemetery on July 13, 2005. *(Courtesy of the Murphy family)*

Lieutenant Michael P. Murphy's headstone at Calverton National Cemetery, located in Section 67, site 3710. (*Photo by the author*)

The reverse side of Michael's headstone, noting his Silver Star and Purple Heart, along with his SEAL Trident. (*Photo by the author*)

Sign welcoming visitors to Navy SEAL Lt. Michael P. Murphy Memorial Park overlooking Lake Ronkonkoma, where Michael served as a lifeguard and beach manager for several years. *(Photo by the author)*

[Center] Dedication of the Navy SEAL Lt. Michael P. Murphy Memorial Park on May 7, 2006. The monument was donated by the Military Order of the Purple Heart. Standing in the back row are Rear Admiral Joseph Maguire and Michael's father, Daniel J. Murphy. In the front row are Michael's younger brother, John, and his mother, Maureen Murphy. *(Courtesy of the Murphy family)*

[Bottom] Lieutenant Murphy's parents with Congressman Timothy Bishop and Rear Admiral Joseph Maguire at the Lake Ronkonkoma park's dedication on May 7, 2006. *(Courtesy of the Murphy family)*

Sailor's Cross dedicated to the memory of Lieutenant Michael Murphy, located in front of the American Legion Post in Patchogue, New York. *(Photo by the author)*

Dan Murphy prays at the grave of Chief Warrant Officer 4 Chris Scherkenbach, the helicopter pilot from the 160th SOAR who lost his life on June 28, 2005, during the Murphys' visit to Arlington National Cemetery on October 21, 2007, the day before Lieutenant Murphy received the Medal of Honor. *(Courtesy of the Murphy family)*

Lieutenant Mike McGreevy's widow, Laura, and daughter, Molly, accompanied the Murphys on their visit to Arlington National Cemetery. *(Courtesy of the Murphy family)*

Escorted by a Navy honor guard, the family of Lieutenant Michael Murphy places wreaths at the graves of those lost in Operation Red Wings interred at Arlington National Cemetery. *(Courtesy of the Murphy family)*

Lieutenant Michael Murphy's parents being escorted by a Navy and Army honor guard during the wreath-laying ceremony at the Tomb of the Unknowns at Arlington National Cemetery. *(Courtesy of the Murphy family)*

Lieutenant Michael Murphy's parents standing at the Tomb of the Unknowns. *(Courtesy of the Murphy family)*

Maureen Murphy holds the Medal of Honor presented to her and Dan by President Bush. *(Courtesy of the Murphy family)*

Michael's parents stand with President Bush as a military aide reads the Medal of Honor citation. *(Courtesy of the Murphy family)*

A Navy honor guard stands at the display table in the Pentagon's Hall of Heroes during Lieutenant Michael P. Murphy's induction ceremony on October 23, 2007. *(Courtesy of the Murphy family)*

The program for the induction ceremony in the Pentagon's Hall of Heroes. *(Courtesy of the Murphy family)*

The Murphys being interviewed by members of the media following the Hall of Heroes induction ceremony. *(Courtesy of the Murphy family)*

The parents of Lieutenant Michael Murphy stand with Secretary of the Navy Donald C. Winter during the Medal of Honor Flag ceremony at the Navy Memorial in Washington, D.C., on October 23, 2007. *(Courtesy of the Murphy family)*

A U.S. Navy honor guard prepares to fold Michael's Medal of Honor Flag. *(Courtesy of the Murphy family)*

Admiral Gary Roughead, the chief of naval operations, presents Lieutenant Michael Murphy's Medal of Honor Flag to his mother, Maureen. *(Courtesy of the Murphy family)*

Dan Murphy prays at the grave of Lieutenant Commander Erik Kristensen at the U.S. Naval Academy Cemetery in Annapolis, Maryland, on October 24, 2007. *(Courtesy of the Murphy family)*

Four-foot-diameter granite marker located in the Serenity Plaza, Navy SEAL Lt. Michael P. Murphy Memorial Park, Lake Ronkonkoma, New York. *(Courtesy of the Murphy family)*

Rear Admiral Edward Kristensen, USN (ret.), and Suzanne Kristensen visit the grave of Lieutenant Michael P. Murphy at Calverton National Cemetery on October 31, 2008. *(Photo by the author)*

On November 1, 2008, Michael Murphy's parents visit the New York City Fire Department station "adopted" by their son. *(Photo by the author)*

The reflection of Michael Murphy's mother in the large display honoring him at FDNY Engine Co. 54, Ladder Co. 43—"El Barrio's Bravest." Michael's funeral prayer card is in the upper left corner, and the actual station patch worn by him on June 28, 2005, is under his picture, as is his SEAL Trident. *(Photo by the author)*

Oil portrait of Lieutenant Michael P. Murphy painted by New York artist Gerald Slater and presented to the family on May 7, 2008. Replica prints now hang in several places around the country that have been named in honor of Lieutenant Murphy. *(Courtesy of Gerald Slater)*

Every muscle in his body tightened; his teeth clenched, and his jaws began to ache from the tension. The rock-hard muscles of his physically fine-tuned body became clearly defined. To Michael Murphy, this was personal.

The instructor walked toward the front of the classroom while he muted the sound with his remote control. The sudden silence mentally snapped Michael to attention. As the instructor reached the front center of the classroom, he turned sharply, facing the class. Without looking behind him, he pointed to one of the television screens and in a low stern voice stated, "Gentlemen, this changes everything. We're going to war!" But Ensign Michael Murphy was not *going* to war—he was already there.

After several more minutes of discussion, the class assembled back outside to complete their PT before going on to reconnaissance training. As the PT repetitions were being counted, the men's voices were louder and crisper. Ben Sauers noticed a visible change in Michael: "Michael always had a smile on his face, was intense but very easygoing; after 9/11 something changed in him. You could see it. While he was still very personable and went out of his way to help anyone and everyone, his intensity changed. It's like he became quieter. To those who didn't know him, they would have noticed nothing out of the ordinary, but having been with him since his rollback, I could see it. He internalized 9/11."

Top Gun and Beyond

With the resolve of the class having changed, the men's last day at La Posta began with familiarization shooting without scores to get ready for the Top Gun competition, a single-elimination tournament with members going one-on-one on the range. Each member contributed $10 for the Top Gun Trophy, a KA-BAR knife engraved with the class number.

Each shooter possessed an M4, ten rounds, and an extra magazine. On command the trainees dropped to a kneeling position and fired rounds at the target at twenty-five meters, then shifted to a prone position and fired at the target at fifty meters. They could fire as many rounds as they liked, and the first shooter with a hit on each target was the winner and progressed on to face another opponent.

After La Posta, the students of Class 236 traveled to Camp Pendleton, California, the U.S. Marine Corps' 125,000-acre facility, where the students utilized the Edison Range, one of the most complete shooting-range training facilities anywhere. There they continued to hone their shooting skills using the entire SEAL arsenal, but with special emphasis on their M4A1.

The next two weeks found them back at the NSW Center for demolitions training. A SEAL must be very familiar with a variety of military and other types of demolitions, and must be able to safely detonate explosives both on land and at sea. While the basics of priming both electrical and nonelectrical demolition charges were covered at Coronado, the majority of demolition training was conducted during four weeks of field training on San Clemente Island.

San Clemente Island

Michael and his class loaded their equipment into a McDonnell Douglas C-9 for the short flight to the "Rock," San Clemente Island. Upon arrival they unloaded their weapons and personal gear into an old white bus for the two-mile drive to the training facility.

San Clemente Island is the southernmost of the Channel Islands off California. Officially uninhabited, the twenty-one-mile-long island hosts an active sonar base, a simulated embassy, and a rocket-test facility. Known for its high winds, dangerous terrain covered with scrub grass, ice plants, and prickly pear and golden snake cactus, it is the home of the Camp Al Huey SEAL training facility, located just north of the runways of the Naval Auxiliary landing field. Built in 1989, Camp Al Huey was named after a Vietnam-era master chief petty officer who had dedicated many years to both the SEAL teams and the training of SEALs. It is a complete training facility containing barracks, chow hall, armory, weapons-cleaning stations, classrooms, shooting, demolition, and hand grenade ranges, and an O-course.

During their last four weeks of Third Phase training, the students began to work seven days a week from 6 AM to 8 PM without a break, until their BUD/S graduation.

Flight Training

One of the more lighthearted but extremely challenging exercises performed by Michael's class was "flight training." Flight training for BUD/S candidates involved the frequent running up and down of the steep hills of San Clemente while carrying a large heavy wooden pallet over their heads. With the very strong winds coming off the Pacific, it was more than a challenge for the SEAL candidates to maintain their balance and footing. It was not uncommon for the winds to lift them off the ground, which slowed their "flight" time. As in every training evolution, there was a precise procedure to flight training, including a prearranged "flight pattern" and "maneuvers," as well as proper "landing instructions." Failure to follow instructions resulted in another "flight."

Chow PT

In life, nothing is free. The same is true in BUD/S. At Camp Al Huey, to earn breakfast, the trainees had to perform maximum push-ups and sit-ups in two-minute timed intervals with full H-gear and full canteens. Before lunch they completed a two-hundred-meter run up a steep hill to "Frog Rock"; this was also made in full H-gear with full canteens, and it had to be completed in ninety seconds. The price for their evening meal was fifteen pull-ups and fifteen dips—also with full H-gear and canteens.

Land-Warfare Skills

Having familiarized themselves with the SEAL weapons arsenal earlier at the Naval Special Warfare's Mountain Warfare Training Facility, Michael and the other students learned combat shooting techniques with both the M4A1 and the SIG SAUER pistol. Combat shooting involved fast and accurate shooting as well as changing magazines while continuing to get rounds on target. The trainees then progressed to immediate-action drills (IADs), which taught the men how to break contact in a firefight or quickly assault an enemy position. During these drills they learned how the leapfrog maneuver, in which one element of the combat unit moved while the other provided covering fire. This meant that someone off to a trainee's side and behind him was firing at a target in front of him. Class 236 first walked through the IADs, then ran through them at full speed, both in daylight and then at night. Other land-warfare skills learned were ambushes, structure searches, handling of prisoners, reconnaissance techniques, and raid planning—again, each skill was taught in the classroom and then practiced in the field, both in daylight and at night. The trainees learned the skill of holding one's breath and diving twenty feet to place demolitions on obstacles submerged off the island's coast. Using the hydrographic reconnaissance skills learned in First Phase, the class conducted a simulated night-combat beach reconnaissance, prepared a hydrographic chart, and returned the following night to place the charges and blow them up.

Class 236's final field training exercise (FTX) problem was conducted over a five-day period. First, the men were divided into squads, upon which each squad entered a period of isolation to begin mission planning. Each squad then conducted four consecutive night operations utilizing the skills they learned during the previous six months at BUD/S.

These separate and exhausting exercises made it a sobering but exciting time for Michael and his classmates, because they saw their months of training begin to gel and pay off. They knew these skills would be utilized in the months and years ahead.

Graduation Week: Final Training Evolutions

Back at the NSW Center, their last graded physical evolution was the SEAL Physical Readiness Test (PRT). The test began with the maximum number of push-ups, sit-ups, and pull-ups in timed two-minute intervals, then continued with a three-mile timed run and a half-mile timed swim. It was not uncommon for individual scores to seem unbelievable by civilian standards, with the number of push-ups exceeding 200, sit-ups exceeding 150, and pull-ups exceeding 30, with near fifteen-minute three-mile runs and twelve-minute half-mile swims.

After the men successfully completed their SEAL PRT, only two physical evolutions remained before graduation. The first, Hooyah PT, consisted of a run through the O-course, a seven-mile beach run, and then another run through the

O-course. The other was the Balboa Park Run, a ten-mile run from Balboa Park in San Diego back to Imperial Beach.

With one day left in their training, the students completed their BUD/S checkout briefing, received their orders, and spent time rehearsing for the event they had been working toward for the previous nine months—graduation.

Graduation

On the Friday of Class 236's final week at BUD/S, the grinder was transformed with flags, rows of chairs, a small stage, a microphone, and colorful and patriotic bunting. With family, friends, SEALs, and the entire NSW command in attendance, and after remarks by invited guests, each graduate received a certificate of completion. Having threatened to resign their positions with the New York City Police Department if not permitted to attend their best friend's graduation, Jimmie and Owen O'Callaghan joined Michael's parents, Maureen and Dan, and his brother, John, as they watched Michael receive his certificate of completion.

Ben Sauers remembered him as "the guy that always had a smile on his face and words of encouragement for everyone. And he was always the guy that during our rare time off could be seen running with full combat gear and doing extra PT. He was not the fastest. He was not the strongest, but very smart and very determined. No one had more determination than Ensign Murphy. I would follow him anywhere."

On October 18, 2001, Ensign Michael P. Murphy signed his Fitness Report and Counseling Record for BUD/S. The written comments about his performance read as follows: "Completed 25 weeks of instruction in physical conditioning, surface swimming, small boat handling, hydrographic reconnaissance, weapons training, small unit tactics, demolition training, and open and closed circuit scuba. His professional performance was outstanding during this physically and mentally demanding course of instruction."

For Murphy and the rest of his class, it was a bittersweet moment. The cost had been high, with the loss of Lieutenant Skop, and Michael's near loss of both his lower legs and feet. Although they had graduated, Michael Murphy and each of the other members of BUD/S Class 236 realized that his certificate of completion was merely a ticket of admission to the next phase of their training.

The *agoge* was the warrior-training program utilized by the ancient Spartans. NSW had its own version of the *agoge* to train modern-day warriors for a nation at war.

CHAPTER NINE

Agoge: Earning the Trident

I expect you to lead at the upper levels of your knowledge, skill, and authority.

—ADMIRAL ERIC OLSON, quoted in Dick Couch, *The Finishing School*

Sparta was a city-state in ancient Greece, located on the Eurotas River in the southern part of the Peloponnese. It rose to become the dominant military power in the region in 650 BC due to its military efficiency and its social structure, unique in ancient Greece. In 480 BC a small force of Spartans, along with allies from Thespiae and Thebes, led by King Leonidas made the legendary last stand at the Battle of Thermopylae against the massive Persian army, inflicting very high casualty rates on the Persians. The weaponry, strategy, and bronze armor of the Greek hoplites and their phalanx proved far superior to that of their opponents. The phalanx was a military formation in which the soldiers would lock shields and project their spears over the shields and progress in a fashion that all but prevented a frontal assault, making the phalanx greater than the sum of its parts.

The *agoge*, a rigorous training regimen for all Spartan male citizens, involved stealth, cultivating loyalty to one's group, military training, hunting, dancing, and social preparation. The *agoge*, first introduced by the Spartan lawgiver Lycurgus in the first half of the seventh century BC, was designed to train male citizens from the ages of seven through twenty-nine. The goal was to produce physically and morally strong males to serve in the Spartan army by encouraging conformity and stressing the importance of the Spartan state over one's own personal interest, and so generating the warrior elites of Sparta.

When a boy reached his seventh birthday, he was enrolled in the *agoge* under the authority of the *paidonomos*, or magistrate, charged with supervising education. This began the first of three stages of the *agoge*: the *paides* (ages seven to seventeen), the *paidiskoi* (ages eighteen to nineteen), and the *hebontes* (ages twenty to twenty-nine). The boys were given one item of clothing per year and expected to make or acquire other needed clothing. They were also deliberately underfed, and taught to become skilled at acquiring their food.

At the beginning of *paidiskoi*, around the age of eighteen, the students became reserve members of the Spartan army. At the beginning of *hebontes*, roughly at the age of twenty, the students became full part of the *syssitia*, the obligatory daily meal for men and youths in the army, and were finally permitted to marry, although they continued to live in barracks, and continued to compete for a place among the Spartan *hippeis*, the royal honor guard. The modern-day SEALs view their training, community, and tactics as being very similar to that of the ancient Spartans, so it is not uncommon to see and hear references to Spartans and the Battle of Thermopylae in many SEAL training evolutions, events, and ceremonies.

With his college education at Penn State, Officer Candidate School, and BUD/S behind him, Ensign Michael Murphy had earned the right to progress to the next level in the SEAL *agoge*: SEAL Qualification Training, or SQT.* Before getting there, he had five different applications or prepatory schools to complete.

Army Jump School: The "Air" in Sea, Air, Land (SEAL)

Following a week of well-earned leave, Ensign Murphy reported to Fort Benning, Georgia. Successful completion of the Army Airborne School, more commonly known as jump school, would result in military certification and the awarding of silver jump wings for completion of five static-line jumps. Conducted by the 1st Battalion (Airborne), 507th Infantry Regiment, U.S. Army Infantry School, jump school was designed to qualify students in the use of the parachute as a means of combat deployment, and to develop leadership, self-confidence, and an aggressive spirit through mental and physical training.

The instructors were known as Black Hats because of the black baseball caps they wore, along with their dress uniforms, rank insignia, and parachutist badges. All students were required to call them "Sergeant Airborne" (or "Petty Officer Airborne" in case the instructor was from the Navy). At jump school, the instructors were from not only from the Army, but also the Air Force, the Marine Corps, and the Navy. Because trainees from all four main branches of the military are able to attend jump school, each branch insists that it have at least one representative present to ensure quality instruction.

Compared to the physical-training demands at BUD/S, the Army's requirements at jump school might have seemed like nothing more than a mere warm-up to Michael and other prospective SEALs; however, the students were expected to remain professional and respectful in their attitude toward their classmates from

---

* For a complete and detailed description of of SEAL Qualification Training, read Dick Couch's *The Finishing School: Earning the Navy SEAL Trident* (New York: Crown, 2004).

the other service branches, as well as the instructors. The three-week program was designed to teach the basics of successful military static-line jumping and mass troop evacuation of an aircraft, and was broken down into three distinct phases, each of which had to be successfully completed before progression to the next phase was permitted.

Ground Week

During Ground Week students began an intensive program of instruction designed to build individual airborne skills, which prepared them to make a parachute jump and land safely. The students simulated jumping from an aircraft using a mock airplane door and practiced parachute landings through controlled falls from a thirty-four-foot tower. To successfully complete Ground Week, each trainee had to qualify individually on all of the training appratus and pass all PT requirements.

Tower Week

During Tower Week the element of teamwork was added to the training with the introduction of mass-exit techniques. The apparatuses used for this training were the 34-foot tower, the mock airplane door, a suspended harness, and a 250-foot free tower. The students completed their individual skill training and built team-effort skills during this week. To move on to the final week of training, each trainee had to master mass-exit procedures and pass all PT requirements. Although SEALs do not use mass-exit procedures in tactical applications, Michael and other SEAL trainees were required to successfully complete this part of the course.

Jump Week

During the final week of training Michael made five parachute jumps into the drop zone (DZ), the area in which training parachute jumps are conducted. Michael and his class were required to run to the airfield, conduct pre-jump training, and then get into their harnesses and wait their turn to jump. Two of these jumps were combat-equipment jumps, in which the jumper carried a rucksack and a dummy weapon. The other three jumps were "Hollywood jumps," meaning that the jumper only wore a parachute and a reserve. In addition, one jump was made at night.

Ensign Murphy successfully completed all requirements and was awarded his silver jump wings. Upon completing five additional jumps, he was awarded his gold wings. His next duty station was back at the NSW Center in Coronado.

Junior Officer Training Course (JOTC)

Throughout BUD/S each trainee is expected to assume a leadership role. Petty officers and officers are rightfully held to a higher personal standard and also responsible for ensuring their respective boat team is up to standard. Failing to ensure the readiness of their men results in discipline of the entire team. For Michael Murphy, having the bar raised was not a matter for concern—for him, the higher the better. In the SQT course to follow there would be an increased dichotomy of training between the enlisted men and their officers. Enlisted men would be expected to become experts in communications, diving, air operations, weapons, and reconnaissance, as well as all of the specific technical specialties required by the SEAL teams. The officers would be primarily responsible for mission planning and tactical decision making.

In NSW there are two primary leadership development courses: Junior Officer Training Course (JOTC) and Senior Petty Officer Training Course (SPOTC). The JOTC is for new officers through the rank of lieutenant. The SPOTC is for team petty officers with two or more deployments who are being groomed for leading petty officer (LPO) or chief petty officer (CPO) duties.

The JOTC is a five-week training program conducted at Naval Amphibious Base, Coronado. The first three weeks consist of a comprehensive group of leadership seminars covering topics such as NSW history, command relationships, enlisted performance evaluation, and public speaking, as well as presentations from SEALs, both active and retired. Students also are schooled in the other special operations forces (SOF), such as the Army's Rangers, Special Forces (Green Berets), and 1st Special Forces Operational Detachment-Delta (Delta Force), the Marine's Force Recon, and the Air Force's pararescue jumpers, known as PJs.

Ensign Murphy and the others learned where NSW falls in the chain of command in a special operations mission involving another service branch as well as in a special operations combined and/or joint task force. There were also classes on their administrative and legal responsibilities as officers. As in BUD/S, each day started with a rigorous PT session and an ocean swim.

Their leadership classes featured case studies of actual events, battles, and operations involving SEAL teams during deployment. They learned quickly that in combat situations there are few instances of black and white, but rather all varying shades of gray. It is these shades of gray that required true leadership. Michael Murphy would learn that lesson all too well.

The first three weeks were full of guest speakers describing deployments in the combat theaters of Vietnam, Grenada, Panama, the Persian Gulf, Bosnia, Somalia, Afghanistan, and Iraq. Michael's class also received several presentations by the commanding officer of NSW. In one such presentation, Admiral Olson had this to say:

> I expect you to lead at the upper levels of your knowledge, skill, and authority. Be a teammate. What's good for the team has priority over what's good for you. Demonstrate professionalism in all that you do. Be sharp, look sharp. Teach, coach, guide, and mentor your force, but don't claim experience that you don't have.

Never sacrifice what you know is right for what is convenient or expedient. Live the life of a leader—one of values, character, courage, and commitment. What you do and what you tolerate in your presence best demonstrates your standards.

Empower your subordinate leaders to work at the full level of their authority. Encourage your subordinate leaders; train them, trust them, hold them to standard. Remember—the prime measure of your performance is the performance of your men.

The fourth week of training was also classroom based, with the emphasis on mission planning, using the most current mission-planning software and the SEAL Mission Support Center (MSC). Ensign Murphy learned the mission-planning platform known as SOMPE-M (Special Operations Mission Planning Environment-Maritime). The Mission Support Center was utilized by deployed teams to allow them to interact with rear-echelon support units for logistical support and tactical information on a real-time basis.

Again Admiral Olson addressed the class, providing a firsthand account of the fight in Mogadishu, Somalia, in October 1993. His insights turned his session into a series of lessons learned.

Amid all the heroics and the carnage, and yes, the mistakes, we found out some things that may help us the next time. And these lessons did not come cheap. Two hundred men from Task Force Ranger were involved start to finish. We suffered ninety-nine casualties—sixteen dead. No SEALs were lost, but we did collect some Purple Hearts. So what did we learn? . . .

There are some macro issues, like the lack of armored vehicles and the non-availability of an AC-130 gunship, but there are times when you simply may not have the assets available you would like to have for a mission or for mission contingencies. We also had a mission statement focused on capturing a single personality—the warlord General Muhammad Farrah Aideed. Our mission statement in Somalia was to get General Aideed, which meant that we could destroy his infrastructure, nab his top lieutenants, restore global peace, and solve world hunger, but it would have still been mission failure if we didn't capture Aideed. So, although we had many tactical successes, we still didn't get Aideed, so we failed our mission. Aside from those terrible twenty-four hours, since we didn't get him, our mission was a failure in that regard. The lives we lost in Mogadishu drove our national policy regarding the use of the military up until 9/11. That's why we fought the conflict in Bosnia with air power alone from twenty-one thousand feet. No one wanted to accept the political risks of another Mogadishu. A policy that involves a single personality sets you up for failure. Much the same thing could be said in Afghanistan because we did not get bin Laden. However, in Afghanistan, we successfully routed a brutal regime.

In answer to the question "Sir, what should our mission be in these situations?" the admiral responded:

They should be as general as possible. In Somalia, to go after the clan infrastructure that was opposing our humanitarian efforts there. In Afghanistan, it is al-Qaeda and those who support terrorism. I think our failure to find bin Laden cost us something in the eyes of those who oppose our interests in the area. But these are big issues, well above your pay grade and mine.

Let's talk about things we can do—what you can do as future naval leaders as you train and prepare your platoons for special operations. First of all, you cannot do enough medical preparation and training. Every man in the squad file has to be medically competent. You don't always want to send your corpsman to drag the wounded out of the line of fire, but the men you do send must have the medical skills to deal immediately with the life-threatening injuries. You have to be prepared to carry on the fight and the mission while you treat your casualties. We had some problems with communication in Mogadishu. We cluttered up the nets when things got hot and didn't use proper call signs. Keep your comms clean and stay with procedure. That said, train for this. In all your scenario-based training, have a man go down; have your radio malfunction. Train for the worst-case scenarios.

As Admiral Olson continued, he began to pace around the room.

If it's a daytime mission, plan for what will happen if you have to stay out after dark, and for the reverse as well. In Mogadishu, when we went back in that evening with the relief convoy, it was to be a daytime mission, in and out quickly. We didn't get out until the next morning. One of my SEALs handed me a night-vision optic right before we left. As it worked out, I would have been hard-pressed to do my job without it. Close air support. Know your fire support platforms; know how to use them. Our special operations pilots are the best in the world. We had pilots flying continually for fifteen hours in a very dangerous environment. They were magnificent. Know what they can and they can't do; don't misuse these brave and talented airmen. Body armor. It's heavy and that day it was very hot, but some of those sixteen good men we lost could have been saved if they had worn body armor with ballistic plates. Your SEALs might complain, especially during training on a hot day, but in an urban environment, it's a life saver. You are leaders; do the right thing. Train like you intend to fight. See that you and your men train *exactly* as if you were doing it for real.

After a deliberate pause, and looking into the eyes of the junior officers, he continued:

One last thought concerning Somalia. In Mogadishu, we put men at risk and remained in harm's way to bring back the bodies of those we could. We have to bring them back; it's part of who we are. It's the right thing to do for ourselves and for the families of our fallen comrades, but it also affects policy. If we are involved, it's a tough mission and we are on the world stage. The bodies of those Americans they dragged through the streets of Mogadishu changed American policy for more than a decade. It will always be a judgment call, risking lives to bring home the remains of our own, but it's something we must do if at all possible. Someday it may be your call. Think about it ahead of time, because if that decision falls on you, it will be in the heat of battle under the worst possible conditions. Good luck to all of you. Take care of your men.

Little did anyone in that classroom realize that Admiral Olson's words were not only reflective, but prophetic as well.

The final week was field based, at the NSW La Posta training facility, conducting leadership quick-reaction drills. These fast, hard-hitting drills were designed to teach tactical decision making in a simulated combat environment. The training was essentially continuous for five days, with the officers eating and sleeping in the field.

While Ensign Murphy finished the JOTC with great anticipation of SQT, he had to complete three more courses before getting there.

Range Safety Officer Course

The range safety officer (RSO) course taught the essentials of using firearms in a safe and effective training environment. Conducted over a one-week period on multiple firing ranges, the training was designed to familiarize the students with all NSW shooting and training regulations and instruct them how to comply with those standards.

Dive Supervisor Course

This one-week course emphasized compliance with all NSW training and diving regulations. While actual diving was an important aspect of this course, Michael and each of his fellow classmates also had to establish and supervise a diving evolution. This involved making sure that all of the students under their charge were properly checked out before entering the water.

Survival, Evasion, Resistance and Escape (SERE)

Established by the Air Force at the end of the Korean War, SERE was extended during the Vietnam War to Army and Navy personnel. A course common to nearly all SOF operators, it is conducted by the naval aviation community at Warner Springs, California.

Survival and Evasion

The majority of the SERE training focused on survival and evasion. Woodcraft and wilderness survival techniques in all types of climates were taught, including emergency first aid, land navigation, camouflage techniques, methods of evasion, communication protocols, and the making of improvised tools.

Resistance and Escape

This segment was designed based on the experiences of former prisoners of war. It included training on how to resist the enemy and survive in the event of capture. The majority of this training is classified.

After spending five days in the classroom learning survival skills, assisting rescuers in the event they are caught behind enemy lines, and learning the U.S. military code of conduct as it pertains to prisoners of war (POWs), Michael and his class were placed in the field. There, for five more days, they applied the skills they had learned in the classroom. In a simulation of an actual event, they engaged in combat and were captured and detained as as POWs. Through this both physically and psychologically demanding course, Michael and his classmates got a small glimpse as to what might be in store for them as POWs.

SEAL Qualification Training (SQT)

Considered the capstone course, more money, time, resources, and talent are given to SQT than any other program conducted at NSW. As such, the pace and schedule are elevated several levels. Successful completion of all training up to this point does not guarantee a student his Trident. Only after succeeding in the fifteen-week SQT course is a student awarded the coveted Trident, the symbol of the SEALs.

For Michael and his classmates, after PT, the first evolution was combat medicine, called tactical combat casualty care, or TCCC. Here they learned how to treat combat casualties, prevent additionial casualties, and still complete their assigned mission. Overall, the best battlefield medicine is superiority in firepower. TCCC required the SEAL trainees to use BATS, a procedure that focused on bleeding, airway, tension pneumothorax, and shock, rather than the civilian ACLS (advanced cardiac life support) protocol. After Michael and his class successfully completed their classroom instruction and passed a written examination, they were placed in simulated combat positions under simulated fire conditions with single as well as multiple combat casualties with varing degrees of injury. The skills Michael Murphy learned during this training would serve him well in the years ahead.

Next was the land-navigation evolution, which began with two days in the classroom learning map reading and land-navigation techniques that include the use of a compass. During this phase of their training, Michael and the other students were also taught how to classify their equipment.

First line gear was what they wore: camouflage uniforms (known as cammies), boots, hat, and whatever they carried in their pockets, which should include a pencil, a notebook, a waterproof penlight, a map, a compass, a pocketknife, a strobe light, emergency rations (usually a PowerBar or two), and a survival kit. Primary and backup weapons were also considered first line gear.

Second line gear, also known as operational gear, was all the equipment carried on their H-gear. This included ammunition and grenades, a personal medical kit, a PRC-112 survival radio, twenty-four hours' worth of rations, and two quarts of water. Also on the H-gear should be a weapons cleaning kit, insect repellent, water purfication tablets, a snap link, an IV pouch and extra field dressings, and a battle-field knife.

Third line gear consisted of their rucksack and its contents, which should include a sleeping bag, a ground pad, rations, water, socks, extra ammunition, demolitions, and grenades.

The students were taught to pack and secure all three levels of their gear to ensure it made absolutely no noise when walking, running, or jumping. Each of them was issued a basic set of first, second, and third line gear.

Following land navigation, they headed off to the NSW Mountain Warfare Training Facility in La Posta, California, to become combat shooters. Sight picture (properly aligning the target within the weapon's sights) and trigger control were stressed, as well as the combat stance: feet apart, knees bent slightly, arms straight, shoulders rolled forward, elbows in tight. Thousands of rounds were fired by each student as he learned to get rounds downrange and on target.

From La Posta they traveled to the firing range at Camp Pendleton, California. Here they learned marksmanship for five days. Again, thousands of rounds were fired by each student, with minimum scores required.

After these evolutions the students moved on to Close Quarters Defense (CQD) training back at NSW. During this phase of their training, only a few hours were spent in the classroom; this training was all hands-on. Here they learned to manage and utilize aggression for self-protection in what are called Box Drills. Box Drills were one-on-one training exercises utilizing the hand-to-hand combat skills they had been taught. The action continued until one of the contestants was knocked out of the box. This training was all about the student dominating his space and fighting to win in a tactical situation. The instruction also included several sessions on prisoner control. Following their week of CQD, Michael's class prepared for the next evolution, at Camp Billy Machen, NSW's Desert Training Facility, located about 135 miles east of the Special Warfare Center. Camp Billy Machen is a Navy SEAL desert training facility located at the edge of the Chocolate Mountains in southern California named after the first Navy SEAL killed in Vietnam.

At Camp Billy Machen, Michael and his classmates began a three-week evolution that required them to demonstrate sound judgment, teamwork, and physical stamina. The first week was spent at the range for weapons training. During week two the men engaged in night evolutions, practiced hand and arm signals, and had a day of rocket firing training, They also had to survive the combat conditioning course, which included a thirteen-mile run that began at 3:00 AM, with full gear and weapons. Several days of practice with military demolitions were followed by immediate-action drills, or IADs. Combat search and rescue (CSAR) was also covered. The last three days were devoted to the final mission problem, or final field training exercise. The final field training exercise was a full-scale exercise that required Michael to use all of the skills he had learned.

Camp Billy Machen was followed by the two-week Combat Swimmer Course (CSC). In a stark change from the desert heat, the students now endured the 60° waters of the Pacific. Here, they would learn about the placing of mines and the vulnerabilities of a ship's hull, master underwater navigation, and hone their knot-tying and diving skills. To successfully complete this evolution, a dive pair swam into a harbor, attacked two ships with limpet mines, and exfiltrated to a pickup point without being detected from the surface.

On April 4, 2002, Ensign Michael P. Murphy acknowledged and signed his SQT Fitness Report and Counseling Record. The report noted Michael's "solid performance as a student in SEAL Qualification Training (SQT) learning the full spectrum of Naval Special Warfare tactics, techniques, procedures, and equipment. He had participated in Medical Training, Land Navigation, Parachuting, Live-fire Weapons and Demolition Scenarios, Combat Diving, and Maritime Operations. He performed well in all aspects of this training and successfully completed all graduation requirements and was recommended for full duty at a SEAL team."

SQT Graduation

With his family present, Ensign Michael Murphy graduated from the Naval Special Warfare Command Center wearing his golden Trident, the symbol of a Navy SEAL. It had taken him nearly six years of education, dedication, and training to get here.

No one graduated from SQT without the the approval of the officer in charge, Chief Warrant Officer 2 Mike Loo. At SQT he was referred to as "the Warrant." Before graduation he provided each student with a handout that was headed "Rules to live by in Naval Special Warfare."

1. Congratulations. You guys have completed a major milestone in your Special Warfare career. Here at the Naval Special Warfare Center you have completed BUD/S, Army airborne training, and SQT, and you have been awarded the NSW SEAL insignia, the Trident. SQT has taught you the SEAL tactics, techniques, and procedures required to successfully integrate into a SEAL platoon. You are now prepared to go in "harm's way" as an operational SEAL. This course has laid the foundation of warfighting knowledge and skills you will use for your entire Special Warfare career. Mastering these skills should be your primary mission. Your lives and the lives of your teammates depend on it.

2. Don't forget that Special Warfare is the number one maritime Special Operations Force in the world and arguably the number one Special Operations Force in the

world. Being number one in the world in anything means *paying a very high price.* You have to be more focused, smarter, work harder, and have more desire than anyone else in other SOF units. Accomplishing the many tasks and difficult assignments that are thrown our way requires great effort, dedication, and persistence.

3. When you get to your team you need to work extremely hard to prepare yourselves for real-world operations. You must be physically and mentally prepared—trained to win the gunfight and accomplish the mission. Stay focused, train hard, and be the professionals we expect you to be. Always maintain your own integrity and the integrity of the teams. This handout contains, in no particular order, a list of lessons learned and rules to live by in Naval Special Warfare. Some of these are my personal rules for success and others are from great leaders in NSW who have been mentors and role models in my life. Keep this handout! Refer to it now and then. Never forget that you are the future of Naval Special Warfare. Talk is cheap; action is everything. Put out the effort and take the action needed to keep our force the best in the world.

A. Master the basics and you will be a good operator. Take care of your equipment and always have your operating gear complete, in good working order, and ready to go to the field. Forgetting a flashlight or having a dead battery in your strobe may cost lives and/or the mission. Pay attention to the basics, in training and real-world. Be the consummate professional whether in the water, in the air, or on land. Practice good noise discipline and situational awareness—360-degree security. Know your duties and responsibilities.

B. Never make the same mistake twice. You are your best critic! When you make a mistake or do something wrong, take it onboard and take it seriously. Be hard on yourselves. Do what you have to do in order to not make the same mistake twice.

C. Strive for perfection. You'll never get there; perfection doesn't exist for SEALs, but we can ALWAYS do better. Being number one in the world is a heavy burden. You will often feel that you are not ready—that you haven't trained enough in a certain area or you're not in top physical shape or there are shortfalls in your gear. Take action. At anytime you could have to risk your life on a dangerous, real-world mission. Knowing this will happen in advance, like right now as you read this, will make you train that much harder to get to the highest possible level of readiness. Put out 110 percent in every endeavor. Identify your weak points, tackle them aggressively, and make them your strong points.

D. The SEAL work ethic. Our job is not eight to five. You cannot be number one in the world and not put in extra hours. Don't be lazy; it is infectious. If some part of your platoon's training is not working, perhaps it's a matter of command and control or a gear problem or a tactical maneuver; fix it now! Don't let it go or put it off to the next training day. As a new guy in the platoon you have the right to speak up and take action on issues like this.

As a new guy, you'll find the learning curve more steep and difficult. You will be required to know and perform a number of tasks to a high operational standard. You will have to master specific assigned duties in the platoon organization. This means working overtime to get the job done. This will not end, even when you have a deployment or two under your belt. It is the SEAL work ethic.

E. Responsibility/Accountability. Ultimately, you have a responsibility to the chain of command and to this country to be prepared to risk your life and the lives of your teammates as you go into harm's way to successfully complete the mission. You are accountable to do what is necessary to make this happen. That is the big picture. On a smaller scale, take your responsibilities seriously and be accountable for your actions.

F. Be a subject-matter expert in your field. We are a small community and we rely on in-house subject-matter experts in communications, ordnance, air operations, diving operations, intelligence, etc., to accomplish our missions. Strive to be the "go to" guy in your field—the one they come to for the right answer. Know all the references, know what other service/units are doing in your field; strive to know everything there is to know about your department or area of expertise.

G. Train as you would fight. An old Army saying but a good one. When possible, train with all the gear you will use in real combat. Train as hard and as realistically possible. That means don't cut corners. During your platoon training, if you accomplish everything successfully, then the training needs to be more challenging. Never say, "If this was real, I'd have this piece of gear with me, or we'd do it this way." Train as you would fight. Use Simunitions as much as possible in urban, CQC, VBSS, and land-warfare training. Whenever possible use role players and other SEALs to oppose you. You may learn that tactics you used for shooting paper targets or bullet traps in the kill house may have to be changed or modified.

H. Don't get cocky; stay humble. Remember the disadvantages we always face:
   • Fighting in an unfamiliar foreign country—someone's backyard.
   • Bad guys who are highly trained. They may have a lot more real-world combat experience than you do, have top-of-the-line gear, and may know our tactics.
   • Bad guys who are passionate about their cause and want to kill you in the worst way.
   • Remember, wearing a Trident doesn't make you invincible.

I. Think ahead and stay organized.

J. When you have a good idea that benefits your platoon/team, share it with other teams.

K. Officers and petty officers need to be administratively savvy; be proficient with awards and evaluations; take care of your men.

L. Look out for your buddies on and off duty.

M. Stay physically fit; be just as smart as you are tough.

N. You are an ambassador of NSW wherever you go. You enjoy a reputation that was earned by the blood, sweat, and toil of the true frogmen of old.

You haven't earned this; you have inherited it, based on the good faith that you will further the tradition. Do nothing to tarnish something you haven't earned by thought, word, or deed.

O. If you don't know or didn't understand, ASK! It's your responsibility to find out. Research; demonstrate an unquenchable desire to know everything about your job.

P. If something is broken or not right, take the initiative to fix it or make it right! Don't wait for someone else to take action.

Q. Always check your equipment again before going into the field. Make sure you have everything and that it's serviceable. LPO and CPO inspections are to make sure this happens.

R. Listen and take notes during all Patrol Leader Order. Prior to going into the field, know the minimum:

- Routes in and out. Have a map and compass.
- Rally points.
- Basic communications plan, call signs, and frequencies.
- Actions at the objective.
- Your platoon's medical plan.
- Your E&E [evasion and escape] plan.

S. ALWAYS rehearse/Dirt Dive everything. Plan the dive (operation). Dive the plan.

T. Mobility. Take only what you absolutely need in the field. When the shit hits the fan, you want to be as light as possible and fast on your feet. You need energy and mobility to win and survive.

U. There is no second place in a gunfight. Winners kill, losers get killed. Fight to win. Train to live.

V. All encounters during a mission are a threat to your team. Never drop your security and always expect contact. Never turn your back on a threat.

W. It takes a shooter to lead a shooter.

X. The easy way out may not be the safest way out.

Y. If the enemy is in range, so are YOU!

Z. Tracers work both ways.

Conclusion: You are a U.S. Navy SEAL, feared by the enemy and respected as the best maritime warrior in the world. Others envy your iron willpower and superior physical toughness. Countless men have dreamed they would become SEALs. Thousands have tried, but only a select few ever earn the right to wear the Trident. Wherever you go, whatever you do, whomever you meet, remember this: you are responsible for your actions. You must protect and defend your country to the best of your ability and uphold the honor of the U.S. Navy and the Navy SEAL Teams. There is no "I" in SEAL team.

You exist to serve the mission. No one owes you anything. You are always on duty, every moment of your career. Your responsibility to be fit and ready to fight never ceases. A crisis will not wait until you complete your next training cycle or recover from a hangover. A warrior's responsibility to be ready for combat never goes on liberty or leave. Think positive mission accomplishment at all times. Synchronize and train your mind and your will just as you train your body. Discipline yourself. Study tactical and leadership material daily. It is only a matter of time before you will engage the enemy in a gunfight. SEAL operations mean you may have to stand toe to toe with an enemy. For those who want to win, there is never enough time to train. Aggressively seek any knowledge that will assure mission accomplishment and make you a survivor and a winner. Never lose the desire to find a new tactic or technique that will make the difference for you and your teammates.

Be openly patriotic. You pay for that right. Wear your uniform proudly and with the same precision and quality with which you would execute a mission.

Live the legend of the teams every day. NCDUs, UDTs, and SEALs have been decorated for incredible acts of valor and accomplished seemingly impossible feats in combat. You are responsible for carrying the SEAL reputation above and beyond your predecessors. Carry yourself with SEAL confidence and professionalism. Leave all who come in contact with you with a positive sense of your combat skills, your loyalty, and your tactical savvy. Make the Trident stand out as the most select special operations insignia in the world.

Be passionate in the pursuit of excellence. Be cautious when working with those who are not. Never allow another man's attitude to jeopardize the mission [or] your teammates' lives. Look for the best in your teammates, not the worst. There are plenty of flaws within each of us. Look for the positive; help and assist those with weaknesses. Openly build and cultivate the close esprit-de-corps that has made the teams famous.

Never show weakness or dissension to anyone outside the teams. When you speak, you learn nothing; you learn only by listening. Listen, then speak, and speak from the heart. Take only those actions that make you a stronger SEAL or strengthen the teams. Think before you act. If an action does not make you or the team better, then don't take it. You must use every precious moment of training to move forward and prepare for combat. You must always be aware that your every action affects the reputation of the team. Never lose the physical and mental courage that you discovered in yourself in BUD/S. You will fail at many things as an individual during your career but you will always face combat as a member of a team. Never be a loner; never leave a teammate alone. Rely on your teammates and never let them down. You are a member of the Naval Special Warfare community; you are the teams.

Looking back on the good times, the bad times, and the hard times in my career in the teams, it has been challenging, rewarding, and fun. If I had to do it all over again, I would relive my career in the teams. The experiences and the lifetime friends I have made are priceless.

Have fun, train hard, and when the time comes, kick ass. It was great working with you.

Cold-Weather Training—Kodiak Island, Alaska

Even though he now wore the Trident, Ensign Murphy was still assigned to the NSW Center for another mandatory training course. Like each of his previous training courses, it would offer new challenges and require the acquisition of an entirely new and different set of skills.

After twenty-four hours of well-deserved leave and another twenty-four hours of preparation, Ensign Murphy found himself on Kodiak Island, Alaska. Claiming more American bald eagles than seagulls, Kodiak is the largest island in the United States outside of the Hawaiian Islands. The SEAL training compound was located at Camp Spruce, home of the Naval Special Warfare Detachment, Kodiak, and consisted of two steel buildings that contained sleeping facilities, a classroom, equipment bays, a galley, and a small clinic. A third building served as a boat barn, an indoor climbing facility, and a smaller storage area.

This three-week training evolution was designed to train Michael and his classmates how to survive in some of the harshest conditions and terrain. This training had become vital because SEALs might find themselves involved in operations in the highest elevations of the Hindu Kush mountain range in Afghanistan.

The first few days were spent in the classroom, where the students received medical, nutritional, and environmental briefings and learned about cold-weather gear—how to use and care for it. They were issued their protective combat uniform (PCU), the cold-weather garment issue that formed an entire clothing system, consisting of multiple layers of special fabric and outer materials to protect the wearer in temperatures as low as 50° below zero Fahrenheit. The system had seven separate layers of varying thickness to permit the wearer to mix and match the layers to fit the environment.

They were also issued their field equipment, called personal environmental protection and survival equipment (PEPSE), which consisted of a sleeping bag, a sleeping shelter, ground pads, cooking utensils, water bottles, a portable stove system, boots, balaclavas (knit caps), several hats, and six pairs of gloves and mittens, as well as a water-filtration system, a pack shovel, a folding saw, and a climbing harness. For mobility they were issued snowshoes, crampons, and folding ski poles.

Their last issue was the military assault suit (MAS). A lightweight dry suit designed for surface swimming in frigid waters, it featured latex wrist and neck seals and a waterproof zipper. With built-in feet, it could be worn with sneakers or boots.

Upon completing a few days of classroom preparation, the new SEALs were off to the field. Their first exercise occurred over three days and two nights. The objective of this exercise was to familiarize the men with the equipment. Drills were conducted at low elevations in which the men used altimeters and contour maps to navigate their way through the rough terrain. During this first exercise they carried only sixty-five pounds of gear—no operational equipment or weapons. The first night was spent near sea level. The second day found them operating at an elevation of twenty-one hundred feet, and spending the night at fifteen hundred feet.

On the third day, the SEALs returned to sea level, where they developed a real appreciation of the equipment they were issued earlier. In what was called the rewarming exercise, each man stripped down to his underwear and waded into the 42° water up to his neck and remained there for ten minutes. The objective was to lower the body temperature several degrees. The men all knew that after those ten minutes they had exactly six minutes—a period known as the six golden minutes—to get warm. They were taught that their low core body temperature would go even lower as they began to move about and blood flow was restored to their arms, hands, fingers, legs, feet, and toes. It was imperative that the SEALs get warm quickly. Working in pairs, they dried off with one layer of their PCUs while putting on another. After putting on a balaclava and a stocking cap, one got the stove going and began to heat water while the other erected a sleeping shelter. Both got quickly into their sleeping bags and then went into their shelter while the water heated up. The objective was to get warm liquids and a hot meal prepared.

After this training evolution, Michael and his classmates received a day off to reassemble and repack their equipment, then went back into the classroom, then went back out for another field training evolution. Before their three weeks of training were complete, they had practiced climbing and rappelling on dangerous cliffs in the most brutal of weather conditons with full gear, during both day and night, when the only light is that from the moon and the stars. Their final training evolution was conducted in weather conditions common to Kodiak Island—a full blizzard that delayed their flight back to NSW for two days.

After returning to Coronado, the men were released and dispatched to their teams. Those reporting to SEAL Delivery Vehicle Teams, including Ensign Michael Murphy, would remain at the NSW Center.

SEAL Delivery Vehicle (SDV) Training

Volunteering for the SDV Teams placed Ensign Murphy at the apex of the NSW teams. He participated in an intensive three-month program conducted at the NSW Command Detachment SDV in Panama City, Florida, which taught SEALs how to operate the MK-16 mixed-gas dive rig and to pilot and navigate the MK-8 SEAL Delivery Vehicle. The SDV is a "wet" submersible used to conduct long-range underwater missions. Much of the training and information regarding the MK-8 as well as the new Advanced SEAL Delivery System (ASDS) remains classified.

Graduating on July 1, 2002, Ensign Michael P. Murphy again signed for his Fitness Report and Counseling Record, which stated in part: ". . . completed two weeks of MK 16 Underwater Breathing Apparatus Operator course with 80 contact hours of instruction including maritime Combat Swimmer operations during day and night environments. Completed 10 weeks of SEAL Delivery Vehicle (SDV) Operator/Navigator course consisting of 64 hours of high risk diving operations, 548 contact hours of instruction in basic pilot and navigator skills, SDV subsystems, maintenance procedures and mission planning."

Having been promoted to lieutenant (junior grade), Michael Murphy served as the assistant operations officer, assisted with schools management, field training, and exercise planning and execution. During the period of July 3–10, 2002, he deployed to Central Command (CENTCOM) as an assistant operations officer. His Fitness Report and Counseling Record covering the period of July 3, 2002 to January 2, 2003 stated as follows:

> LTJG is a model SEAL Officer. Possesses the superior leadership, creative ability and self-confidence traits to excel in any wardroom assignment. Deployed to CENTCOM AOR filling a Key 04 billet as a Joint Operations Center Commander. Assistant Operations Officer for Exercise Early Victor 02, involving five CNSWTGs, and one SDV Task Unit. Expertly coordinated eight full mission profiles and produced 35 daily situational reports and a detailed after action report. Tactical Operations Center Watch officer for a 14-day submarine underway period. Served as key information relay between underway SSN and SEAL Platoon in the field resulting in five successful at sea rendezvous and certification of the SSN/NSW/DDS package. Extremely fit. Regularly scores outstanding on NSW SEAL physical readiness test. Junior officer mentor. Developed electronic notebook of NSW Warfare PQS study materials and requirements greatly increasing junior officer readiness for oral and written boards. Expertly coordinated five Combat Capability Demonstrations for VIPs including COMNAVSPECWARCOM and Secretary of the Air Force. Hard charging Officer with unlimited potential. Unquenchable thirst for knowledge of NSW. Recommended for early promotion, assignment as a Platoon OIC, and follow-on Post Graduate education.

Michael's Fitness Report and Counseling Record for the period of January 13–April 9, 2003 revealed the following:

> Ranked # 1 of 3 outstanding LTJGs. Proven Wartime performer! Flawlessly performed as SOCCENT Joint Operations Center maritime Operations Officer, a position normally filled by an O4/O5. Provided operational-level coordination, support and overwatch for highly successful maritime SOF missions in the opening phase of the Iraqi campaign. These operations were vital to securing southern Iraq oil infrastructure, directly supporting of the achievement of COMUSENTCOM strategic military objectives.

Chosen for advance party to establish transition of SOCCENT operational control into the CENTCOM AOR. Helped ensure a seamless shift of SOCCENT CO of ongoing operations.

Single-handedly developed mission tracker used by SOCCENT to monitor special operations missions. Tracked and facilitated combat operations in support of Operations ENDURING FREEDOM and IRAQI FREEDOM. These operations involved more than 15,000 special operations forces from a variety of Coalition countries. Created flag-level briefings for COMSOCENT and COMUCENTCOM.

LTJG Murphy is one of the finest junior officers I have ever worked with. A rising star in Naval Special Warfare, his work ethic, devotion to duty, and overall professionalism far exceeds that of his peers. Detail to only the most demanding assignments. Promote now!

The following assessment of Michael's performance comes from his Fitness Report and Counseling Record for the period March 1–July 3, 2003, during which he served with SDVT-1.

INTELLIGENT AND FOCUSED! LTJG Murphy excels in critical position of responsibility.

AGGRESSIVE OPERATOR. As ALFA Platoon AOIC, LTJG Murphy deomonstrated superior operational acumen and led 12 SEALs in executing five high-risk at-sea maritime/air training evolutions and twenty arduous combat swimmer diving profiles.

DEDICATED PROFESSIONAL. Hand-selected to deploy as Future Operations Officer for NSWTG-HOA. Led real world operational planning for sensitive and highly classified intrusive ISR operations, which encompassed three large surface combatants, a nuclear submarine, a P-3 squadron, for NSW RIBs, three SEAL platoons and an NSW Task Group. His efforts facilitated mission success and positively impacted the War on Terror!

Meticulous manager. LTJG Murphy's skill with administrative technologies and attention to detail ensure accurate accountability for 16 platoon members and over $8M in material and equipment.

Personable mentor. Recognizes potential leaders and continualy challenges junior personnel to reach for new heights and apply for commissioning programs.

LTJG Murphy is a mature and motivated NSW Officer whos sound judgement and operationasl expertise foretell a highly successful NSW career. PROMOTE EARLY AND ASSIGN AS PLATOON COMMANDER!

CHAPTER TEN

Warrior Community and Structure

Only as a warrior can one withstand the path of knowledge. A
warrior cannot complain or regret anything. His life is an end-
less challenge, and challenges cannot possibly be good or bad.
Challenges are simply challenges.

—CARLOS CASTANEDA, *Journey to Ixtlan*
(New York: Simon & Schuster, 1972)

Overview

The NSW Command was commissioned April 16, 1987, at the Naval
Amphibious Base in Coronado, California. As the Naval special operations component in the United States Special Operations Command
(USSOCOM), headquartered at MacDill Air Force Base in Tampa, Florida, it is
responsible for providing the vision, leadership, doctrinal guidance, resources, and
oversight needed to ensure that its units are ready to meet the mission requirements of commanders.

The mission of the commander of the Naval Special Warfare Command is to
prepare NSW forces to carry out assigned missions and to develop maritime special operations strategy, doctrine, and tactics. It exercises operational control over
all U.S.-based NSW Command training, has operational control over all U.S.-
based Naval Special Warfare forces, and is responsible for training, equipping, supporting, and providing trained and ready forces to the combatant commanders.
The commander of NSW Command is a Navy flag officer, Rear Admiral Edward
G. Winters III.

The Naval Special Warfare Center serves as the schoolhouse for much Naval
Special Warfare training. It is a major component of the Naval Special Warfare
Command and is commanded by an NSW captain. In addition to the twenty-six-
week BUD/S and nine-week Special Warfare Combatant-craft Crewman (SWCC)
courses, the Center also conducts advanced maritime special operations training
for NSW and other service-component SOF personnel. The Center maintains a

detachment at the Naval Amphibious Base, Little Creek, in Virginia, for selected training of personnel assigned to commands on the East Coast.

There are three types of personnel assigned to NAVSPECWARCOM: NSW officers, Navy enlisted SEALs, and Special Warfare Combatant-craft Crewmen.

Mission

The NSW mission areas include unconventional warfare, direct action, combating terrorism, special reconnaissance, foreign internal defense, information warfare, security assistance, counterdrug operations, personnel recovery, and hydrographic reconnaissance. NSW forces can operate independently or integrate with other U.S. special operations forces or within U.S. Navy carrier battle groups and amphibious ready groups.

Naval Special Warfare units are organized, trained, and equipped to conduct special operations in maritime and riverine environments. They are deployed in small units around the world in support of fleet and national operations. They provide an effective means to apply an effective counterforce in conjunction with national policy and objectives in peacetime and across the spectrum of hostilities from peacetime operations to limited war and to general war.

Structure

NSW is a highly structured and close-knit organization. The major operational components of Naval Special Warfare Command include Naval Special Warfare Group One and Special Boat Squadron One, located in Coronado, California, and Naval Special Warfare Group Two and Special Boat Squadron Two, stationed in Little Creek, Virginia. These components deploy SEAL teams, SEAL Delivery Vehicle Teams, and Special Boat Units (SBUs) throughout the world.

Naval Special Warfare Groups (NSWGs) are major commands led by a Navy captain that provide command and control as well as trained and ready SEAL and SDV platoons and forces to specific geographic areas. NSW Groups One and Two are organized into (1) three SEAL teams, consisting of six sixteen-man platoons, which conduct reconnaissance, direct action, unconventional warfare, foreign internal defense, and other operations in maritime or riverine environments; (2) one SDV Team, which operates and maintains submersible vehicles that deliver and recover SEALs in hostile areas and conduct reconnaissance and direct-action missions; and (3) NSW Units, which are small command-and-control elements located outside the continental United States used to support other NSW forces assigned to theater special operations commanders (SOCs) or components of naval task forces.

A Naval Special Warfare Command Combat Service Support Team (CSST) is assigned to each NSW Group and provides a full range of support for designated SEAL teams, Special Boat Units, NSW Task Groups/Task Units, and/or special mission units. Special Boat Squadrons, also commanded by Navy captains, equip, support, and provide trained and ready special operations ships and craft to the assigned geographic areas of operations. Each command is comprised of one or more active or reserve component Special Boat Units (SBUs) and *Cyclone*-class Patrol Coastal (PC) ships.

SEAL Delivery Vehicle Team

Although SEALs are expert combat swimmers, there are times when the distances they must swim would be too great for them to remain effective, or when they have too much gear to transport to the site themselves. SDV Teams use underwater SDV craft to increase the areas in which SEALs can operate. SDV Teams usually deploy from submarines, but when necessary, they can also deploy from shore-based stations or surface ships. The SDV provides life support for the embarked SEALs. The older boats allow each SEAL to plug into an onboard air source and are flooded during operations, but the new Advanced SEAL Delivery System (ASDS) carries the SEALs in a dry compartment, keeping them warmer longer and increasing their effectiveness once they reach their drop-off point. Each type of SDV is powered by batteries and offers navigation and communications equipment in addition to the propulsion and life-support systems.

The primary SDV used by SEALs currently is the MK-8 Mod 1. At 22 feet, it is rated to carry six SEALs (two operators and four passengers). It can travel at about six knots out to a range of about seventy miles, although in many cases the effects of water conditions on the crew is more of a limitation than the battery power of the SDV. The MK-9 SDV was developed to carry a crew of two SEALs and two MK 37 torpedoes for use in standoff attacks against enemy shipping but has been superseded by the MK-8.

The MK-8 is used to conduct long-range submerged missions as well as deliver SEALs or other agents onto enemy territory from a submarine or other vessel at sea. Mission usage would include underwater mapping and terrain exploration, location and recovery of lost or downed objects, offshore and in-port intelligence collection, and infiltration or exfiltration of personnel on direct-action missions.

The latest addition to the delivery vehicles is the new Advanced SEAL Delivery System. It is a dry, 65-foot mini submersible used for long-range insertion of SEALs from a larger platform, either a surface ship or a submarine. Along with its increased range, speed, and capacity above that of the MK-8, it has the distinct advantage of keeping the SEALs dry, thereby minimizing their exposure to cold and fatigue while being transported to their target. The ASDS can also be transported by land, sea, or air by C-5 or C-17 aircraft.

Two *Los Angeles*–class submarines, the USS *Greenville* and the USS *Charlotte*, have been structurally modified to carry the ASDS, which is connected to the ship by a watertight hatch. With a sophisticated sonar and hyperbaric recompression chamber and operating with a sixty-seven horsepower electric motor, the ASDS is manned by a crew of two and can carry eight SEALs.

There are two SDV Teams. SEAL Delivery Vehicle Team One (SDVT-1) is based at Pearl Harbor, Hawaii, and operates in the Pacific Command and Central Command geographic areas. Team Two is based at Little Creek, Virginia, and conducts operations throughout the Atlantic, Southern, and European Command areas.

SEAL Team

Currently there are ten SEAL teams, each under the leadership of a Navy commander, consisting of six operational SEAL platoons with a headquarters element and support personnel.

SEAL Platoon

A SEAL platoon is the largest operational element that will normally be used to conduct a mission. A Navy lieutenant normally commands a SEAL platoon. A platoon consists of sixteen SEALs—two officers, one chief petty officer, and thirteen enlisted men. The senior officer is the platoon commander or officer in charge, the junior officer is his assistant, the senior enlisted man is the platoon chief, and the next senior enlisted man is the leading petty officer. The LPO is in charge of the day-to-day management of the enlisted platoon members.

A platoon may divide into two squads of eight or four elements of four. All SEALs are dive, parachute, and demolitions qualified. They can destroy or sabotage enemy shipping, port and harbor facilities, bridges, railway lines, communications centers, and other lines of communication, or infiltrate and exfiltrate selected personnel by submarine, surface vessel, aircraft, or land vehicle. They also can conduct reconnaissance and surveillance in multiple environments, and organize, train, and assist U.S., allied, and other friendly military or paramilitary forces in the conduct of special operations.

Primary or Core Missions

Regardless of whether a SEAL team is working strictly for the Navy or as a component of a joint task force operating within the USSOCOM, SEALs have nine primary or core missions:

1. *Direct action (DA)*. Direct action refers to small-unit, short-duration strike operations designed to destroy, seize, capture, recover, or inflict damage on facilities or personnel in denied overseas areas. This type of mission can take

place on land or at sea against all types of fixed or mobile targets, and may take the form of a raid, an ambush, sabotage, or a direct assault, which may be accompanied by explosives or handheld weapons. SEALs also conduct standoff attacks from the ground, water, or aircraft, and employ handheld laser devices to guide aircraft or weapons strikes. Their targets are always of strategic, operational, or tactical importance, and may be hit well in advance of declared or formal hostilities.

2. *Counterterrorism (CT).* Increasing in importance is counterterrorism, which refers to offensive action taken to preempt, deter, or respond to terrorism. This is a highly specialized mission type requiring specialized courses and training for those who perform it. Certain special operations forces from the Army, Navy, and Air Force are assigned full-time to this primary mission throughout the world. Maintaining a high state of readiness, they can deploy overseas on short notice. CT activities may include attacks on terrorist organizations and facilities having strategic importance to those groups.

3. *Foreign internal defense (FID).* This primary mission type involves active assistance by U.S. military and civilian government agencies in aiding a foreign country in its efforts to fight subversion, lawlessness, or insurgency. The SEALs' primary contribution to this mission type is to train, advise, and assist the host nation's military and paramilitary forces. They also assist in the development of their host's maritime capabilities and instruct its forces about tactical operations on its rivers and along its coastlines.

4. *Unconventional warfare (UW).* In contrast to direct action, UW involves a long-duration, covert or clandestine military or paramilitary operation conducted by local or surrogate forces overseas. SEALs and other SOF and certain government agencies organize, train, equip, and support these forces to varying degrees to achieve U.S. strategic objectives.

5. *Special reconnaissance (SR).* SR is performed when intelligence-gathering activities are best accomplished by humans on the ground with their eyes on the target. It is conducted to collect information on the capabilities, intentions, and activities of the enemy. SR is also conducted to provide vital weather, hydrographic, and geographic information about a specific target. Prestrike SR is done to accomplish target acquisition, while poststrike SR assesses the battle damage inflicted against targets identified. SR can also be done to assess chemical, biological, nuclear, or environmental hazards.

6. *Psychological operations (PSYOPS).* Psychological operations are conducted to influence the emotions, motives, objective reasoning, and ultimately the decision-making processes of foreign governments, organizations, groups, and individuals. This is accomplished through dissemination of selected

information or disinformation distributed by a wide variety of means, such as radio, media, or leaflets dropped by aircraft.

7. *Civil affairs operations (CAOs).* Capitalizing on U.S. relationships with foreign military forces, government organizations, and the civilian population, these civil affairs operations are conducted by specially trained and equipped units. These operations could be conducted in friendly, neutral, or hostile areas before, during, and after military action. A civil affairs operation could include setting up and managing a hospital, a school, or other local government functions.

8. *Information operations (IOs).* These operations are conducted to affect an enemy's technological and information infrastructure, such as computers, command and control, and sophisticated weapons systems, while at the same time defending our own systems.

9. *Counterproliferation (CP) of weapons of mass destruction (WMD).* This mission type encompasses actions taken to seize, destroy, render safe, capture, or recover WMD. Special operations forces provide unique capabilities to both monitor and support foreign countries' compliance with arms control treaties or agreements.

SEAL Missions

SEALs have performed these core or primary missions around the globe. An integral part of SEAL training is studying previous missions. During this process they not only analyze what went right and what went wrong, but also, more important, why and how to prevent errors from reoccurring on future missions. Michael Murphy and his classmates examined numerous previous SEAL missions.

- Operation Urgent Fury. In October 1983 President Ronald Reagan sent U.S. forces to the island of Grenada to obtain the release of U.S. students being held hostage. SEAL Teams Four and Six were attached to U.S. forces to aid in the assault.

- Operation Earnest Will was in effect from 1987 through 1989. SEALs were part of a policing force that was to prevent Iranians from seeding mines in a maritime seaway used by many of the world's oil tankers. SEALs participated in an assault on the ship *Iranian Air*, which U.S. Army scout helicopters had found laying mines. The ship fired on the helicopters when ordered to stop. The ship and crew were captured without U.S. casualties.

- On April 14, 1988, the USS *Samuel B. Roberts* hit a mine placed by the Iranians. On April 18, SEALs took part in Operation Praying Mantis in retaliation.

- Operation Just Cause. In December 1989 SEALs were charged with two missions; both involved preventing Panamanian dictator Manuel Noriega's escape. One team was assigned to disable two fast boats while the other disabled his Learjet at the Patilla Airfield near Panama City. Four SEALs were killed, and eight seriously wounded.

- Operation Desert Shield. SEALs were present in the Persian Gulf when Iraq invaded Kuwait on August 2, 1990. Following the invasion, SEAL Team Five and Navy Special Boat Units were able to cross the Kuwaiti border before it was sealed off by the invading Iraqi forces. In addition to Team Five, Teams One and Three were in the country on various missions.

- Operation Desert Storm. On February 23, 1991, SEALs were the first into Kuwait City, racing ahead of Allied forces to scout Iraqi resistance in Fast Attack Vehicles, and later escorted the U.S. ambassador to the U.S. embassy and provided perimeter security.

- In February 2000 the Russian-flagged *Volgoneft-147* was forcibly boarded by fast rope by SEAL Team Two after it had failed to stop for boarding and inspection under suspicion of smuggling Iraqi oil, in violation of U.S. sanctions.

- Operation Restore Hope. In 1993 SEALs were involved in the peacekeeping missions in Somalia, initially providing beach hydrographic reconnaissance for Marine units that would be landing. SEALs were subsequently involved in the Battle of Mogadishu on October 3–4, 1993.

In any trouble spot throughout the world, wherever and whenever American interests are threatened, SEALs are most likely involved. In most cases SEALs are in and out before the main combat action begins, a role requiring a special breed of warrior.

SEAL "Community"

There are just over two thousand active-duty SEAL operators, comprising about one-tenth of the U.S. Navy's personnel. Because of the nature of their highly specialized training and missions, members of the SEAL community tend to be very close-mouthed and guarded. The elite of all special operations forces, SEAL operators are fully mindful of their training, responsibilities, and, most important, their ethos. SEALs effectively "police" themselves and are hesitant about, if not resistant to, non-SEAL or -NSW attempts to penetrate their community.

While some may view this reluctance as being aloof or arrogant, it is neither. The SEAL bond and sense of community is developed in and through BUD/S training. While the first law of nature is self-preservation, the metamorphosis, the fundamental rewiring, of those who successfully complete BUD/S brings the SEAL to realize that any one of his teammates is more important than himself. It is this fundamental mind-set that separates SEALS from all other military units and that is foreign to most non-SEAL operators. It is the mind-set of a warrior.

Having completed BUD/S, each and every SEAL knows what every other SEAL knows. In the civilian workplace many people with many different thought processes, training, capabilities, and character intermingle with varying degrees of attitude and commitment, if any, to the overall mission of the enterprise. In all too many cases, most believe that what is best for them is what is best for everyone else and the workplace.

However, as a member of the warrior community, all SEAL operators know each other's thought processes, endurance, training, capabilities, and character. They know that their lives are in their teammates' hands. This knowledge of each other is necessary to accomplish their core missions, and it is this stark distinction from the civilian world that may appear to isolate SEAL operators from others.

SEALs are fully aware that they are the most highly trained and specialized military unit in the world, and that SEAL missions are, in most cases, beyond the level of training and capability of any other military unit. With that awareness comes an underlying level of confidence that is clearly visible in how SEALs talk, act, and carry themselves, as well as in their interaction with the civilian populace. It is this fundamental difference that may lead some to view SEAL operators as distant and overbearing.

But there is a difference between confidence and conceit, commitment and convenience, and character and contrition. It is the SEALs' fundamental difference in thought process and attitude that provides them with confidence, commitment, and character. Thankfully, conceit, convenience, and contrition simply do not apply to the warrior community.

Unlike the mission statements framed on many corporate walls, but in most cases totally unknown to their workers, the SEAL Creed is ingrained into every aspect of a SEAL's being. The SEAL Creed is not simply words. SEALs eat it, breathe it, and live it—every minute of every day:

> In times of war and uncertainty there is a special breed of warrior ready to answer our Nation's call. A common man with uncommon desire to succeed. Forged by adversity, he stands alongside America's finest special operations forces to serve his country, the American people, and protect their way of life. I am that man.
>
> My Trident is a symbol of honor and heritage. Bestowed upon me by the heroes that have gone before, it embodies the trust of those I am sworn to protect. By wearing the Trident I accept the responsibility of my chosen profession and way of life. It is a privilege that I must earn every day.

My loyalty to Country and Team is beyond reproach. I humbly serve as a guardian to my fellow Americans, always ready to defend those who are unable to defend themselves. I do not advertise the nature of my work, or seek recognition for my actions. I voluntarily accept the inherent hazards of my profession, placing the welfare and security of others before my own.

I serve with honor on and off the battlefield. The ability to control my emotions and my actions, regardless of circumstance, sets me apart from other men. Uncompromising integrity is my standard. My character and honor are steadfast.

My Word is my Bond.

We expect to lead and be led. In the absence of orders I will take charge, lead my teammates and accomplish the mission. I lead by example in all situations.

I will never quit. I persevere and thrive on adversity. My Nation expects me to be physically harder and mentally stronger than my enemies. If knocked down, I will get back up, every time. I will draw on every remaining ounce of strength to protect my teammates and accomplish our mission. I am never out of the fight.

We demand discipline. We expect innovation. The lives of my teammates and the success of our mission depend on me—my technical skill, tactical proficiency, and attention to detail. My training is never complete.

We train for war and fight to win. I stand ready to bring the full spectrum of combat power to bear in order to achieve my mission and the goals established by my country. Execution of my duties will be swift and violent when required yet guided by the very principles that I serve to defend.

Brave men have fought and died building the proud tradition and feared reputation that I am bound to uphold. In the worst of conditions, the legacy of my teammates steadies my resolve and silently guides my every deed. I will not fail.

SEALs are not maniacal individuals hell-bent on self-destruction. They have hopes and dreams for themselves and their families just like each of us do. However, SEALs are acutely aware that freedom is not free. They understand better than most that everything has a price that must be paid. Like the Spartan warriors described in Steven Pressfield's *Gates of Fire*, SEALs know that their "seasons are marked . . . not by calendared years themselves, but by battles. Campaigns fought and comrades lost; trials of death survived. Clashes and conflicts from which time effaces all superficial recall, leaving only the fields themselves and their names, which achieve in the warrior's memory a stature ennobled beyond all other modes of commemoration, purchased with the holy coin of blood and paid for with the lives of beloved brothers-in-arms."

SEALs give all and ask for nothing. Their reward is coming home to their families and friends, watching them and others enjoy the freedoms they helped secure, ever vigilant that for as long as the Lord tarries, the fight is never complete.

Thank God for America's warriors. We continue to enjoy our freedoms because of men such as these.

CHAPTER ELEVEN

Deployment Work-up

The only easy day was yesterday.

—SEAL motto, quoted in Richard Schoenberg,
The Only Easy Day Was Yesterday

SEAL platoons operate on a twenty-four-month cycle. Of those twenty-four months, eighteen consist of training work-up followed by a six-month deployment overseas in an operational status. The type of training work-up is dictated by three major factors: advanced individual and platoon-level skills that will be necessary for the conduct of all special operations, the anticipated methods of delivery (insertion) and extraction most likely to be used while on deployment, and the geographical area of operations.

The West Coast (odd-numbered) teams are primarily responsible for the Pacific Rim, the Far East, Africa and the Middle East, and eastern bloc regions; the East Coast (even-numbered) teams are responsible for South and Central America, the Mediterranean and Caribbean areas, Europe, and Russia. Even though the teams have primary areas of responsibility, the Global War on Terror (GWOT) dictates that each team be utilized to maximum efficiency, thereby necessitating an overlapping of geographic regions of responsibility.

In the teams SEAL operators are either on a mission or preparing for the next one. It is a constant cycle. The predeployment work-up is divided into three distinct phases: professional development (PRODEV), Unit Level Training (ULT), and Squadron Integration Training (SIT).

Professional Development (PRODEV)

PRODEV is a six-month training block in which individual SEALs attend a number of schools and courses, leading to individual qualifications and designations that, when combined with the other SEALs, allow the platoon to operate as an effective operational combat team. Depending on the operational needs of the overall team, or platoon, SEALs acquire any number of advanced skills: sniper; breaching; surreptitious entry; electronic and media exploitation; technical surveillance; high-threat protective security; advanced weapons training; advanced driving skills (rural, urban, security); advanced climbing and rope skills; advanced air operations, including high-altitude, low-opening (HALO) and high-altitude, high-opening (HAHO) parachute jumping; parachute rigging and packing; diving supervisor; range safety officer; instructor school; leadership school; foreign weapons; unmanned aerial vehicle and precision bombing operator; language school; and advanced special operations.

Unit Level Training (ULT)

ULT is the following six-month training block that follows PRODEV. It allows individual SEALs to perfect the skills they obtained during PRODEV and incorporate them into the platoon/team core mission areas: land warfare; close-quarters combat; urban warfare; maritime interdiction; combat-swimmer operations; long-range interdiction; air operations; special reconnaissance and maritime operations; and combat operations involving advanced marksmanship and heavy weapons.

The first ninety days of ULT is commonly spent on getting back to basics, such as hydrographic reconnaissance combined with underwater demolition of submerged targets. Another twenty-one days are spent on air training, including several "Duck drops" from different aircraft during both day and night. "Duck drop" is a term used to describe the practice of dropping inflatable watercraft from aircraft. Other training includes combat equipment jumps, fast-roping, rappelling, and SPIE (Special Purpose Insertion/Extraction) rig techniques.

Mission planning is conducted in the classroom, followed by intelligence gathering and reporting. This is followed by Intel Week, when a platoon will reconnoiter a local utility facility, gathering photographic and sketch data, and then compile a comprehensive report on the facility's strengths, weaknesses, and vulnerabilities.

Mission planning is followed by the Combat Swimmer course (CSC) over the next twenty-one days. The platoon will execute over thirty dives in this course, including a full mission profile, in which SEALs are inserted by aircraft or surface vessel at a predetermined location for a thirty-mile "over-the-horizon" transit in a vehicle. This is followed by a "turtleback," which is a surface swim in full dive gear, then a four-hour multileg dive into the enemy harbor to place limpet mines on the hulls of designated target ships, and then evasion of the antiswimmer measures put in place by the trainers.

The platoon then moves on to land warfare. Here they again start with the basics of small-unit tactics, building to a full mission profile in simulated combat situations. Here the training takes place nearly twenty-four hours a day. One of the

SEALs' favorite and most intensive training exercises is the immediate-action drill (IAD). Although IADs are classified, it is safe to say that they are so effective that they can totally mislead the enemy into believing that they are up against a whole company (one hundred men) of soldiers. Special attention is given to the use of small arms, including pistols and sniper rifles. Skills needed for sniper and countersniper operations and close-quarters battle are all emphasized.

The advanced land-warfare phase includes training in intelligence gathering; structural penetration; long-range reconnaissance and patrolling; close-quarters combat; sniper/countersniper skills; advanced driving skills; edged weapons; hand-to-hand combat; extreme environment survival; field medicine; explosives; small-unit tactics; infiltration and exfiltration; snatch-and-grab missions, and prisoner handling.

The teams responsible for areas often covered with snow conduct extreme cold-weather and winter-warfare training, usually in Alaska, Montana, New York, Norway, and Canada. This training covers mountaineering, free climbing, mountain patrolling and raiding, arctic survival and navigation, high-altitude mountaineering, camouflage, concealment and cover techniques, fire and manuvering techniques on skis and snowshoes, winter orienteering, cross-country skiing, evasion and escape, extreme cold-weather diving, snowshoeing, building snow caves and shelters, winter survival, heavy weapons management, and avalanche survival.

The teams responsible for the parts of the world covered by dense jungle and swamp conduct their training in the sweltering and treacherous jungles of Panama or Pineros Island in Puerto Rico.

Squadron Integration Training (SIT)

During the third six-month training block, six platoons, along with their supporting SEAL squadron, Special Boat Squadrons, medical teams, explosive ordnance disposal (EOD) detachment, interpreters, intelligence unit, and cryptological support team, conduct coordinated advanced training under simulated battlefield conditions. A final intense, graded certification training exercise (CERTEX) is then performed by the entire SEAL team using battlefield conditions. The purpose is to coordinate platoon operations under a task force group umbrella while using live ammuition. After successfully completing the CERTEX, the SEAL team becomes a SEAL squadron and is scheduled for deployment.

The Dangers of SEAL Training

Ensign Andy Haffele, a graduate of the U.S. Naval Academy who had recently earned his Trident, arrived at SDVT-1 in Pearl City, Hawaii, in 2003. He was slated to become the third officer in charge in Alfa Platoon, behind the platoon commander, Lieutenant George Stahl, and the assistant platoon commander, Lieutenant Michael Murphy. Murphy and Haffele quickly became good friends—as Haffele described them, "two peas in a pod."

Approximately four months after joining Alfa Platoon, Michael and Haffele were leading their platoon in conducting live-fire immediate-action drills (IADs) on Point Man Range at Schofield Barracks. Haffele later described IAD as being "as close to actual combat as you're going to get without being there." IADs were necessary, according to Haffele, because "when bullets are flying for real in bad guy country, that is not the time to be involved in live fire for the first time. When it all hits the fan, you will fall back on your muscle memory. Muscle memory is developed in training. Live rounds coming out the end of your weapon are completely different than blanks. You have to train as you will fight. Live fire is necessary."

Alfa Platoon had been conducting IADs several times a day for the previous week or so. On March 18, 2004, Alfa Platoon had divided into two squads. The second squad consisted of Chris Hall, Dan Healy, Andy Haffele, Shane Patton, Michael Murphy, and Matthew Axelson. Both squads had walked through the exercise without gunfire, and the first squad had completed the live-fire IAD. At about 2:45 PM the second squad, led by Michael, was in squad formation patrolling the assigned training area. Suddenly the range safety officer detonated an explosive charge and fired live rounds behind the squad. The squad's rear security officer, Chris Hall, yelled, "Contact rear!" Hall, Healy, Haffele, Patton, Murphy, and Axelson, who was on point, came toward the rear to meet the threat. Murphy yelled, "Center peel!" the correct tactical manuever for the situation.

The center peel is designed with human psychology in mind. This tactical manuever is utilized by modern-day military units when a smaller group of troops needs to withdraw from an engagement with a much larger force. Generally it is a sloped or diagonal retreat from the enemy utilizing suppression fire. The diagonal motion of the manuever gives the impression of increasing numbers of soldiers joining the battle, a psychological move designed to demoralize the opposition. The slanting motion also has the benefit of keeping open the field of fire. Retreating directly backward would put the soldier too closely behind his own men, severely limiting his field of fire.

All members of the squad went into their field of fire, the target area directly in front of them. Chris Hall was the first to get his weapon firing downrange; he was followed by Dan Healy. Once Healy began firing, that was the signal for Hall to stop firing, put his weapon on safe, get up, and retreat, tapping Haffele on the shoulder as he passed. That was the signal for Haffele to begin firing. Healy then stopped firing, put his weapon on safe, got up, and retreated, tapping Shane Patton on the shoulder as he passed. That was the signal for Patton to begin firing. When Patton began firing, Haffele stopped firing, put his weapon on safe, got up, and turned to retreat. He was immediately hit by a .556 green-tip round from Murphy's M4 and went down to the ground, unable to breathe.

Murphy was the first to get to Haffele, followed within seconds by Chris Hall. With Haffele remaining fully conscious, Michael immediately placed a trauma dressing and direct pressure over the now profusely bleeding wound in Haffele's right upper chest. The bullet had pierced the right axillary artery, resulting in a tension pneumothorax. Marcus Luttrell, the medic, and Corpsman John Dane quickly arrived and started lifesaving treatment. Dane began inserting intravenous lines into both of Haffele's arms while Luttrell conducted a head-to-toe emergency assessment. The fact that he might well have been dying never crossed Haffele's mind until Commander Todd DeGhetto, the commanding officer of SDVT-1, asked for his wife's contact number. Andy and Chrissy had only been married for seven months and lived near the base. He was loaded onto a backboard and placed in a transport truck and rushed to the helicopter landing area and the awaiting Blackhawk medevac helicopter. Luttrell ordered the pilot to head to Queen's Medical Center, Oahu's only Level I Trauma Center. Andy made it through five hours of surgery, fifty units of blood, and the administration of last rights, Chrissy at his side. The next twelve hours resulted in additional surgeries and an additional twenty units of blood.

Following four weeks of hospitalization, Haffele's attention turned to the physical and occupational rehabilitation of his right arm, which was now non-functional. During this time Michael Murphy was a frequent visitor. On several occasions Andy and Michael had heart-to-heart conversations, with Michael expressing extreme remorse for what had happened. During the subsequent investigation by the judge advocate general, Commander DeGhetto repeatedly interviewed Michael Murphy and reported the following.

> Mike was a young officer with limited experience and it is part of growing and learning, and unfortuately it had dire—almost dire consequences for Andy Haffele. Over the years there have been numerous close calls when conducting live fire exercises, that after the fact everyone looks around wipes their brow and says, "Thank God nobody got hurt." Everything we do is high risk. Mike was learning. They were doing a closed terrain manuever. I was with the patrol at the time, maybe three or four feet away from Mike who was the squad leader on this iteration. They had a contact rear, a center peel was called, because there was no other tactical manuever you could do. Everybody goes down into their field of fire. When Andy steps down into his field of fire, there is very tall elephant grass, perhaps five or six feet tall between Mike and Andy. As the guys were center peeling back, Mike went down on his four power scope. As soon as he went down on that scope, he lost situational awareness, as Andy stood up. Being three feet away, I saw Mike fire—I saw the muzzle flash, I looked at Andy's chest and didn't see any blood, I then looked in his eyes and I could tell he was hit. I told the Range Safety Officer that he had a man down and the medical safety procedures were put into action.

Ironically enough, two days before the shooting I had fired the corpsman and replaced him with Marcus Luttrell, the lone survivor. Make no mistake, Andy Haffele is alive today because of Marcus Luttrell.

After the incident, I sat down with my Command Master Chief, my Operations boss, senior leaders, my XO my executive officer, the senior guys especially in the training department that saw Mike and his abilities day in and day out. As a community, sometimes we "eat our own" in situations like this. It is easy to fire somebody, throw them by the side of the road and say you are not worthy to wear that Trident. Mike made a mistake. He lost situational awareness for a split second, but he would never, ever do that again. I made the decision, I briefed my Admiral [Maguire], he backed me up, because I told him point blank that Mike would never make that mistake again, as this was a mistake that you learn from.

Every single person I talked to recommended keeping Mike, putting him back on the horse and keeping him in ALFA Platoon. He was that good. It was not a easy decision, because I knew that a lot of people would second-guess my decision, but it was the right thing to do. We all make mistakes, and it was a mistake. Granted, it cost Andy his career, but it <u>was</u> a mistake. Mike took this incident to heart and he learned from that mistake. He was a smart kid.

Commander DeGhetto related that he had absolutely no mental hesitation in making his decision, and stated that had he had any reservations or reason to believe that Mike had not learned from his mistake, he would have been "sent packing," either back to the fleet or to the street.

Michael Murphy's Fitness Report and Counseling Record covering the period from March 1, 2004, to January 31, 2005, filed by his commanding officer, documented the following:

LT Murphy was a LTJG for 10 months of this reporting period. O-3 effective 01JAN05. CONFIDENT, INTELLIGENT, SOLID PERFORMER. LT Murphy's care for subordinates and loyalty to superiors are second only to his relentless drive for NSW knowledge and combat effectiveness.

MISSION FOCUSED. Demonstrated exceptional tactical leadership and situational awareness through thirteen months of pre-deployment training. Safely conducted 306 hours of high risk SDV, land warfare and special reconnaissance evolutions.

GETS RESULTS. His exemplary performance as SDV Navigator and special reconnaissance team leader for an 80-hour Full Mission Profile in the harsh environment of Puget Sound, WA was instrumental to his platoon's success and combat readiness.

Distinguished himself with his mastery of SDV subsystems, tactical communications, special operations surveillance equipment and the Semi-Autonomous Hygrographic Reconnaissance Vehicle (SAHRV).

Selfless. LT Murphy consistently shifts praise to subordinates and never ceases to secure professional recognition for fellow platoon members, including two NAMs and one command SOY (Sailor of the Year) in less than 10 months. His personable leadership style and mentoring methods have led directly to his platoon's high morale and 100% retention rate.

A TRUE NSW OPERATOR. READY NOW FOR AN ASSIGNMENT AS SEAL PLATOON OIC!

CHAPTER TWELVE

Operation Enduring Freedom

Our war on terror begins with al Qaeda, but it does not end there. It will not end until every terrorist group of global reach has been found, stopped and defeated.

—PRESIDENT GEORGE W. BUSH, State of the Union Address, 2002

At War

The Global War on Terror (GWOT), or War on Terror, is the common term for the military, political, legal, and ideological conflict against terrorism. It is more specifically used in reference to the September 11, 2001, attacks against the United States and their aftermath; however, America was at war for years before its people and leaders recognized the crisis. Al-Qaeda had been carrying out attacks against the United States and its interests and allies since the mid-1990s.

U.S. forces learned on February 24, 1997, that we were at war with al-Qaeda and radical Islam. On that date, Ali Abu Kamal opened fire on tourists on an observation deck atop the Empire State Building. It would take another year before the American people and her political leaders would come to the same conclusion.

Having been emboldened by their successful attacks against U.S. targets overseas, in the fall of 1998 a meeting was held in Afghanistan between Khalid Sheikh Mohammed and Osama bin Laden. During the meeting, Mohammed received bin Laden's permission to proceed with his plan to attack the U.S. mainland. Bin Laden provided the leadership and finances and was involved in the selection of the participants for the attacks.

On the morning of September 11, 2001, al-Qaeda launched the largest and most deadly terrorist attack in history against a sovereign nation, with nineteen hijackers taking control of four commercial airliners en route to San Francisco and Los Angeles from Boston, Newark, New Jersey, and Washington, D.C. At 8:46 AM American Airlines Flight 11 was flown into the north tower of the World Trade Center in New York City. Seventeen minutes later, at 9:03 AM, United Airlines Flight

175 was crashed into the World Trade Center's south tower. American Airlines Flight 77 was crashed into the Pentagon at 9:37 AM. A fourth plane, United Airlines Flight 93, whose ultimate target was the U.S. Capitol, crashed near Shanksville, Pennsylvania, at 10:03 AM when the passengers, aware of the hijackers' plan, tried to retake control of the plane.

The subsequent loss of life was staggering. In the planes, 246 people died; at the Pentagon, 125; and in both towers of the World Trade Center, 2,627. Within hours of the attacks, the FBI determined the identities of the hijackers. The Pentagon/Twin Towers Bombing Investigation, code-named PENTTBOM, was the largest investigation in world history, involving over seven thousand agents of the FBI alone.

The Global War on Terror (GWOT)

After the September 11, 2001, attacks, President George W. Bush set forth a policy regarding the U.S. response to terrorism. In what has become known as the Bush Doctrine, the United States put the world on notice that it reserved the right to aggressively secure itself from countries that harbor or give aid to terrorist groups.

In his address to the nation on the evening of September 11, 2001, President Bush stated this resolve by stating that "we will make no distinction between the terrorists who committed these acts and those who harbor them." In his September 20, 2001, address to a joint session of Congress, President Bush reemphasized this doctrine: "We will pursue nations that provide aid or safe haven to terrorism. Every nation, in every region, now has a decision to make. Either you are with us, or you are with the terrorists. From this day forward, any nation that continues to harbor or support terrorism will be regarded by the United States as a hostile regime."

This doctrine was published by the U.S. National Security Council (NSC) on September 20, 2002, in a text entitled *The National Security Strategy of the United States*. The policies outlined in the NSC document represented a significant foreign policy change, since it was not the Afghanistan government (the Taliban) who had initiated the attacks, and there was no evidence that the Taliban had any foreknowledge of the attacks; however, the Taliban did harbor bin Laden and al-Qaeda, who did commit the attacks.

In a subsequent address to the cadets of the U.S. Military Academy at West Point, New York, on June 1, 2002, President Bush clearly stated the role that preemptive war would play in the future of American foreign policy and national defense: "We cannot defend America and our friends by hoping for the best. We cannot put our faith in the word of tyrants, who solemnly sign non-proliferation treaties, and then systemically break them. If we wait for threats to fully materialize, we will have waited too long . . . Our security will require transforming the military you will lead. A military that must be ready to strike at a moment's notice in any dark corner of the world. And our security will require all Americans to be forward-looking and resolute, to be ready for preemptive action when necessary to defend our liberty and to defend our lives."

President Bush made it clear that the United States should depose foreign regimes that represent a potential or perceived threat to the security of the this country or its national interests, even if that threat was not an immediate one. He further advocated a policy of spreading democracy around the world, especially in the volatile, war-torn region of the Middle East, as an overall strategy of combating terrorism, even if this meant acting unilaterally.

Despite the fact that most Americans believe that the fight against terrorism is limited to a region or area and against a single group, the reality is that the GWOT is global in nature. This is a war being fought on several different fronts on several different continents and against more than one group.

Europe

Operation Active Endeavor, which began on October 26, 2001, in response to the September 11 attacks, is an ongoing naval operation of the North Atlantic Treaty Organization (NATO). NATO, a military alliance established on April 4, 1949, consists of twenty-six independent countries whose members have agreed to participate in a mutual defense in response to an attack by any external party. Operation Active Endeavor operates in the Mediterranean Sea. It is designed to prevent the movement of terrorists or weapons of mass destruction and to enhance the security of area shipping in general, as well as helping Greece with the prevention of illegal immigration.

The Philippine Islands

In January 2002 the United States deployed SOF operators to the Philippines to advise and assist the armed forces of that country in combating terrorism, specifically the Abu Sayyaf Group and Jemaah Islamiyah, which have strongholds on the island of Basilan.

The Horn of Africa

The American effort in the Horn of Africa was initiated in response to the September 11 attacks on the United States. While this effort does not have a specific terrorist organization as a target, it focuses on the detection and disruption of terrorist groups in the region and works with host nations to prevent a resurgence of terrorist cells and activities.

In October 2002 Combined Joint Task Force–Horn of Africa (CJTF-HOA) was established at Camp Lemonier in Djibouti. Approximately two thousand personnel, including SOF and coalition force members, were assigned to a naval task force designated Coalition Task Force 150 (CTF-150). The coalition task force included ships from Australia, Canada, France, Germany, Italy, the Netherlands, Pakistan, New Zealand, Spain, and the United Kingdom. Its primary goal remains as originally stated: to monitor, board, and inspect shipments entering the Horn of Africa and other areas.

Afghanistan

Despite the U.S. government's repeated calls for the Taliban to turn over Osama bin Laden, the Taliban refused. In response, on October 7, 2001, the United States and the United Kingdom led an unprecedented aerial bombing campaign. High-altitude long-range bombers attacked al-Qaeda training camps and Taliban air defense sites. Within days, with the Taliban defenses neutralized, the bombing was concentrated in and around the cities of Kabul, Jalalabad, and Kandahar, taking out command, control, and communications targets, which crippled the Taliban's ability to communicate.

During the intense aerial bombing campaign, the United States had few combat troops on the ground, instead utilizing special operations forces to serve as liaisons with local Afghan militia. Militia units led U.S. forces to the White Mountains (Safed Koh), where al-Qaeda forces had dug into the extensive Tora Bora cave complex and underground bunkers. A continuous targeted heavy bombing of the area ensued. The B-52s that performed that mission were called in and guided by U.S. special operations forces. On December 17, 2001, the defenders were overrun. SOF found thousands of weapons and millions of rounds of ammunition within the cave network. SOF remained in the area and continued to coordinate numerous successful Air Force bombing missions that destroyed the weapons cache. On December 6, 2001, Taliban leader Mullah Mohammed Omar was seen leaving Kandahar, essentially surrendering control of Afghanistan. It is believed that he escaped over the mountains into neighboring Pakistan. As efforts continued in Afghanistan to find and rout out the remnants of bin Laden's al-Qaeda, the United States turned its attention to Iraq.

Iraq

Beginning in 1990, the United States listed Iraq as a state sponsor of terrorism. Moreover, Iraq had strained relations with the United States and the United Nations since the Gulf War. Saddam Hussein remained a threat for his refusal to allow international weapons inspectors to account for his known inventory of known chemical and biological weapons of mass destruction in violation of UN resolutions, and its open support of terrorist activities against Israel and its neighbors.

Central Intelligence Agency (CIA) operators and U.S. special operations forces entered Iraq on July 10, 2002, in an attempt to monitor and verify Iraq's chemical and biological weapons program. On March 20, 2003, the American invasion of Iraq was launched as what the Bush administration said were the "serious consequences" spoken of in UN Resolution 1441. While encountering little real resistance from Iraqi forces, the United States was now fighting the Global War on Terror on several different fronts, thereby straining the capabilities of our military forces. Saddam Hussein's regime was quickly overrun, and George Bush stated on May 1, 2003, that major combat operations in Iraq had ended. But an insurgency quickly arose against the U.S.-led coalition and the newly developing Iraqi military and post-Saddam government.

During the ensuing years, the war in Afghanistan became a lower priority for the U.S. administration than the war in Iraq. This was confirmed in a July 22, 2008, Jim Lehrer interview with Admiral Mike Mullen, chairman of the Joint Chiefs of Staff. Admiral Mullen said that while the situation in Afghanistan was "precarious and urgent," the ten thousand additional troops requested by the commander there would not be made available "in any significant manner" unless troop withdrawals from Iraq were initiated. He added that "my priorities . . . given to me by the commander-in-chief are: Focus on Iraq first. It's been that way for some time. Focus on Afghanistan second."

The Final Visit Home

After having been promoted to the rank of lieutenant on January 1, 2005, Michael returned home on March 16 for a well-deserved leave. While he was in Patchogue, he visited family and friends, and spent time with his fiancée, Heather Duggan, who was busy making wedding preparations. While Michael was certainly interested in his wedding, he was somewhat distant and appeared preoccupied with others matters.

While visiting John and Maureen Bogenshutz, Michael and his uncle were seated in the living room, talking and enjoying a cold beer. John was fascinated by Michael's chosen profession and had a never-ending set of questions. Michael answered the questions he could and deflected the rest.

After listening to the extended conversation, Maureen interrupted and said to Michael, "So, Michael, how are the wedding plans coming?" Michael looked at his aunt and said, "Fine, I guess." Maureen responded with a puzzled look to which Michael, having experienced the career-ending accident involving his friend Andy Haffele, responded firmly, "Aunt Maureen, I know that Heather is really upset that I am not more involved in the wedding plans, but I can't be thinking like that right now. After I get back, I can take time and think about that, but right now I have got to stay focused and keep my head straight. If I don't, there won't be any wedding. It's as simple as that." Maureen and John looked at each other. Now very uneasy, she nervously smiled and changed the subject.

During his leave, Michael met with the FBI in New York City. He was planning on leaving the Navy after his initial enlistment, and he was considering joining the FBI's elite counterterrorism unit.

With Michael being home, a large family St. Patrick's Day family reunion was held at the spacious McElhone home in Kings Park. As with most large families whose members have hectic individual schedules and may live in different locations, it was difficult, if not impossible, to assemble the extended family. When they got word that Michael would be home and in attendance, his relatives made an extra effort to be present. Many members of his large extended family were there, and Michael was pleased to have the opportunity to see them all again. Naturally, his relatives asked a large number of questions about his military service and activities. Michael answered most, deflected some, and respectfully declined to answer a few. One of the most frequent questions he received was about his next duty assignment. This question, of course, could not be answered, and he gave a vague answer that substantively said nothing but satisfied those asking.

What Michael knew but could not share was that in February 2005, the Taliban had announced their intention to increase attacks on the elected government of Afghanistan and its president, Hamid Karzai, who was in a struggle to maintain control outside Kabul. Even though much of the Taliban leadership was hiding in Pakistan, many rank-and-file Taliban fighters had remained in Afghanistan and launched a series of drive-by shootings and suicide bombings directed at local officials and other progovernment clergy. In southern and eastern Afghanistan they began targeting U.S. troops. Other Taliban fighters would cross the border and hit quickly, then retreat over the mountains or through one of thirteen passes between Afghanistan and Pakistan.

Mullah Ahmad Shah, a key terrorist leader, and his ever-growing band of well-trained fighters had increased their attacks on U.S. and coalition forces. As a result, additional SEALs were requested in both Iraq and Afghanistan. SEAL Team Ten had been ordered to Afghanistan and SEAL Team Three to Iraq. Commander Kent Paro served as SEAL Team Ten's commanding officer, with Lieutenant Commander Erik Kristensen serving as task unit commander and Lieutenant Mike McGreevy as SEAL platoon commander.

Prior to deployment, both Paro and Kristensen requested the additional support of SDVT-1, based in Hawaii, and SDVT-2, based in Virginia. As a result of the request, SDVT-2 initially deployed with SEAL Team Ten to Naval Support Activity (NSA) Bahrain. Included in the SDVT-2 deployment were Danny Dietz and Ben Sauers, both petty officers second class. Sauers had graduated from BUD/S Class 236 with Michael.

Bahrain is a major Middle Eastern U.S. ally approximately four times the size of Washington, D.C. Comprised of thirty-six small islands interconnected by causeways, the country is home to multiple U.S. military facilities, including the Navy's Fifth Fleet.

Paro and his SEALs arrived at Camp Ouellette, located at the air base in Bagram, Afghanistan, on April 1, 2005. Camp Ouellette was named in honor of Petty Officer First Class Brian Ouellette of NSW Group Two, who was killed in action on May 29, 2004, in Afghanistan.

Paro and his team were assigned to a unit comprised of about 1,200 NSW personnel known as Combined Joint Special Operations Task Force–Afghanistan (CJSOTF-A), under the command of an Army colonel, David Pahl. Organizationally, CJSOTF-A was part of Combined Joint Task Force 76 (CJTF-76), which was a subordinate unit of Combined Forces Coalition–Afghanistan (CFC-A), headquartered in Kabul under the overall command of Major General Eric T. Olson. The Southern European Task Force (SETAF) assumed control of CJTF-76 in March 2005. In addition to the Navy's SEALS, the CJTF's 13,000 troops also consisted of Army Rangers, the Delta Force, the Marine's Force Recon, and the Air Force's pararescue jumpers (PJs). After receiving their initial briefing, both Paro and Kristensen renewed their request for SDVT-1, which was approved.

As a result, Michael's next duty station was Bahrain. However, he knew that Bahrain was only a temporary stop. There would be subsequent antiterrorist missions to Qatar, the United Arab Emirates (UAE), Dubai, Jordan, and Uzbekistan. Uzbekistan, which had been a member of the former Soviet Union, bordered Afghanistan. Knowing that he might soon be under fire in one of the world's hot zones, he discouraged further questions at the reunion by reminding everyone that this was a St. Patrick's Day family celebration, to which everyone raised their glasses and cheered.

On March 31, 2005—Easter Sunday—Dan took Michael to LaGuardia Airport, where he departed for what would be his final deployment. Michael had asked his father to take him to the airport so they could discuss investment options Michael wanted to pursue. Learning that Michael was departing on a discount airline to Hawaii, Dan insisted that his son call or text-message both him and Michael's mother when he arrived back in Hawaii.

As promised, when he arrived in Hawaii, he text-messaged his mother, "Momma, home safe and sound. Mike."

CHAPTER THIRTEEN

Afghanistan—Home of al-Qaeda

This is their land and they know every inch of it. So when you're out there and you come across them, or more likely, they come across you, don't freak out or nothing, don't be calling back for a QRF for an extraction. Just assess the situation and go on with the mission.

—BEN SAUERS, interview with author, October 9, 2008

Afghanistan: An Overview

Afghanistan is a landlocked country located approximately in the center of Asia. Bordered by Pakistan in the south and east, Iran in the west, Turkmenistan, Uzbekistan, and Tajikistan in the north, and China in the far northeast, it is a culturally mixed nation that serves as a crossroads to the east and the west. What is now Afghanistan was conquered by Alexander the Great (356–323 BC), one of the most successful military commanders of all time, who had conquered much of the civilized world by 331 BC.

Afghanistan has a continental climate, with very hot summers and bitterly cold winters. It is the site of frequent earthquakes, although these are isolated mainly to the northeast in the Hindu Kush range.

The Taliban, under the leadership of Mullah Mohammed Omar, came to power in Afghanistan in 1998, controlling nearly 90 percent of the country. Once in power they established one of the most oppressive regimes ever established. There were widespread abductions of women and forced prostitution, as well as reports of stonings and lashings for those who refused. Women were barred from attending schools or working outside the home and could only be seen in public fully robed from head to toe. Warlords in the north used property destruction, rape, and murder to discourage displaced Pashtuns from reclaiming their homes, and child labor and human trafficking were common outside Kabul. The Taliban's human rights violations placed them in direct conflict with the world community. A more important consideration from the U.S. policy perspective, however, was the Taliban's role in hosting Osama bin Laden and his al-Qaeda terrorist network. Bin Laden's fanatics bombed U.S. embassies in Kenya and Tanzania on August 7, 1998, killing more than 225 people.

Despite an ultimatum from the United States, the Taliban refused to surrender bin Laden, who was bankrolling their regime. Increased sanctions by the United Nations in 1999, as well as the revocation of Afghanistan's seat at the UN, were also ineffective. The country's increasing international isolation only seemed to embolden the oppressive Taliban, who retaliated against their own people, resulting in mass starvation and over a million refugees who fled into neighboring Pakistan and Iran and other countries ill-equipped to handle the influx.

It was not until the Taliban bombed two monumental sixth-century statues of the Bamyan Buddhas, one nearly two hundred feet high and the other more than half that size, carved out of a mountain in Afghanistan, that there was international outrage. While the international hand-wringing regarding what to do about the Taliban and bin Laden continued, another sinister plot was in its final stages of planning.

Afghanistan in the Wake of the 9/11 Attacks

Even before the fires had been extinguished and the final toll of the dead counted, President George W. Bush demanded that the Taliban surrender bin Laden for his role in the terrorist attacks on American soil. Again the Taliban thumbed its nose at the world.

On October 7, 2001, the United States, leading a small coalition of international forces, unleashed an attack so devastating as to be unprecedented in that part of the world. American forces located and identified many of bin Laden's al-Qaeda camps and destroyed them, along with much of the military infrastructure of the Taliban, in one of the largest bombing campaigns in modern warfare. During this campaign, American air units utilized the BLU-82B/C-130, known as the Daisy Cutter. Twelve feet long and nearly four feet wide, this high-altitude 15,000-pound conventional bomb had to be delivered from the huge MC-130 aircraft, as it was too heavy for the bomb racks on other aircraft. The extensive bombing campaign resulted in bin Laden and the remaining Taliban leadership fleeing into the mountains of neighboring Pakistan. Although bin Laden was in exile, al-Qaeda, with Taliban support, continued its terrorist killings of foreign aid workers and kidnapping of foreign construction workers.

SEALs operated with members of the U.S. Army's 1st Special Forces Operational Detachment-Delta (SFO[D]), or Delta Force, as part of Task Force 11 in hunting down members of the Taliban government and al-Qaeda leadership. In January 2002 a simple twelve-hour planned intelligence-gathering mission turned

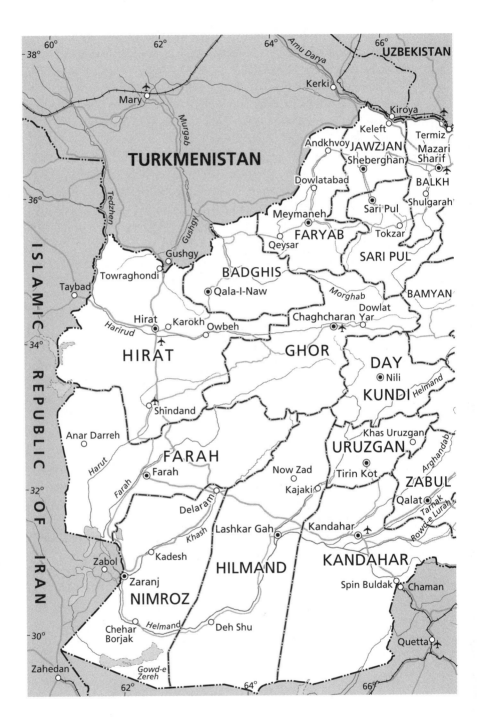

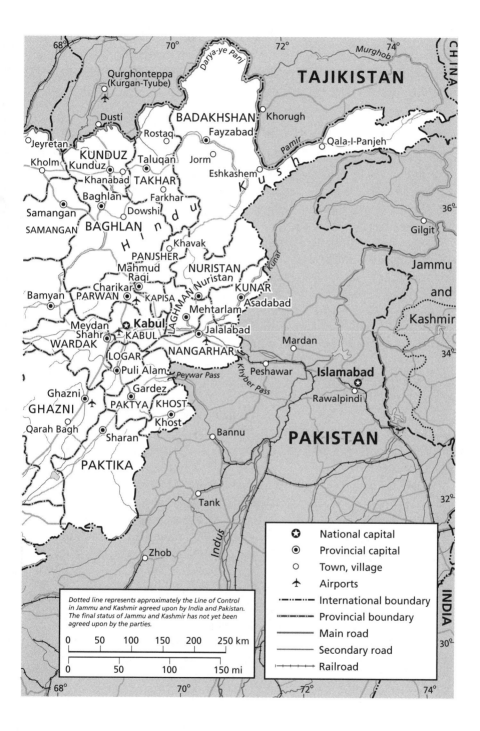

CHINA

Murghob

TAJIKISTAN

68°   70°   72°   74°

Qurghonteppa
(Kurgan-Tyube)

Dusti   **BADAKHSHAN** Khorugh
          Rostaq   Fayzabad
                                        Pamir
Kholm KUNDUZ Taluqan Jorm   Qala-I-Panjeh
  Kunduz   Eshkashem
   Khanabad TAKHAR
   Baghlan   Farkhar   Gilgit
Samangan   Dowshi
SAMANGAN BAGHLAN   36°
                  Khavak   Jammu
         PANJSHER
    Mahmud   **NURISTAN**   and
    Raqi   Nuristan KUNAR
  Charikar   Asadabad   Kashmir
Bamyan PARWAN KAPISA Mehtarlam
                                          34°
Meydan   Jalalabad
Shahr   KABUL   Mardan
WARDAK **Kabul**
   LOGAR   **Islamabad**
   Puli Alam Peywar Pass Peshawar
                  Khyber Pass Rawalpindi
Ghazni   Gardez
GHAZNI PAKTYA KHOST   **PAKISTAN**
Qarah Bagh   Khost
      Sharan   Bannu

PAKTIKA
                              32°
         Tank

     Zhob   INDIA

                                          30°

*Dotted line represents approximately the Line of Control
in Jammu and Kashmir agreed upon by India and Pakistan.
The final status of Jammu and Kashmir has not yet been
agreed upon by the parties.*

✪	National capital
◉	Provincial capital
○	Town, village
✈	Airports
–·–·–·–	International boundary
~~	Provincial boundary
———	Main road
———	Secondary road
╠╪╪╪╪	Railroad

0   50   100   150   200   250 km

0   50   100   150 mi

68°   70°   72°   74°

into a nine-day bonanza of exploration and destruction. Nearly a million pounds of ammunition and equipment was found in an extensive network of seventy caves and tunnels in a narrow valley at Zhawar Kili, in Kunar province in eastern Afghanistan, near the Pakistan border.

Naval Special Warfare Reorganization

Prior to January 2004, twelve SEAL platoons were deployed in various theaters of operation around the globe at any given time. Due to the Global War on Terror, at the beginning of 2004 there was a dramatic need for increased SEAL deployments, necessitating a major realignment of the available resources of both the East Coast and West Coast teams. As a result of the reorganization, a SEAL team now consisted of four platoons instead of the previous six, and commanders were seeking maximum utilization of the two SDVTs with their highly skilled reconnaissance capabilities to augment the efforts of the other SEAL teams.

The day before Easter in 2005, Michael had met with his cousin Kelly at his mother's home before leaving to visit friends before his all-too-short leave was gone. As Kelly and Maureen walked Michael to the door, his cousin gave him a hug and kiss, saying, "See ya later." Michael just smiled and said, "Yeah, I like that. See ya later."

In the spring of 2005, SDVT-1, Michael's unit, had a 2.0 global commitment, meaning that two of its platoons were committed at any one time: one in Pacific Command (PACOM), and the other in Central Command (CENTCOM). The platoon in Pacific Command stayed at SDVT-1's home base in Hawaii on an on-call basis for six months; then, if nothing else required its attention, it deployed to Central Command.

As a result of this policy, ninety-six hours after he had left New York, Lieutenant Michael Murphy and his SDVT-1 teammates had deployed to Naval Support Activity (NSA) Bahrain, located in Manama, as part of Naval Forces Central Command (NAVCENT). They were assigned to NSW Group Two (NSWG-2). NAVCENT shared a commander and its headquarters with the Navy's Fifth Fleet, which was responsible for naval forces in the Persian Gulf, the Red Sea, the Arabian Sea, and the coastal waters off the Horn of Africa as far south as Kenya.

From Bahrain Michael and his teammates were scheduled to go to Qatar, Dubai, Jordan, Uzbekistan, and Abu Dhabi in the United Arab Emirates (UAE) for Joint /Combined Exchange Training (JCET) in each country. While the JCETs were to assist foreign nationals in their own antiterrorism efforts, most of the exercises ended up being foreign internal defense missions.

SDVT-1 was led by Lieutenant Seth Dunn, who served as the task unit commander, and Lieutenant Mark Hernandez, who acted as the platoon commander.

Having been promoted to the rank of lieutenant in January, Michael Murphy now served as the assistant officer in charge (AOIC).

There is no substitute for combat experience for special operations forces. Although his platoon already had scheduled missions to Qatar, the United Arab Emirates, Dubai, and Jordan, Lieutenant Dunn attempted to get it pushed forward and deployed into both the Iraq and Afghanistan theaters of operation. Dunn's SEAL platoon had been conducting predeployment work-ups designed for both Iraq and Afghanistan for the past eighteen grueling months and were in prime operational condition. While not looking for war, all the men were anxious to put their months of intense training to the best possible use and wanted to get their guns in the fight.

After extended conversations with Captain Paul Pfeifer, the NSW commander in Bahrain, Lieutenant Dunn became aware that a new operations officer was needed for SEAL Team Seven in Iraq. Dunn immediately volunteered, hoping that from that position it would be easier to get his men assigned to SEAL Team Seven. His request for reassignment was granted. With Dunn now reassigned, Lieutenant Mark Hernandez assumed command. Lieutenant Michael Murphy remained the assistant officer in charge. Hernandez strongly lobbied Pfeifer into accepting the idea that by splitting his platoon into squads, the unit could "cover down" all of its assignments and still deploy into Iraq.

During the operational planning discussions between Hernandez and Murphy, Commander Kent Paro and Lieutenant Commander Erik Kristensen's priority request for additional SEALs was received by Captain Pfeifer in Bahrain. At a quickly called meeting, Pfeifer informed Hernandez and Murphy that one-half of their platoon was to prepare for deployment to Afghanistan in seventy-two hours.

For a variety of operational reasons, Hernandez and Murphy decided that Senior Chief Petty Officer Dan Healy (referred to as Senior Chief), Petty Officer Second Class Shane Patton, Petty Officer Second Class James Suh, Petty Officer Second Class Matthew Axelson, and Petty Officer First Class Marcus Luttrell would deploy to Afghanistan, with Hernandez as the officer in charge (OIC). Murphy would deploy with the rest of the platoon and cover down on the JCETs. Twenty-four hours before departure, Pfeifer informed Hernandez that if he indeed wanted to show that his platoon could cover down all of the missions for which he had so strongly lobbied, the "senior officer in charge will have to prove that"— meaning that Hernandez would have to remain in Bahrain and deploy on the JCETs and Murphy would deploy to Afghanistan. As Murphy's squad prepared to leave for Afghanistan, Hernandez's squad prepared for deployment to Qatar, then the United Arab Emirates. It was agreed that after Hernandez returned from the UAE the two squads would "switch out," thereby giving the entire platoon live combat experience.

With plans in place, the entire platoon pushed forward and deployed to Qatar. Here, they had a few hours to say their last good-byes, although the mood was upbeat. Knowing all were headed into combat, Senior Chief Healy insisted that each man "pack their stuff" in case the worst happened, so the responsibility would not be left to their remaining teammates. With their "stuff packed," Murphy's squad left for Afghanistan and Hernandez's squad readied for its missions.

April 26, 2005, Bagram Airfield, Afghanistan

Lieutenant Murphy and his SEALs landed at Bagram Airfield, located high in the mountains of Parwan province, seven miles southeast of the city of Charikar and twenty-seven miles north of Kabul. They settled into their B-hut, a forty-foot-by-fifteen-foot semipermanent wooden eight-man structure at Camp Ouellette. After they dropped off their duffel bags, they headed over to the chow hall, then went back to their B-hut for several hours of needed sleep. Prior to their formal orientation briefing, there was an informal gathering of several of those getting ready to depart and Murphy and his five teammates. During this gathering, a very frank and open discussion ensued regarding the terrain and the local goat herders. Murphy and the other new arrivals were told, "Look, these goat herders are everywhere. This is their land and they know every inch of it. So when you're out there and you come across them, or more likely, they come across you, don't freak out or nothing, don't be calling back for a QRF for an extraction. Just assess the situation and go on with the mission."

General Orientation Briefing

The formal briefing was conducted in the Operations Area and included several members of SEAL Team Eight, including Commander Paro, Lieutenant Commander Kristensen, and Petty Officer Second Class Ben Sauers. Representing the new arrivals were Lieutenant Murphy, Senior Chief Healy, and Petty Officer First Class Luttrell. Murphy's unit was assigned to SEAL Team Ten, under Kristensen's command. Kristensen, the son of Rear Admiral Edward Kristensen (ret.), was well known within the SEAL community as a disciplined and highly competent leader. Due to the closeness of the SEAL community, the men were all familiar with each other, their reputations in the teams having preceded them. During the briefing, members of SEAL Team Eight described the terrain, the locals, and the obstacles to be managed. Because of the rugged terrain, many of the missions occurred in the mountains, which were populated with civilian goat herders. These goat herders were very quick covering the rugged terrain and were acutely aware of any changes in the landscape. Any broken twig or branch, overturned rock, bent grass, or new smell would attract their attention.

Due to the frequency of missions into the mountains, the large number of goat herders, and their keen knowledge of the terrain, it was not a question of whether a mission would be compromised; it was only a matter of when and how often. The new arrivals were also informed that most encounters with the local goat herders had been uneventful; despite the language barrier, a PowerBar or other food item usually resulted in them continuing on their way without any trouble. To date, there had been no violent incidents. Everyone looked at each other. No one had to say a word; each knew what the others were thinking.

They were also given the standard operating procedure (SOP) and rules of engagement (ROEs) for such compromises. If the compromise was by known anticoalition militia (ACM), they were to be neutralized. If the compromise was by civilians, they were to be turned loose and moved to a new location.

On the Move

Brought in to accomplish a list of specific tactical missions, Murphy's unit was mission ready and within hours of their arrival and briefing were operational, conducting several snatch-and-grab missions and direct-action assignments. Snatch-and-grab missions were quick missions organized on short notice to secure Taliban and other terrorist leaders. Sauers accompanied Murphy on four such missions, and was pleased to have the opportunity to serve with Michael again. He later related, "I developed a tremendous amount of respect for Lieutenant Murphy when we were in BUD/S, jump school, SQT, and SDV training. My respect for him continued to grow during those four missions. He was a great SEAL leader, always concerned about taking care of his men. Like I said, I would follow him anywhere."

All of the missions were to mountainous eastern Afghanistan near Khost and the Pakistan border, in the areas of Bagram Airfield and two forward operating bases (FOBs), Camp Salerno and Camp Chapman. Camps Salerno and Chapman were about four kilometers apart. On one mission, the men missed their intended target, but obtained actionable intelligence through the target's father-in-law. Plans were made for the target's apprehension or elimination.

Of the four missions that Sauers and Murphy were on together, Sauers related, "the officers took turns being in charge of the mission. Lieutenant Murphy had a lot of confidence in his men. On one mission, he knew that I had completed the basic Emergency Medical Technician course, so when we had a guy injured, he called me forward and told me to take care of the situation. Another time, we were on a mission and he knew that I had extensive training in land navigation and tracking, he again called me forward, had me look at some tracks, and asked for my assessment." As the word got around, the enlisted men began to hold Lieutenant Murphy in very high esteem.

CHAPTER FOURTEEN

When Character Met Circumstance: Operation Red Wings

But how does anyone—Green Beret, Navy SEAL, whatever—
learn to be that brave? I can't explain it. No one can. We are
taught to understand, correctly, that courage is not the absence of
fear, but the capacity for action despite our fears.

—CAPTAIN JOHN MCCAIN, USN (ret.), *Why Courage Matters*

With the frequency of missions, Michael found it difficult to communicate with his family. However, on Mother's Day, Sunday, May 8, he was able to send an e-mail to his mother, including with it a picture of his team holding a cardboard sign that read, "Happy Mother's Day."

Consuming an increasing amount of his team's time was Mullah Ahmad Shah, one of Osama bin Laden's top lieutenants. He commanded the rebel group known as the Mountain Tigers, a militia force with an estimated strength of 40 to 150 men. Shah, who was fluent in five different languages, was constantly on the move, hiding among the civilian populations of the Pashtun villages in the Hindu Kush along the border of Afghanistan and Pakistan in Kunar province.

Kunar Province

Kunar, one of thirty-four provinces in Afghanistan, is located in the northeasternmost part of the country on the border with Pakistan's Bajaur Agency, which is part of the region known as the Federally Administered Tribal Areas. It had long been a favored location of insurgent groups, because of its impenetrable terrain, extensive cave network, and border with the semiautonomous Pakistani North-West Frontier Province. There native Taliban forces mingled with foreign al-Qaeda fighters, while mujahideen militias continued their warring manner with other tribes. As a result of Operation Enduring Freedom, U.S. and coalition forces drove bin Laden and the remainder of his al-Qaeda forces underground in the Kunar cave network and neighboring Pakistan.

One of the primary missions for which Lieutenant Murphy's team was brought to Afghanistan was to utilize their reconnaissance skills to neutralize high-profile al-Qaeda and Taliban targets. On June 3, 2005, Shah's forces ambushed and killed three Marines from Company C, 1st Battalion near Forward Operating Base (FOB) Orgun-E, located outside the town of Orgune in the Paktika province in southwestern Afghanistan along the Pakistani border. Killed were Captain Charles D. Robinson and Staff Sergeant Leroy E. Alexander. Seriously burned was Staff Sergeant Christopher N. Piper, who subsequently died of his wounds. The Marines approached CJSOTF-A's commanders and requested the capture or elimination of Shah. They in turn immediately contacted Commander Kent Paro, who began the initial planning for the mission.

The first planning session held included Paro, Lieutenant Commander Erik Kristensen, Lieutenant Mike McGreevy, and Senior Chief Dan Healy. As task unit commander, the planning effort was the direct responsibility of Kristensen, assisted by McGreevy and Healy. Although not directly involved in the step-by-step planning of the mission, Paro was intimately involved in the overall planning.

The name of this mission was left to the task unit commander, Lieutenant Commander Erik Kristensen. A big hockey fan, Kristensen liked to name SEAL missions after professional hockey teams. The next team on his list was the Detroit Red Wings.

An initial plan and detailed drawings based on the latest intelligence was drawn up. With Paro's review and approval, Kristensen, McGreevy, and Healy approached Major Stephen Reich and Captain Myron Bradley of the Army's 160th Special Operations Aviation Regiment (SOAR), known as the Night Stalkers, and enlisted their help with air operations. During this initial meeting, Kristensen, McGreevy, and Healy huddled with Reich and Bradley in the 160th's Operations Center near the flight line. A large detailed map was laid out, covering the wooden table in the center of the room. At the top of the paper in large red letters were the words "Operation Red Wings." Kristensen and Healy went over their plan in detail and sought the input of Reich and Bradley, which resulted in a few modifications.

With a command change scheduled for the last week in June, CJSOTF-A commanders made it abundantly clear that Shah was the number one target and absolutely must be neutralized before that time. While Shah was a high-profile target, there were several other concurrent operations being both planned and executed. The highly experienced Senior Chief Dan Healy, a recognized expert in counterintelligence, spent hours combing intelligence reports, continually pouring over lists, photographs, maps, and charts, which resulted in the modification of several operational plans, including Operation Red Wings. Due to the terrain, the altitude, and the strength of Shah's forces, attempts to pinpoint Shah's location had proved difficult and at times totally unsuccessful. Petty Officer Marcus Luttrell described the terrain in his book *Lone Survivor:* "The steep, stony mountain crevasses and cliffs, dust-colored, sinister places, were now alive with the burgeoning armies of the Taliban. . . . Up there, complex paths emerge and then disappear behind huge boulders and rocks. Every footstep that dislodges anything, a small rock, a pile of shale, seemed like it might cause an earthshaking avalanche. Stealth, we were told, must be our watchword on the high, quiet slopes of the Hindu Kush."

Operation Red Wings: Planning

Under pressure to neutralize Shah, additional effort and resources were channeled into the planning for Operation Red Wings. On June 10, 2005, Commander Paro was unexpectedly and temporarily reassigned and command of the unit was assumed by Lieutenant Commander Kristensen. However, Paro and Kristensen remained in daily contact about the Red Wings mission planning. Paro later described LCDR Kristensen: "I had every confidence in Erik. He was a highly competent SEAL commander. Highly cerebral, no detail escaped his watchful eye, and he left nothing to chance. He reminded me of someone who in their later years would be in a bulky sweater, smoking a pipe and reading book after book and having highly intellectual discussions with others."

Kristensen was assisted by Lieutenant McGreevy. Paro also described McGreevy: "They simply did not come any better than Mike McGreevy. Honor Man in his class, highly respected in the teams, detail oriented, a highly competent strategic and operation planner as well as an excellent tactician. When you put both Erik and Mike together it simply did not get any better than that."

As the plan continued to develop, others were brought into the planning process. Included from the 160th SOAR were Lieutenant Colonel John Dunson, the commanding officer; Major Steve Reich, the acting task force operations officer; Captain Myron Bradley, the air mission commander; and Chief Warrant Officer 4 Chad Easter, the senior flight lead. Representing the SEALs were Lieutenant Commander Kristensen, Lieutenant McGreevy, Lieutenant Michael Murphy, Senior Chief Healy, and Marcus Luttrell, who served as leading petty officer (LPO).

Actionable intelligence showed that Shah's troop strength numbered between 80 and 200 men, and his force was growing. Although the plan was fully developed, on the day of the scheduled mission it was "taken down" due to the lack of adequate air support and indefinitely postponed as commanders placed other missions higher on the priority list.

Throughout their deployments, Lieutenant Mark Hernandez and Lieutenant Michael Murphy remained in frequent communication and planned and coordinated the remaining missions which they were required to cover down. Mission planning was conducted utilizing the capabilities of the SEAL Mission Support Center (MSC), and the most recent version of SOMPE-E (Special Operations Mission Planning Environment-Maritime), the mission-planning software. A variation of the Microsoft Windows NT Office 2000, it allowed special operations planners a secure platform from which to access information, conduct Web chats and whiteboard sessions, and bring the vast military and special operations databases to operational- and tactical-level planners.

Operation Red Wings: The Mission

Most special operations missions were conducted in a relatively short period of time, several hours at the most. Red Wings would extend over a minimum of three to four days. The mission called for a four-man SEAL reconnaissance element to find Shah and document his troop strength. Once Shah was located, the recon unit was to call in a SEAL team to act as a combined assault and blocking force. They were to surround and neutralize Shah's camp, then perform a combined direct-action assault to neutralize anticoalition militia (ACM) throughout the Korangal Valley.

The Korangal Valley is located on the southern part of the Pech River, a strategic passage the Taliban and al-Qaeda wanted to control. As such, it was among the deadliest pieces of terrain in the world for U.S. forces. Below the Korangal River and across the valley is the dark face of the Abas Ghar ridge and Sawtalo Sar. Sawtalo Sar is a 9,282-foot peak with a ridge that runs north to south and defines the eastern wall of the six-mile-long Korangal Valley. The Taliban essentially owned Abas Ghar and Sawtalo Sar. The Korangal fighters were fierce, knew the terrain, and watched the Americans' every move.

Father's Day

Despite his busy mission planning and execution schedule, on Sunday, June 17, at 4:58 PM, Michael sent a combined e-mail to his father, his mother, his fiancée, Heather, and his brother John.

> Hey All,
>
> I know this is really weak you guys each deserve your own e-mail but I'm really busy. I haven't been able to talk for a while, I have been away. I hope you are all OK and in good health. I pray once in a while that all of you stay safe and are happy. I'm doing fine. My prize possession is this beard I've grown. It's itchy as all hell but . . . whatever. Things are going well, I like it out here and we are doing a lot. I have some funny stories and some sad ones, but all in all things are good. I'll write each of you separate later, I just wanted to let you all know I was OK.

Oh yeah John, it's summer vacation and I know you are working but make sure you start a consistent regimen of physical training. You're going to need it if you want that job. Not to be on your ass, I heard that you did very well in college. Great job and keep up the good work.

After a lengthy delay and with the end-of-June command change just days away, CJSOTF-A commanders placed Operation Red Wings back at the top of their priority list. The four members of Murphy's Alfa Platoon originally selected to serve as the reconnaissance element were Michael, as team leader; Petty Officer Matthew Axelson; Petty Officer Shane Patton; and LPO Marcus Luttrell. Michael was selected based on his previous Fitness Report and Counseling Records, combined with his proven performance in previous missions since he arrived in Afghanistan. However, twenty-four hours before the operation began, the task force's commanders determined that Petty Officer Danny Dietz, currently assigned to SEAL Team Ten from SDVT-2, would replace Patton. Dietz was a communications expert, a skill that was deemed critical on this mission. Luttrell lobbied hard for Patton, who had performed superbly as a communications specialist in his previous missions. Luttrell wanted this to be an all SDVT-1 operation. But the commanders wanted more than one team to have the opportunity to participate in this mission, and so, despite Luttrell's efforts, they went ahead with their decision to replace Patton with Dietz.

On June 25, Shah released a statement threatening U.S. forces. Commander Paro and Lieutenant Commander Kristensen discussed the threats during their daily conversation and determined that his rhetoric was essentially unchanged.

The Reconnaissance Element

Petty Officer Second Class Matthew Gene Axelson, twenty-nine, was born on June 25, 1976, in Cupertino, California, to Cordell and Donna Axelson. After graduating from Monta Vista High School in 1994, he attended California State University, Chico, where he earned a degree in political science. He enlisted in the U.S. Navy in December 2000, entering basic training, or boot camp, at Naval Station Great Lakes, near Waukegan, Illinois. After completing Sonar Technician Surface (STG) "A" school, he was selected to attend BUD/S training and graduated with Class 237.

After BUD/S, he attended Army Airborne jump school, SEAL Qualification Training (SQT), and SEAL Delivery Vehicle (SDV) School. He reported to SEAL Delivery Vehicle Team 1 (SDVT-1) in December 2002 in Hawaii, joining Michael Murphy's Alfa Platoon. Known as "Cool Hand Luke" to his teammates, at six feet four inches tall, he was quick, slim, and a superb athlete, and was considered an expert mountain climber and a SEAL sniper, both skills required on this mission. He and his wife, Cindy, were married in December 2003.

Petty Officer Second Class Danny Philip Dietz Jr., twenty-five, was born on January 26, 1980, in Aurora, Colorado, to Danny and Cindy Dietz. After graduating from Heritage High School in nearby Littleton in 1999, he enlisted in the Navy on August 31, 1999. Following his graduation from Recruit Training Command, Naval Station Great Lakes, on November 27, 1999, he completed Gunner's Mate "A" school at the Naval Air Technical Training Center (NATTC), Pensacola, Florida. From there he transferred to BUD/S and graduated with Class 232 in 2001. He went on to attend the Basic Airborne Course at Fort Benning, Georgia, then SQT and SDV Training.

Immediately upon checking in at SEAL Delivery Vehicle Team 2 in Virginia Beach, Virginia, on November 8, 2001, he was assigned to Task Unit Bravo as the secondary SDV pilot and the Ordnance and Engineering Department head. During a rigorous predeployment work-up he honed his skills and became one of the best pilots in the command. He married his wife, Maria, in March 2003. He leveraged his skills during a six-month deployment to European Command (EUCOM) as the lead pilot in multiple proof-of-concept rehearsals (detailed training exercises under full mission conditions). Upon his return from EUCOM, he was assigned to Task Unit Charlie as a primary Special Reconnaissance Team member and the Communications Department head. During predeployment he focused his attention on perfecting his SEAL sniper, reconnaissance, and field skills. In the barren and forbidding mountains of the Hindu Kush, his communications expertise would be critical.

Leading Petty Officer Marcus Luttrell, thirty, was born in 1975 in Huntsville, Texas. He began training for the SEALs at the age of fourteen with former Green Beret Billy Shelton and joined the Navy in 1999. He started with BUD/S Class 226; however, due to a fractured femur he suffered on the O-course, he graduated with Class 228 on April 21, 2000. After completing BUD/S, he attended Army jump school and SQT. He was then sent to Fort Bragg, North Carolina, for an additional six months of advanced training in conventional and unconventional medical skills, ranging from diagnosis and treatment of nearly every known condition to advanced emergency medicine and battlefield life support.

After SDV Training, he completed a two-year tour in Iraq. A highly competent and battle-proven corpsman, his medical training was a critical element in the preferred four-man SEAL units, although hopefully it would not be needed. If that were the case, he would serve as the backup sniper.

The Plan

The plan seemed simple enough. Murphy and his team were to spend the first day monitoring Shah's location and movements from a concealed position in the hills above Asadabad, the capital of Kunar province. On day two, once Shah's location was verified, SEAL Team Ten had orders to call in the prearranged SEAL assault force designated to neutralize Shah, his headquarters, and his Mountain Tigers. A combined task force of ground troops would then be deployed on the third day to begin conducting mop-up operations throughout the valley. This would, it was believed, neutralize any remaining ACM in the Korangal Valley.

Bagram Airfield, Sunday, June 26, 2005

The air mission briefing was conducted at the 160th SOAR Planning Center. Present from the 160th were Major Steve Reich, the operations officer; Captain Myron Bradley, the air mission commander; Chief Warrant Officer 4 Chad Easter, the senior flight lead; and the pilots and flight crews of the two assigned helos. Attending from the SEALs were Lieutenant Commander Erik Kristensen, Lieutenant Michael McGreevy, Lieutenant Michael Murphy, Senior Chief Dan Healy, and Leading Petty Officer Marcus Luttrell.

During the briefing every aspect of the mission was thoroughly detailed, including the all-important abort criteria. Abort criteria were a predetermined set of circumstances that could cause the immediate cancellation of the mission. The abort criteria for this mission were ACM at the helicopter landing zone (HLZ) and inadequate air support. Captain Bradley later related, "Nothing was overlooked, no detail was too small for consideration, everything was gone over in 'eye-bleeding' detail." Although not openly discussed, all were acutely aware of the insistence from CJSOTF-A commanders for successful completion of the mission. At the conclusion of the one-hour meeting, it was announced that the mission was a go for the next operational period—the next period of darkness.

Operation Red Wings: Execution

Monday, June 27, 2005

Early in the morning of June 27, confirmed intelligence pinpointed Shah's location. By that afternoon, Kristensen and McGreevy had laid out the updated detailed maps and other photographic intelligence of the terrain for Murphy and Luttrell to review. Murphy, highly skilled in land navigation, drew a much smaller version of the map for his use. The target village location contained thirty-two houses—or, more accurately, straw huts.

After two additional delays during the day, Operation Red Wings was on for that night. A couple of hours before the operation commenced, during an electronic conversation with Hernandez, Murphy related that Operation Red Wings was proceeding. He said that this was the operation they had hoped for since their arrival and that it was fitting that this would be their last mission before they left Afghanistan. Both were pleased that the SEALs were being utilized on this mission because it was the type for which they were specifically trained, and their after-action report and direct experience would provide excellent training material for future teams and deployments. Hernandez related that he was "happy for them" and that he was still working on a plan that would allow Murphy's squad to bypass the other cover-down operations and meet up with them in Iraq soon. Both looked forward to the reunion.

Zero Hour: Insertion

Just after dark, two helos were waiting on the flight line. Murphy, Dietz, Axelson, and Luttrell loaded into the lead Chinook MH-47E, which had the call sign Turbine 21, piloted by Easter and Chief Warrant Officer 3 Steve Swartz. Also on board were Captain Bradley; Staff Sergeant Ron Oster, the flight engineer; and three crew chiefs. Kristensen and McGreevy, the mission commanders, and a quick-reaction force (QRF) of twenty-five ground troops loaded into the other helo, which had the call sign Turbine 22. The QRF was a contingency in case there were any problems with the insertion or during the first twenty-four hours while the team was on the move to its target.

The Boeing MH-47E is a derivative of the CH-47D Chinook heavy-duty lift helicopter developed specifically for the 160th SOAR. It is a long-range special operations forces insertion/extraction platform with integral command and control capabilities. With a maximum speed of 154 knots, and a service ceiling of 11,000 feet, it features twin SATCOM (satellite communications) links, and is also equipped with an AN/APQ-174A multilode (terrain following, terrain mapping, air-to-ground ranging) radar, an AN/AAQ-16 forward-looking infrared (FLIR) system, and the integrated GPS-based scrolling map display system. The FLIR uses the detection of thermal energy to create a "picture" assembled for the video output that helps pilots and drivers steer at night, in fog, or detect warm objects against a cold background when it is completely dark.

Also equipped with two pintle mounts, one located at the right-side crew door and the other on the left-hand side at the first window, the MH-47E is capable of accepting a single machine gun, either an M60D single-barrel 7.62-mm medium machine gun or a single M134 7.62-mm six-barreled Minigun capable of firing two thousand to four thousand rounds per minute. With two guns up front at the cabin door and the left-side gunner's window (M134s) and two guns in back at the machine-gun cutouts (M240 7.62-mm machine guns), it is a well-armed aerial platform.

After the flight-readiness check, Easter took the lead helo, Turbine 21, skyward. Turbine 22 followed. Both helos headed northeast toward the treacherous and unforgiving Hindu Kush range, a sixty-two-minute trip by air. To decrease the signature, or noise, of approaching forces, Turbine 22 broke formation at a pre-designated point and proceeded to Asadabad to wait, then relocated to the forward operating base (FOB) at Jalalabad (J-bad), about a fifteen-minute flight from the designated insertion point. There, commanders monitored both the reconnaissance element insertion and the first twenty-four hours of the mission. In a cold, driving rain, Turbine 21 continued up Sawtalo Sar on its seven-minute trip to an altitude of nine thousand feet in search of its landing zone (LZ). The engines struggled in the thinning atmosphere and driving rain, and the helo lurched to the left and right, shuddered, and vibrated. As they gained altitude and headed away from the lights of J-bad, Easter, Bradley, and Swartz noticed the ominous camp-fires and lights of local villagers and ACM.

"Ten minutes!" yelled Oster as he turned toward the SEALs. Murphy acknowledged and gave a thumbs-up. The SEALs reviewed their plan of operation, equipment, and communications. Murphy and his team mentally prepared for their insertion. Bradley heard a radio communication from an AC-130 gunship circling overhead stating that it was "breaking station"—leaving its assigned area due to low fuel. Although another AC-130 was on its way, it had not arrived, thereby depriving the helo of air support, one of the all-important abort criteria. As the air mission commander, Bradley had a decision to make: abort the mission, or continue on and hope the relieving AC-130 arrived quickly. Aware of the critical importance of the mission to CJSOTF-A commanders, Bradley requested a status report on the primary helicopter landing zone, Nez Perce, and the alternate, Neka. Bradley was informed that LZ Nez Perce was clear but infrared sensors placed four individuals at LZ Neka. The two LZs were about 3.2 miles (5 kilometers) apart. Bradley informed the flight crew and the SEALs of the situation and his decision to continue with the mission. Murphy nodded affirmatively.

"Six minutes!" Murphy again acknowledged as Oster opened the rear ramp and both he and the crew chiefs prepared the aircraft for landing. "Three minutes!" Murphy again acknowledged, then he and the SEALs got on their feet and checked their equipment to ensure it was secure. Oster noticed Murphy communicate with each of his teammates, who all responded with an affirmative nod. As the helo approached, LZ Nez Perce was covered with fifteen-to-twenty-foot-tall trees, large tree stumps, thick brush, and large boulders. Easter tried repeatedly to find a safe "sweet spot" to set the helo down but was unsuccessful, which necessitated a fast-rope insertion. Oster immediately pulled the 1¾-inch-diameter nylon fast rope down from the fast rope insertion/extraction system (FRIES), secured it to the helo's frame, and kicked it out the door. He then turned to Murphy and said, "One minute."

Easter handed off the visual control to Oster, who obtained a direct visual of the LZ. Oster acknowledged visual contact: "Roger, Budweiser!" Oster gave Murphy a thumbs-up, which he returned.

Easter performed a flare maneuver by pitching the nose up, which would normally cause the helicopter to gain altitude, while at the same time reducing power to prevent a climb from occurring. This allowed the aircraft to hover over a suitable site. With the rear ramp down, Oster monitored the fast rope dangling from the back of the aircraft to the landing zone some thirty feet below and ensured that the rope reached the ground. Two crew chiefs manned the helo's Miniguns and kept an eye on the LZ for enemy activity and fire. Oster gave Murphy another thumbs-up, which he again returned. The SEALs walked toward the rope with their hands over their heads, hanging onto the overhead FRIES support bar. Murphy and his men were dressed in full combat gear—knee and elbow pads, weapons, helmet, goggles, a rucksack containing about eighty-five pounds of food, ammunition, communications, and other supplies—and were wearing their all-important Kevlar Cobra tactical gloves, which prevented friction from burning their hands as they rapidly descended the rope. As the cold driving rain continued, the first one down was Dietz, followed by Luttrell, Murphy, and Axelson.

During the insertion Oster communicated with the crew: "First man on the rope . . . second man . . . third man . . . last man on the rope . . . last man on the ground." The precision fast-rope insertion took approximately fifteen seconds. Without the weight of the SEALs on the rope, the prop wash of the helicopter's rotor blades caused the fast rope to snake around a small tree and become entangled in the heavy brush, which anchored and threatened the aircraft. With everyone on the same communication frequency, Oster informed both Easter and the SEAL team about the fast rope. Easter carefully maneuvered the helo in an attempt to free the rope, but without success. Although it was not part of the operational plan, Oster advised both the SEALs and Easter that cutting the rope was the only way to free the helo. Dietz acknowledged and Oster cut the fast rope. Looking down from the ramp, Oster saw Dietz and Axelson run toward and secure the rope as Murphy and Luttrell monitored the perimeter. Dietz acknowledged possession of the rope. The ramp was raised, and Easter pointed his helo back down the mountain toward J-bad airfield. Dietz and Axelson covered the rope with brush, weeds, grass, sticks, rocks, and dirt, then each member of the team moved about twenty yards apart and froze into the landscape for fifteen minutes in total silence—no movement, no communication.

By this time, Easter had returned the helo to J-Bad. Upon entering the Operations Center, Lieutenant Colonel John Dunson and Captain Bradley were approached by Lieutenant Commander Kristensen and Senior Chief Healy, who had monitored mission communications regarding the cutting of the fast rope. All agreed that it was not part of the operational briefing. After the Army officers described the situation at the LZ and the reason for cutting the rope, Kristensen and Healy accepted the explanation, but inquired as to the possibility of the 160th returning and retrieving the rope to prevent its detection by ACM. Their thinking was that due to the size of the rope, the SEALs would be unable to carry it with them.

Bradley explained that the only way to retrieve the rope in that terrain was to lower a man by hoist, find the rope, which had been hidden, and then extract it. Bradley also explained in detail the difficulties they had just encountered with the insertion and that such an attempt could bring unwanted attention to the SEAL team. Dunson concurred and voiced his concern about such a return mission. Kristensen and Healy recognized the danger in such a mission and withdrew their request.

Flight crews and mission commanders in the Operations Center were able to monitor the team's progress because it was carrying a tracking beacon. As the SEALs moved slowly toward their target objective in the cold, driving rain, they counted two fires or lanterns in the village below, an estimated mile away, and reported "eyes on" several local goat herders as they progressed toward their layup (LUP) position. The terrain to the right featured huge, thick trees; to the left were the forbidding mountains, low tree stumps, and thick foliage. The men were soaked and worked to keep their body temperatures up by remaining in constant motion. Although on the ground, the team was far from its planned area of operation. Dietz established quick communication with an AC-130 gunship arriving high overhead, and the team prepared to move on its preplanned four-mile journey along Sawtalo Sar's ridge, which stretched into a long right-handed dogleg. Conditions for the team were so bad that despite being expert mountain climbers, each member fell back down the mountain within the first half hour. Murphy periodically radioed back to Kristensen with news of their progress as they slowly reached each predesignated checkpoint.

Exhausted after the seven-hour trip, the men rested and Dietz radioed J-bad headquarters that they were "good to go." Murphy informed Kristensen that even though they were not at their intended layup point, he believed they had reached an even better one than anticipated and were going to lay up for the day. Hearing that, Kristensen turned to Bradley and said, "We are at a stopping point here. They are going to lay up for the day. We are good here." The QRF loaded back up in the two helos and returned to Bagram to prepare for the assault of Shah's compound during the next operational period. As a planned contingency, Marine forces and helos were placed on ready alert as a QRF in case Murphy's SEALs needed them.

After a short rest, Murphy and his SEALs relocated against some trees and rocks; however, due to an incoming fog bank, their view of the village was severely limited—only two huts were visible—resulting in the team relocating yet again. After an hour-long reconnaissance by Murphy and Axelson, a perfect location was found to observe the village; however, it provided little cover. Although the new site was only about a thousand yards away, it took the team over an hour to cover the treacherous and sheer terrain.

Location Compromised

The team's new location was over the brow of the summit, approximately eighty feet from the uppermost escarpment at an altitude of about nine thousand feet. As daylight approached, they determined that their current location was too dangerous to stay there. Despite the fact that SEALs lie low in the daylight and move at night, Murphy ordered the team to "move in five." The men retraced their route about a hundred yards and found a prime location in the trees that overlooked the target village. The village was nearly a mile and a half away, but their location provided a clear line of sight with good concealment. With their specialized equipment, the distance proved no obstacle to their reconnaissance efforts.

In perfect hiding locations, they waited in full combat gear, soaked from the night's rain, baking in the searing Afghan sun. In a tactical diamond-shaped formation about thirty yards apart, each was waiting with heightened vigilance and in perfect silence when a man carrying an ax and accompanied by about a hundred goats was spotted by Axelson. In perfect silence, he placed the goat herder in the crosshairs of his weapon as he approached Luttrell's position. As the goat herder jumped down from the log under which Luttrell had positioned himself, the petty officer broke cover and the man nearly stepped on him. Immediately upon seeing Luttrell, the man tossed his ax on the ground in front of him. While Luttrell took control of the man, Axelson signaled that two more goat herders were closing in on his position. As they neared, they appeared to the carefully observing SEALs to be a father and his young son. It was clear to the team that despite the fact the first goat herder had been carrying an ax, these individuals were civilians, not ACM members. The SEALS were now in a situation known as a soft compromise. Not knowing if the entire team's presence had been compromised, the SEALs could not afford to allow the other two herders to proceed unchallenged. The other three SEALs also broke cover as the man and his son reached their position.

The two goat herders were startled as the SEALS surrounded them. They stood motionless alongside the first man, just staring at the four Americans. In response to the team's questions, the goat herders replied in heavily accented, broken English, "No Taliban! No Taliban!" The goat herders were directed to sit together on a nearby log as the team engaged in several minutes of discussion, followed by attempts at interrogation, which failed. Although they acknowledged understanding the team's questions, the goat herders gave the SEALs no information and continued to stare at them. Luttrell gave the young boy a PowerBar. Without taking his eyes off Luttrell, the boy accepted it, but placed it on a rock beside him instead of eating it.

Despite the sometimes-blurred lines between different-ranking members of a SEAL team, each of the men understood the chain of command and would follow orders without question. Despite their open discussion that day,* each man understood that the team structure was not a democracy—there was to be no consensus, and there would be no voting. After requesting and receiving appropriate and valuable input from the other members of his team, the final decision unquestionably would be made by the team leader, Lieutenant Michael Murphy. He was acutely aware of their situation and reminded his team of several important pieces of information.

1. These three individuals were clearly civilian goat herders.
2. If they aborted every mission in which they were compromised, no mission would ever be completed.
3. The SOP and ROEs for this situation were clear.
4. If they were to eliminate these three civilians, who would do the execution, how would they dispose of the bodies, and what would they do with more than a hundred goats with bells around their necks?
5. CJSOTF-A commanders were insistent on mission completion before command change.
6. Shah's forces were continuing to inflict U.S. causalities.
7. This might be the best chance to neutralize Shah.
8. This was their last scheduled mission before deploying to Iraq.
9. This mission was why they had come to Afghanistan.

Utilizing his innate leadership and interpersonal skills, and after listening to the input of his team, Michael Murphy explained the situation and shared each of the items of concern and led his team to the only acceptable option: to set the civilian goat herders free. Murphy then gave the order. While they watched the goat herders run up the mountain and disappear out of sight, Michael ordered the team to prepare to move to a new location. Again, trained to move only at night, the team found itself in a catch-22. Within twenty minutes the men were on the move. As the OIC, Murphy understood the essence of leadership: in any moment of decision, doing the right thing was always the right thing to do . . . regardless of the consequences.

The team headed for the best defensive position it could find—up the mountain. Approximately forty yards from the summit was a location with tree cover and concealment that made them nearly impossible to see. Their immediate strategy

---

* Their discussion is detailed in Marcus Luttrell's book *Lone Survivor: The Eyewitness Account of Operation Redwing and the Lost Heroes of SEAL Team Ten* (New York: Little, Brown, 2007).

was to remain in defensive positions until the cover of darkness, then relocate. Murphy reminded his men to remain on high alert. They took up a defensive diamond position with each member about thirty yards apart. Axelson was charged with the responsibility of using binoculars and a scope to watch for Taliban fighters and monitor the village. About twenty minutes later Luttrell assumed the watch; Murphy followed him. More than an hour later, they were still in their new position, and all remained quiet.

The Battle for Murphy's Ridge

Suddenly the silence was interrupted. "Sssssssst. Ssssssssst." It was Lieutenant Murphy's warning sound—a familiar one to his men. He began calling out orders, among them instructions to Dietz to call for immediate reinforcements from HQ. As Murphy directed the team's attention up the mountain, they saw about eighty to one hundred heavily armed Taliban fighters, each with an AK-47 pointed in their direction and several carrying launchers for the all-too-familiar shoulder-fired rocket-propelled grenades (RPGs). Within minutes the Taliban worked their way down the mountain on three sides, including the team's left and right flanks. The team was sure that Axelson and Dietz's position had in all likelihood not been compromised, but the same could not be said about Murphy and Luttrell's. If spotted, they were trapped, with the only avenue of escape down the near-vertical nine thousand feet to the open valley below.

Up to this point, no shots had been fired. Dietz established radio contact with the J-bad communications center just as gunfire finally erupted and the sound of AK-47s filled the mountain air. A fierce firefight ensued between the four SEALs and the much larger enemy force. J-bad relayed the information to Bagram. Despite being flanked on both sides, the SEALs kept fighting. However, the sheer number of Taliban closing in on them, as well as the intensity of the gunfire and the frequent explosions of RPGs, made remaining in their current position impossible.

Nearly thirty minutes into the firefight, Dietz and Axelson had each received multiple wounds and Murphy had suffered a bullet wound to the abdomen. The wounded men began bounding down the mountain's steep sides, making blind leaps of thirty to fifty feet into the trees, rocks, boulders, and thick shrubbery below, all the while providing each other with alternating cover fire. During their leaps downward, each man had lost his rucksack and Luttrell all of his medical supplies.

About forty-five minutes into the fight, the severely wounded Dietz sought open air space to place another distress call back to the base, but before he completed his call, he suffered another gunshot wound, this one to his right hand, shattering his thumb. Their ammunition was running low, and Dietz, Axelson, and

Murphy had been severely wounded by gunfire or RPG rounds. Someone yelled, "I'm hit!" Murphy yelled back, "We're all hit! Keep moving!"*

"Iron-Souled Warrior"

More than an hour into the fight, Dietz was dead and Axelson was suffering from multiple gunshot wounds, including one in his head. Despite being severely wounded with multiple gunshot wounds himself, Lieutenant Michael Murphy, in a last-ditch effort to save his men, broke cover and deliberately walked onto open ground in one final attempt to acquire a cell-phone signal. Recognizing the desperate condition of his team, he made the conscious decision that the only way any of his men were going to survive was to call in reinforcements. And the only way to do that in this rugged mountain terrain was to get to open ground, regardless of the cost.

Murphy used his encrypted Iridium satellite cell phone and called back to the Operations Center at J-bad. Luttrell yelled at Murphy to take cover, but he kept walking and finally made contact. Luttrell described Murphy's actions: "He walked until he was more or less in the center, gunfire all around him, and he sat on a small rock and began punching in the numbers to HQ. I could hear him talking, 'My men are taking heavy fire . . . we're getting picked apart. My guys are dying out here . . . we need help.' Right then he took a bullet straight in the back. He slumped forward, dropped his phone and his rifle, but then he braced himself, grabbed them both, sat upright again, and once more put the phone to his ear. I heard him speak again. 'Roger that, sir. Thank you.'"

Having completed his call, he knew help was on the way. Luttrell saw Murphy pick up his weapon and flank to his left out of the line of sight. Luttrell then saw Axelson take another round and rushed over to him, but he could do nothing to help without his medical supplies. Axelson was unable to hold his weapon, but despite his mortal wounds, he placed his weapon on a rock and continued to return fire. Luttrell moved to another location and continued to fight on.

After about another thirty minutes the sound of gunfire diminished. Luttrell heard only the familiar sound of the AK-47s, which continued to fade, then ceased altogether. All around him Luttrell heard enemy voices yelling, screaming, and chanting. After several minutes, he heard several more rounds from an AK-47, followed by dead silence. He was alone.

---

* Luttrell, the only remaining eyewitness, described the epic battle in graphic detail as only a battle-tested eyewitness can in his best-selling book *Lone Survivor*.

CHAPTER FIFTEEN

Rescue Mission

Despite the urge to avert your eyes from the suffering, the only way to really appreciate the nobility of courage is to familiarize yourself with its costs so that you will come to understand how rare a thing it really is.

—CAPTAIN JOHN MCCAIN, USN (ret.), *Why Courage Matters*

I n response to Michael Murphy's call for assistance, the Marine QRF at J-bad loaded onto four aircraft, two UH-60 Blackhawks and two Apache assault helos. As they awaited orders to deploy, the four aircraft sat on the tarmac with rotors turning. Having monitored the radio call from Lieutenant Murphy to J-bad, Lieutenant Commander Kristensen ordered the assault force (AF) troops to extract his fellow SEALs. Senior Chief Healy located Petty Officer Second Class Ben Sauers and told him, "Our guys are in a TIC, we gotta go . . . now!" (TIC is an acronym for troops in contact or combat.) Sauers ran for the line of B-huts and alerted the SEALs, who immediately began preparations while the call went out to the flight crews of the 160th Night Stalkers.

Not scheduled in the rotation for another three hours, Captain Bradley was asleep in his B-hut when he was awakened by his maintenance officer. "Sir, you gotta get up, we have to go get those SEALs you dropped in, they're in real trouble." After springing from his bed, Bradley quickly dressed. He then ran out the door to the next B-hut to awaken Platoon Sergeant Michael Russell, who immediately got up, dressed, and began to muster the flight crews. After awakening Russell, Bradley ran to the Operations Center. First to arrive at the flight line was Sergeant First Class Marcus Muralles, a senior combat medic preparing for his last mission before going home. He opened each helicopter and prepared for the rescue attempt by loading the medical supplies he hoped he would not need.

In the Operations Center Kristensen met Major Reich and other mission commanders. After a brief discussion, Kristensen, Lieutenant Mike McGreevy, and

Reich came to the conclusion that this was not a QRF mission, but rather an acceleration of the planned mission. The plan in place was quickly adapted. Quite simply, the revised plan was for the rescue team to take the high ground at the point of insertion on Sawtalo Sar and fight its way down to the SEALs. The original plan had been to move in that night; however, waiting until the cover of darkness was not an option.

While the rescue plan was being finalized, Chief Warrant Officer 3 Cory Goodnature worked with Senior Flight Leader Chad Easter and made the required adaptations and calculations. The responding assault force consisted of thirty-two troops, sixteen in each helo. With the heat of the day exceeding 100° and the thin atmosphere at ten thousand feet, the helos would not be able to carry such loads to the insertion point on Sawtalo Sar. In addition, anticipating that they would find wounded SEALs, medics were needed to treat the injured.

Reich and McGreevy decided to drop half of the AF at the forward operating base (FOB) at J-bad, then proceed to the extrication site, locate and extract Lieutenant Murphy's SEALs, return to J-bad, pick up the remaining troops, and finally come back to finish off Shah and his militia. Additional plans would be made in the air. Kristensen, Reich, and McGreevy then began the short trip to the flight line, where the flight crews had already loaded each helo with eight Night Stalkers. They were ready for take off and the chance to prove the Night Stalkers slogan: "If we put them in, we take them out."

The lead helo, an MH-47E Chinook, call sign Turbine 33, was piloted by Chief Warrant Officer 4 Chris Scherkenbach and copiloted by Chief Warrant Officer 3 Cory Goodnature, both Night Stalkers. Standing directly behind Scherkenbach was Captain Bradley, the air mission commander. The other Night Stalker crew members were Sergeant First Class Marcus V. Muralles, Master Sergeant James W. "Tre" Ponder, Platoon Sergeant Michael Russell, Staff Sergeant Shamus Goare, and Sergeant Kip Jacoby.

Coordinating the SEAL boarding of Turbine 33 was Chief Petty Officer Jacques Fontan. As the SEALs ran for the helos, Fontan directed Jeffrey Lucas, Jeffrey Taylor, Michael McGreevy, and Ben Sauers on board, then climbed on himself. After boarding Fontan recognized Sauers and yelled, "You're SDV. You're in the other helo." Sauer exited and ran toward Turbine 34, another Chinook.

Senior Chief Healy directed SEALs James Suh and Shane Patton to board Turbine 34.* Just as Healy was about to climb on board, he heard Sauers yelling. Healy stopped and motioned for Sauers to get on board, then climbed on himself and secured the side door behind him.

---

* The flight crew and other 160th SOAR special operators on board Turbine 34 will remain anonymous.

As the two helos sat fully loaded and running on the tarmac, Kristensen and Reich boarded the lead helo, Turbine 33. Reich approached Captain Bradley behind the cockpit and said, "What's your plan, Captain?"

Bradley responded, "Insert the QRF on the high ground near the insertion point and work our way down to our guys."

"Excellent, but this isn't a QRF. We've accelerated the planned mission. I've got this one. You stay here!" Bradley insisted on going as the air mission commander, to which Reich responded, "Captain, I said I've got this one. You're staying here."

Although frustrated, Bradley acknowledged Reich's order: "Yes, sir. Good luck."

"Thanks."

Bradley gathered his weapon and jumped off the helo. At a safe distance from the aircraft, he turned and saw the helos reach skyward, then ran to the Operations Center and assumed command. As the operations officer, he would monitor the rescue effort.

After the sixty-minute flight to J-bad, as planned, both helos flew over the still waiting QRF and touched down on a different flight line. As Sauers and some of the SEALs and Night Stalkers jumped off, they were told, "Don't go anywhere, we'll be back for you in ten minutes." While both aircraft rested on the tarmac, Healy, Suh, and Patton exited Turbine 34 and ran and boarded Turbine 33. Once the two helos had taken off again and gained altitude, the QRF commander ordered his units into the air, but by that time the two MH-47Es were well out in front as they raced toward the LZ.

While Scherkenbach and Goodnature flared and maneuvered their Chinook over the landing zone, Turbine 34 did a quick flyby to check out the area. Because the area was heavily forested, very little, if anything, could be seen on the ground. As Scherkenbach and Goodnature held their position at an altitude of about fifty feet and with the ramp open for deployment of the fast rope, the call came: "Thirty seconds!" At that, the others on board lined up for the insertion.

The Loss of Turbine 33

On the ground almost directly below and slightly behind Turbine 33, an RPG was fired. It penetrated the middle of the aircraft on the underside, creating an instant fireball and causing the aircraft to turn on its right side. Within seconds it crashed into the side of the nine-thousand-foot mountain. The entire incident was captured on both video and still photography by an MQ-1 Predator.

Back at the 160th's Operations Center, Captain Bradley was stunned. He knew that Major Reich and the other fifteen men on board Turbine 33 were gone. He also realized that Major Reich's assuming command of the mission had saved him.

On the ground, Luttrell heard cheers and yelling from the Taliban. He knew that something had happened, but he had no idea what had caused the fighters' excitement. In his critically wounded state, however, he was in no condition to investigate.

On board Turbine 34, the crew was also stunned. The pilot radioed back to both J-bad and Bagram: "Turbine 33 is down. Repeat, Turbine 33 is down!" Turbine 34 and the four QRF aircraft requested permission to insert, check for survivors of the crash, and locate the SEALs. The commanders back at Bagram denied the request. Despite calls from the troops in the rear of the remaining aircraft, the pilots followed orders and aborted the mission. The helos started on their way back to J-bad.

Back in the Operations Center, Bradley had sent for Chad Easter, who was in disbelief when he arrived. They heard the commanders order Turbine 34 to abort the mission and return to J-bad just as Lieutenant Colonel Dunson arrived. Dunson, Bradley, Easter, and several other SOF operators loaded into a helo and departed for J-bad to link up with the returning helos and their crewmen.

On the tarmac at J-bad, Sauers and the others learned of the shootdown. Sauers immediately asked, "Before or after the QRF insertion?" "Before," they were told. Incensed, the entire group demanded to be flown to the crash site and inserted so they could look for and treat survivors and to find the SEALs. They were ordered to stand down and directed into the Operations Center, where they monitored the actions on the ground through the video and photographs sent by the MQ-1 Predator. As they watched the video of the shootdown, they knew that little hope existed for those on board Turbine 33. However, they remained optimistic about the four SEALs in Murphy's team, although no communication had been received from them for several hours.

Rescue to Recovery

Upon arriving at J-bad just before dark, Dunson, Bradley, Easter, and other operational planners assembled in the Operations Area and developed a plan to go back up the mountain. Easter then went outside and advised the waiting troops from the QRF and Turbine 34. Everyone headed to the flight line and loaded into the five awaiting MH-47Es, designated Turbines 41, 42, 43, 44, and 45. The helos then took off.

Turbine 41, the lead helo, piloted by Easter, headed up the mountain with the other aircraft close behind. Soon they found themselves in an ever-thickening fog bank and heavy rain. As the aircraft neared the crash site, the fog was so thick and the visibility so poor that the pilots were flying blind, unable to see the other aircraft, the mountains, or the ground below. Back at Bagram, the commanders monitoring the radio traffic aborted the mission. All pilots acknowledged the abort order. Easter and the other pilots now faced making a 360-degree turn in formation with no visibility, an extremely dangerous maneuver that increased the already high level of tension in the aircraft. All five aircraft performed the difficult maneuver without incident and returned safely to J-bad.

At the start of the next operational period twelve hours later, the same five aircraft headed up the mountain toward a new LZ just south of where they made their last attempt. In addition, Marine ground forces were dispatched on foot up the mountain toward the crash site from the southeast.

The aircraft split formation and headed for their designated LZs. The mood of the men on the flight was somber and intense. All contact with Murphy's SEALs had been lost, and sixteen of their fellow special operators had died the previous day.

The two LZs for this mission were called Napier and Stork. Turbine 41, Turbine 42, and Turbine 45 approached LZ Napier, while Turbine 43 and Turbine 44 headed to LZ Stork. The LZs were along the Sawtalo Sar ridgeline above the crash site. The crewmen of Turbine 41 utilized the FRIES and dropped its ninety-foot rope to the ground below, then dispatch the assault force. Turbine 42 and Turbine 45 followed suit. At LZ Stork, the troops on board Turbine 43 and Turbine 44, piloted by Captain Bradley, were similarly inserted.

July 3, 2005

The assault force began the treacherous decline toward the crash site, which took them just over three hours. After they reached the crash site, they secured both the inner and outer perimeters. The remains of all eight SEALs and all eight Night Stalkers were recovered. The Marine ground forces coming from the southeast, who were still several hours from the site due to the terrain, were instructed to abort and return to J-bad.

Due to the terrain, no suitable LZ was available in which to land the helos. To accommodate the aircraft, the AF detonated several large charges and cleared a functional evacuation LZ, which was given the code name Thresher.

The remains of all sixteen American troops were evacuated back to Bagram Airfield on Turbine 41 and Turbine 42. Escorting the fallen was the air mission commander, Captain Myron Bradley.

At Bagram, Commander Kent Paro and all of the remaining special operations forces were waiting on the flight line to meet Captain Bradley and the sixteen lost SEALs and soldiers. While the remains were being transferred into waiting ambulances, Petty Officer Second Class Eugene Bryant ran toward Paro holding a piece of paper. As Bryant got within hearing distance, Paro heard him yell, "They've got him sir, they've got him. Marcus has been found. He's in pretty rough shape, but he's alive. We have him." Paro's spirits were lifted by the news. Perhaps the other three missing SEALs were also alive. He then redirected his attention to the remains of the sixteen men being transferred from the helos.

CHAPTER SIXTEEN

Answering the Call

Enduring an inescapable fate stoically is admirable, but it is not the same thing as courage. Suffering stoically a terrible fate that you could have escaped, but that your convictions, your sense of honor, compelled you to accept, is.

—CAPTAIN JOHN MCCAIN, USN (ret.), *Why Courage Matters*

The core concept of the SEALs is TEAM. To a SEAL, nothing is more important than his teammate. It is that mind-set that keeps all SEALs as safe as possible. It is that mind-set, and the level of training that goes with it, that makes the Navy SEALs the most formidable fighting force on Earth.

While this work would embarrass Michael Murphy, it would be a grave disservice to his legacy not to remember here those members of the SEAL community and the 160th Special Operations Aviation Regiment (SOAR), the Night Stalkers, who answered his call for assistance on June 28, 2005. Those sixteen men willingly ran to their helicopters to undertake their dangerous rescue mission.

Michael was all about TEAM. The following pages are dedicated to the memory of those who paid the ultimate price answering his call. Truly, to paraphrase President Abraham Lincoln's famous words, these men gave their last full measure of devotion.

Erik S. Kristensen, Lieutenant Commander, U.S. Navy

The only child of retired Navy rear admiral Edward Kristensen, Erik was born on March 15, 1972, in Portsmouth, Virginia. He was accustomed to life on the road, having lived in Japan, Guam, and Washington, D.C. Known as "Spider" to his teammates, he considered Washington, D.C., his home, and graduated from Gonzaga High School in 1990 with academic honors. While at Gonzaga he excelled at football and lacrosse and was musically gifted as a trumpet player, having earned the ranks of first chair, section leader, and co-concert master. An Eagle Scout, he earned numerous academic awards that he never picked up.

Following high school, he attended the academically challenging Phillips Andover Academy in Andover, Massachusetts, for a year before attending and subsequently graduating from the U.S. Naval Academy in Annapolis, Maryland, in 1995 with academic honors. During his time at the Academy, Erik majored in English and minored in French, and earned his varsity letter in heavyweight crew.

Following his graduation from the Naval Academy, he was commissioned as an ensign and served in the engineering department of the USS *Chandler*, a now-decommissioned guided missile destroyer, in Everett, Washington, as fire control officer. While in the *Chandler*, he earned his surface warfare officer designation. He subsequently served as an officer in the Fleet, with tours as the officer in charge of the Rigid Hull Inflatable Boat Detachment at Naval Special Warfare Boat Unit Twelve (SBT-12) in 1999. After his tour of duty with the SEALs, he returned to the Naval Academy and taught English and began graduate studies at St. John's College in Annapolis.

In 2000, after five years of service, Erik knew he wanted to be a Navy SEAL but was told that he was too old and would not be able to make it. Instead of listening to those who said he could not make it as a SEAL, he chose instead to redouble his efforts to achieve his goal. After failing once to make the SEALs, he tried again. As the oldest member of Class 233 at age twenty-seven, he graduated BUD/S in March 2001.

Overcoming numerous injuries and obstacles, he finally realized his dream and became a SEAL. His first assignment was as the officer in charge of a sixteen-man SEAL platoon at SEAL Team Eight. He then deployed to Afghanistan as a task unit commander for SEAL Team Ten in support of the U.S. Global War on Terror. In that position, he was not obligated to board the rescue helicopter that fateful day in June 2005; however, consistent with the SEAL Creed, there was absolutely no way that he would permit the rescue team to leave without him and his weapon downrange. Erik would never send his men into harm's way without leading them.

Single and fluent in French, Erik had been selected by the George and Carol Olmsted Foundation as an Olmsted Scholar to attend graduate school at the Institute of Political Studies in Paris, France, and was scheduled to begin his schooling there in 2006.

Military Awards and Decorations
- Bronze Star Medal with "V" device
- Purple Heart
- Combat Action Ribbon
- Afghanistan Campaign Medal

- Navy and Marine Corps Commendation Medal (3 stars)
- Navy and Marine Corps Achievement Medal (1 star)
- National Defense Service Medal (1gold star)
- Global War on Terror Service Expeditionary Medal
- Global War on Terrorism Service Medal
- Sea Service Deployment Ribbon (1 star)
- Expert Rifle
- Expert Pistol

Burial and Memorials

With full military honors, the funeral of thirty-three-year-old Lieutenant Commander Erik S. Kristensen was conducted at 10:00 AM on July 19, 2005, in the chapel at the U.S. Naval Academy in Annapolis, Maryland. He was buried in the Academy's cemetery, located on the peninsula overlooking the Severn River and College Creek. There, he remains on permanent station in Section 01-008.

Michael M. McGreevy Jr., Lieutenant, U.S. Navy

The Honor Man of BUD/S Class 230, Lieutenant Michael M. McGreevy Jr. was born in Milwaukee, Wisconsin, on April 24, 1975. His family moved to Portville, New York, a small town just north of the Pennsylvania border, soon after he was born. While attending Portville High School, he was involved in everything, including the student council, the National Honor Society, wrestling, soccer, ice hockey, and track, setting a school record for the eight-hundred-meter run. While in high school he wanted to take the state Regents exam in German, but his school did not offer that language. Undaunted, he bought German-language books and taught himself so well that he passed the exam. Tall and very thin, he ran more than three miles to school each morning to be there by 6:00 AM so that he could get in a session of strength building before classes started. Accepted for early admission to the U.S. Military Academy in West Point, New York, he declined, seeking instead a spot at the U.S. Naval Academy in Annapolis, which he received. He served as secretary of his class, graduating in 1997 with a B.S. in mechanical engineering.

Upon receiving his commission, he served aboard USS *Oak Hill* (LSD-51), a *Harper's Ferry*–class landing ship, as the surface warfare officer. His passion was to become a SEAL, however, and so he entered BUD/S training in late 1999, graduating with Class 230 in August 2000 after his second attempt. Known as "Groove" by his friends, he served with SEAL Team Four, volunteered to attend the Army Ranger School, and graduated as Top Ranger, the Rangers' equivalent of Honor Man.*

---

* The author is unaware of any other member of the U.S. military to have achieved "Honor Man" status in both BUD/S and Ranger School.

He then deployed to Southern Command and conducted foreign internal defense missions and multiple joint-combined exercises with several foreign special operations forces. Upon returning from this deployment, he volunteered for an emergent deployment with SEAL Team Eight to the Crisis Response Element, Joint Special Operations Task Force–Horn of Africa as the assistant officer in charge. Following that tour he transferred to SEAL Team Ten as officer in charge (OIC) of Echo Platoon. As OIC, he deployed in April 2005 to Bagram Airfield, Afghanistan, in support of Operation Enduring Freedom.

Military Awards and Decorations

- Bronze Star Medal with "V" device
- Purple Heart
- Combat Action Ribbon
- Navy and Marine Corps Commendation Medal
- Navy and Marine Corps Achievement Medal (2 stars)
- Navy Meritorious Unit Commendation Medal
- National Defense Service Medal (1 star)
- Armed Forces Expeditionary Medal
- Global War on Terrorism Expeditionary Medal
- Global War on Terrorism Service Medal
- Sea Service Deployment Ribbon (1 star)
- Navy Expert Rifle
- Navy Expert Pistol

Burial and Memorials

Lieutenant McGreevy is survived by his wife, Laura, and his daughter, Molly. A private funeral service was conducted at the St. John the Apostle Church in Virginia Beach, Virginia. Lieutenant Michael McGreevy Jr. was laid to rest with full military honors in Arlington National Cemetery, "Where Valor Proudly Sleeps," on October 20, 2005, in Section 60, along with several other of his comrades who perished on June 28, 2005.

Daniel R. Healy, Senior Chief Petty Officer, U.S. Navy

Senior Chief Petty Officer Daniel R. Healy was born on January 17, 1968, in Exeter, New Hampshire. He was the first of five children of his parents, Henry and Natalie Healy. He graduated from Exeter High School in June 1986. After exploring his entrepreneurial spirit by owning his own landscaping business and working as a journeyman electrician for four years, he enlisted in the Navy in 1990, graduating from BUD/S in 1992 with Class 196.

He was assigned to SEAL Delivery Vehicle Team One (SDVT-1) at Pearl Harbor, Hawaii, from 1992 to 1996. A year of intensive language training at the Defense Language Institute in Monterey, California, followed. He then served at SEAL Delivery Vehicle Team Two at Little Creek, Virginia, before returning to SDVT-1 at Pearl, where he led a training platoon.

Military Awards and Decorations

- Bronze Star Medal with "V" device
- Purple Heart (1 star)
- Afghanistan Campaign Medal
- Navy and Marine Corps Commendation Achievement Medal
- Joint Meritorious Unit Award
- Meritorious Unit Commendation
- Good Conduct Medal (3 stars)
- National Defense Service Medal

Burial and Memorials

On July 9, 2005, Senior Chief Daniel R. Healy was buried with full military honors at Fort Rosecrans National Cemetery in Point Loma, California. His funeral was attended by Admiral Joseph Maguire, along with many of his SEAL brothers stationed at Naval Special Warfare Command in Coronado and his teammates from SDVT-1 in Pearl Harbor.

Dan's family organized an East Coast memorial service at Rye Harbor State Park, five miles from Exeter, overlooking the turquoise blue waters of the Atlantic Ocean. More than a thousand people, including Judd Gregg, U.S. senator from New Hampshire, and his wife, Kathy, attended the event, which was held on Sunday, July 17, 2005, beneath a beautiful cloudless sky.

In his memory, Dan's mother established the Daniel R. Healy Memorial Foundation to assist a graduate from Exeter High School who was entering the military or the building trades.

In 2008 the bridge on New Hampshire Route 101 between Manchester and Hampton Beach was renamed the Senior Chief Daniel R. Healy, U.S. Navy SEAL Bridge. That same year the pool in the local park in Exeter was renamed the Senior Chief Daniel R. Healy Memorial Pool.

Eric Shane Patton, Petty Officer Second Class, U.S. Navy

Eric Shane Patton, born on November 15, 1982, at the Balboa Naval Hospital in San Diego, California, was the second of six children of Valerie and "JJ" Patton. When his parents divorced in 1994, Shane and his brothers moved to Boulder City, Nevada, with their father, a Las Vegas Municipal Court marshal and a former Navy

SEAL. At Boulder City High School, he was a member of the baseball team and played guitar in a band called True Story. He also enjoyed skateboarding and surfing. Immediately upon graduation, he enlisted in the Navy with the goal of becoming a SEAL like his father. He graduated with BUD/S Class 239.

He was assigned to SEAL Team One in Pearl City, Hawaii, before his deployment to Afghanistan in April 2005. Originally scheduled to be part of Lieutenant Murphy's four man reconnaissance unit, he was on the rescue helicopter struck by the RPG in the Korangal Valley on June 28, 2005. His remains arrived under military escort at McCarran International Airport on Thursday, July 6, 2005. Visitation was held on Friday, July 7, 2005, at the Palm Mortuary in Boulder City.

Military Awards and Decorations

- Bronze Star Medal with "V" device
- Purple Heart
- Navy and Marine Corps Achievement Medal (3 stars)
- Combat Action Ribbon
- Afghanistan Campaign Medal
- Global War on Terrorism Service Medal
- Rifle Expert
- Expert Pistol
- National Defense Service Medal
- Armed Forces Service Medal

Burial and Memorials

With full military honors, Shane Patton was buried at the Southern Nevada Veterans Memorial Cemetery in Boulder City, Nevada, on Saturday, July 9, 2005.

Jeffrey Allen Lucas, Petty Officer First Class, U.S. Navy

Electronics Technician First Class Lucas was born on September 17, 1971. While growing up in Corbett, Oregon, he chose his career path early—in the fourth grade, when he wrote a paper about the Special Forces (Green Berets), the Rangers, the Marine Corps' Force Recon, and the SEALs. He had his eyes set on the SEALs because "they were the best." After graduating from high school in 1989, he immediately enlisted in the U.S. Navy. Upon completing recruit training and Electronics Technician school, he transferred to Naval Submarine Training Center Pacific, Pearl Harbor, Hawaii. From there he transferred to the Branch Medical Clinic, San Diego, California, from May 1991 to June 1993.

He entered BUD/S in June 1993 and graduated with Class 191 in January 1994. Upon completing his SEAL training, he reported to SEAL Team One in Coronado, California, where he was stationed from 1994 to 1999, before transferring to the

East Coast in 1999 to Naval Special Warfare Development Group (DEVGRU) in Dam Neck, Virginia. He then transferred to SEAL Team Eight for a year before again transferring to SEAL Team Ten in March 2002. A leading petty officer (LPO), he had ten years of experience as a SEAL, allowing him to create an extensive list of qualifications, including sniper, sniper instructor, and military free-fall parachutist.

He was married to his wife, Rhonda, for twelve years. They had one son, Seth, who was four years old when his father was killed in action.

Military Awards and Decorations
- Bronze Star Medal with "V" device
- Purple Heart
- Navy and Marine Corps Achievement Medal (3 stars)
- Combat Action Ribbon
- National Defense Service Medal (1 star)
- Armed Forces Service Medal
- Kosovo Campaign Medal
- Afghanistan Campaign Medal
- Global War on Terrorism Service Medal
- Humanitarian Service Medal
- Sea Service Deployment Medal (3 stars)
- NATO Medal
- Rifle Expert
- Expert Pistol

Burial and Memorials
With full military honors, Petty Officer Jeffrey Allen Lucas was laid to rest in Section 60, site 8229, in Arlington National Cemetery, "Where Valor Proudly Sleeps."

The Jeff Lucas Memorial Fund was established by his family as a 501(c)(3) corporation to construct a lasting memorial to Jeff. A stadium grandstand and football sports complex will be built at Corbett High School. It will be dedicated as the Jeff Lucas Memorial Veterans Stadium. In addition, family and friends have established the Seth A. Lucas Fund.

Jacques Jules Fontan, Chief Petty Officer, U.S. Navy

Chief Fontan was born on November 11, 1968, in New Orleans, to Earl and Hazel Fontan. After graduating from Brother Martin High School in 1986, he attended the University of Louisiana at Lafayette prior to enlisting in the U.S. Navy on March 7, 1989. Following graduation from the Recruit Training Command at Naval Station Great Lakes, he completed Fire Controlman "A" school at Fleet Combat Training Center, Dam Neck, Virginia. He then transferred to the USS *Nicholas* (FFG-47),

Charleston, South Carolina, and then to Helicopter Anti-Submarine Squadron One in Jacksonville, Florida. After graduating from BUD/S on October 23, 1998, he was assigned to SEAL Team Eight, Little Creek, Virginia, then to Naval Special Warfare Group Two, and subsequently to SEAL Team Ten, Little Creek, Virginia.

Military Awards and Decorations

- Bronze Star Medal with "V" device
- Purple Heart
- Joint Service Commendation Medal
- Navy and Marine Corps Commendation Medal with "V" device
- Combat Action Ribbon
- Joint Meritorious Unit Award
- Navy Unit Commendation Ribbon
- Navy "E" Ribbon
- Good Conduct Medal (4 stars)
- National Defense Service Medal (1 star)
- Southwest Asia Service Medal (2 stars)
- Afghanistan Campaign Medal
- Global War on Terrorism Service Medal (2 stars)
- Military Outstanding Volunteer Service Medal
- Sea Service Deployment Ribbon (2 stars)
- NATO Medal
- Kuwait Liberation Medal
- Expert Pistol
- Sharpshooter M4 Rifle

Burial and Memorials

Chief Fontan was buried with full military honors. He is survived by his parents, his wife, Charissa, and his daughter, Jourdan.

Jeffrey Scott Taylor, Petty Officer First Class, U.S. Navy

Jeffrey S. Taylor was born on May 18, 1975, in Beckley, West Virginia. He attended Independence High School in Coal City, West Virginia, before enlisting in the Navy on June 20, 1994. His duty assignments included the Recruit Training Command, Naval Station Great Lakes, in Illinois; Naval School of Health Sciences, San Diego, California; Naval Medical Center, Portsmouth, Virginia; Field Medical Service School, Camp Lejeune, North Carolina; SEAL Team Eight, Little Creek, Virginia; USS *Theodore Roosevelt* (CVN-71), Norfolk, Virginia; John F. Kennedy Special Warfare Center and School, Fort Bragg, North Carolina; and SEAL Team Ten, Little Creek, Virginia.

Military Awards and Decorations

- Bronze Star Medal with "V" device
- Purple Heart Medal
- Navy and Marine Corps Commendation Medal with Combat "V" (1 star)
- Citation
- Navy Unit Commendation (1 star)
- Meritorious Unit Commendation
- Navy Battle "E" Ribbon
- Good Conduct Medal (3 stars)
- Navy Fleet Marine Force Medal
- Armed Forces Expeditionary Medal
- National Defense Service Medal (1 star)
- Afghanistan Campaign Medal
- Global War on Terrorism Expeditionary Medal
- Global War on Terrorism Service Medal Navy and Marine Corps Achievement Medal
- Combat Action Ribbon
- Presidential Unit
- Sea Service Deployment Ribbon (2 stars)
- Expert Rifle
- Expert Pistol

Burial and Memorials

Jeffrey Taylor's wife Erin scattered his ashes over Section 60 at Arlington National Cemetery.

James E. Suh, Petty Officer Second Class, U.S. Navy

James Erik Suh was born in Coronado, California, but later moved with his family to Deerfield Beach, Florida. James and his sister Claudia were raised by their single-parent father, Solomon Suh, a Korean immigrant. James excelled in all of his academic subjects in school and was placed in a program for gifted students. He was especially strong in math, but also proved to be a talented artist and athlete. James graduated from high school in June 1995, but as he prepared to enter the University of Florida, he also began thinking seriously about joining the Navy SEALs.

After graduating with a bachelor's degree in statistics in 1999, James enlisted in the Navy in January 2001. He began his BUD/S training with Class 237 in July and received his SEAL Trident in February 2001. Following successful completion of SEAL Delivery Vehicle training, he was assigned to SDVT-1 in Hawaii in December 2003. In April 2005 he and his teammates of Alfa Platoon went to Afghanistan on what was his first deployment. Petty Officer Second Class James E. Suh was killed while serving as a member of the QRF in Operation Red Wings on June 28, 2005.

Military Awards and Decorations
- Bronze Star Medal with "V" device
- Purple Heart
- Afghanistan Campaign Medal

Burial and Memorials
James E. Suh was buried with full military honors in Forest Lawn Cemetery in Hollywood, California, on July 30, 2005. His funeral was attended by fifty of his SDVT-1 teammates. James' father, Solomon, was presented the burial flag by Rear Admiral Joseph Maguire, Commander, Naval Special Warfare.

Stephen C. Reich, Major, U.S. Army

Stephen C. Reich was born on May 22, 1971, in Cleveland, Ohio. His family moved to Washington, Connecticut, when he was four years old. His father was a teacher and coach and his mother a nurse at the local community hospital. At Shepaug Valley Regional High School, he was a triple-sport standout in wrestling, basketball, and baseball. After high school, he received an appointment to the United States Military Academy in West Point, New York, receiving his commission in 1993. While at West Point, he set numerous pitching records for the baseball team, several of which stand today. Reich graduated with dual degrees in Arabic and Spanish.

Following his commissioning, he received permission to play baseball for Team USA during the summer of 1993, receiving the honor of carrying the American flag in the opening ceremonies of the World University Games at Buffalo New York's Rich Stadium. After initial flight qualification school, he was assigned to the University of Kentucky's Reserve Officers' Training Corps (ROTC) and played professional baseball in the Baltimore Orioles organization, having received a waiver from the Army. Reich entered the Army's World Class Athlete Program in 1995 to train for the 1996 U.S. Olympic team trials.

In 1996, after receiving UH-60 Blackhawk transition training, he was ordered to Germany, where he served as platoon leader in Company A, 5th Battalion, 158th Aviation Regiment. While in Germany he became fluent in German, his third foreign language. During his subsequent tour with the 12th Aviation Brigade, he served in Operation Allied Force, deploying to Hungary, Bosnia, Albania, and Kosovo.

Returning from Germany in 2000, Reich attended the Infantry Captains Career Course at Fort Benning, Georgia, followed by the Combined Arms and Services Staff School at Fort Leavenworth, Kansas. Upon arrival at the 160th

Special Operations Aviation Regiment (SOAR) in 2001, he deployed with the 2nd Battalion to Operation Enduring Freedom as a battle captain in support of Task Force Dagger, a special operations unit seeking the capture or death of Osama bin Laden in the Tora Bora mountain cave network of Afghanistan.

In December 2001 he served as operations officer for the 2nd Battalion's detachment of MH-47E aircraft in Afghanistan. He commanded Headquarters Company, 2nd Battalion from February 2002 through May 2003. Having been promoted to major, Reich then completed a one-year deployment to Daegu, Republic of Korea, as the operations officer for E Company, 160th SOAR. Other specialized military training consisted of the Survival, Evasion, Resistance and Escape (SERE) Level-C course, the Army Airborne School, and the Air Assault School.

Two weeks after his marriage to his wife, Jill, on March 19, 2005, he deployed to Bagram Airfield for his fourth tour of duty in Afghanistan.

Military Awards and Decorations
- Bronze Star Medal with "V" device, two oak leaf clusters
- Meritorious Service Medal, oak leaf cluster
- Purple Heart
- Air Medal with "V" device
- Army Commendation Medal
- Army Achievement Medal
- Afghanistan Campaign Medal
- Global War on Terrorism Expeditionary Medal
- Global War on Terrorism Service Medal
- Overseas Service Medal
- Korean Defense Service Medal
- Meritorious Service Medal
- Joint Meritorious Unit Award
- Humanitarian Service Medal
- Senior Aviator Badge
- Airborne Badge
- Air Assault Badge
- Combat Action Badge

Burial and Memorials

A private military ceremony was conducted at Hunter Army Airfield in Georgia on July 7, and a memorial service was also held in Washington, Connecticut, at the Bryan Memorial Town Hall on July 10, which was attended by more than a thousand family members, friends, and town residents.

Although he was extremely confident, he was soft-spoken and never arrogant. In fact, his parents and bride did not know the actions for which he had received his first two Bronze Stars until after his death. Unfortunately, all are acutely aware of the actions that resulted in his third.

Each year on July 4, the Steve Reich Memorial Freedom Run is conducted in Washington, Connecticut, with proceeds going to the Steve Reich Memorial Scholarship Program benefiting students at his high school alma mater.

Chris J. Scherkenbach, Chief Warrant Officer 4, U.S. Army

The youngest of eight children of Elmer and Marjorie Scherkenbach, Chris was born on November 3, 1964, in Des Plaines, Illinois. He graduated from Prospect High School in 1982, then moved with his parents to Palm Harbor, Florida, following his father's retirement from Ford Motor Company. The elder Scherkenbach had previously served as a decorated B-17 bomber pilot in World War II.

Chris graduated from the St. Petersburg Junior College and immediately enlisted in the U.S. Army as a communications specialist. He completed basic training at Fort Jackson, South Carolina, in April 1987 and his training as an automatic data telecommunications center operator at Fort Gordon, Georgia, in July 1987. He then transferred to his first duty station in Germany.

Upon his return he was accepted into the Warrant Officer Program at Fort Rucker, Alabama, in 1990. After graduating that same year, he was immediately sent to the Aviation Warrant Officer Basic Course and Initial Entry Rotary Wing (helicopter) training. After completing his CH-47D aircraft qualifications at Fort Rucker, he was assigned to Company B, 2nd Battalion, 159th Aviation Regiment, Hunter Army Airfield, Georgia. He was then assigned to Camp Humphreys in South Korea as an MH-47D Chinook pilot. After completing his tour there, he returned to the 159th Aviation Regiment.

While on a fitness run in a local Savannah, Georgia, park, he met his future wife, Michelle, a physician's assistant at the Mayo Clinic in Jacksonville, Florida. They were married on September 20, 1997.

Chris was selected for the Army's Degree Completion Program, graduating magna cum laude with a B.S. in aeronautics from the prestigious Embry-Riddle Aeronautical University in Daytona Beach, Florida, the world's largest aerospace university in March 2005.

His final assignment was Company B, 3rd Battalion, 160th Special Operations Aviation Regiment at Hunter Army Airfield, Georgia. On Friday, May 27, 2005, he deployed to Afghanistan. He was the pilot of the MH-47D shot down while attempting the midday rescue in Operation Red Wings.

Chris and Michelle were in the final stages of adopting an infant from China. On the day he was killed, Michelle had sent him an e-mail message confirming travel arrangements to China. That e-mail was found in the pocket of his flight suit after his body was recovered.

Military Awards and Decorations

- Bronze Star Medal with "V" device
- Purple Heart
- Air Medal with "V" device, 1 oak leaf cluster
- Army Commendation Medal
- Army Achievement Medal
- Army Good Conduct Medal
- National Defense Service Medal
- Armed Forces Expeditionary Medal
- Afghanistan Campaign Medal
- Iraq Campaign Medal
- Global War on Terrorism Expeditionary Medal
- Global War on Terrorism Service Medal
- Humanitarian Service Medal
- Army Service Ribbon
- Senior Army Aviator Badge
- Meritorious Service Medal
- Combat Action Badge
- Master Army Aviator Badge

Burial and Memorials

Chief Warrant Officer Chris Scherkenbach was buried with full military honors in Section 60, site 8200, in Arlington National Cemetery, next to a teammate, Sergeant First Class Marcus Muralles. Approximately thirty days after Chris's death, Michelle traveled to China and brought home their daughter, Sarah Grace Xiaomei Scherkenbach.

Sadly, Chris Scherkenbach never had the opportunity to meet his daughter. Nevertheless, if he had known in advance what the outcome of his mission that fateful day would be, he still would have gone, epitomizing the inscription on the Night Stalker Memorial Wall at Fort Campbell, Kentucky: "I serve with the memory and pride of those who have gone before me, for they love to fight, fought to win and would rather die than quit." Sarah may not understand now why her father died, but the example of his courage will light her path for a lifetime.

Cory J. Goodnature, Chief Warrant Officer 3, U.S. Army

Born February 13, 1970, in Clarks Grove, Minnesota, to Donald and Deborah Goodnature, Cory was driven to become a military pilot and changed his plans more than once as a young man to realize his goal. After graduating from Albert Lea High School, where he participated in wrestling and track, he enrolled in the University of Minnesota and its Air Force ROTC program. Due to funding problems, the program was cut. He then transferred to the Marine Corps and had a pilot's slot in the ROTC, but that program was also cut. He graduated from the University of Minnesota with an associate's degree in aerospace engineering in 1991 and enlisted in the Army in October 1991.

Though his earlier efforts to become a pilot had been derailed, he was undeterred and worked his way up in the Army to achieve his goal. He served as a parachute rigger at the U.S. Army John F. Kennedy Special Warfare Center and School at Fort Bragg, North Carolina, and the Warrant Officer Basic Course at Fort Rucker, Alabama. Upon graduation from flight school in 1995, his first assignment was flying UH-1s (Hueys) in Korea, and in 1996 was assigned to Wheeler Army Airfield, Hawaii. He tested for the 160th Special Operations Aviation Regiment in 1998 and was assigned to the 3rd Battalion, 160th SOAR at Hunter Army Airfield, Georgia, as an MH-47D Chinook pilot. Having served one tour in Iraq, he was on his fourth deployment in Afghanistan when he died. He leaves a wife, Lori, and two teenage boys, Shea and Brennan.

Military Awards and Decorations

- Bronze Star Medal with "V" device
- Purple Heart
- Air Medal with "V" device, 1 oak leaf cluster
- Army Commendation Medal
- Army Achievement Medal
- Good Conduct Medal
- National Defense Service Medal
- Armed Forces Expeditionary Medal
- Global War on Terrorism Expeditionary Medal
- Global War on Terrorism Service Medal
- Meritorious Service Medal
- Iraq Campaign Medal
- Afghanistan Campaign Medal
- Korean Defense Service Medal
- Overseas Service Ribbon
- Senior Army Aviator Badge
- Airborne Badge
- Air Assault Badge
- Rigger Badge
- Combat Action Badge

Burial and Memorials

A memorial service for Cory Goodnature was held on Friday, July 8, 2005, at the Isle of Hope Methodist Church in Savannah, Georgia. His funeral service was conducted at the Albert Lea United Methodist Church in Albert Lea, Minnesota, on July 16, 2005. With full military honors, he was buried at Graceland Cemetery in Albert Lea, where he remains on permanent station.

Each year the Isle of Hope Methodist Church hosts more than two hundred runners in the Cory Goodnature Run for Missions. The Cory Goodnature Memorial Scholarship Program is funded by an annual Golf Classic in Albert Lea.

James W. "Tre" Ponder III, Master Sergeant, U.S. Army

James "Tre" Ponder was born June 24, 1969, in Alabama, and was a resident of Clarksville, Tennessee. He joined the Army in March 1990 as a Chinook helicopter repairer. After graduating from basic training at Camp Eustis, Virginia, he was assigned to Camp Humphreys, Korea. He arrived at the 160th Special Operations Aviation Regiment in December 1992 and served in a variety of positions in the 2nd Battalion, including flight engineer instructor, standardization instructor, and regiment standardization instructor. He was on his fourth deployment to Afghanistan in June 2005.

His military education consisted of the Primary Leadership Development, Combat Lifesaver, Survival, Evasion, Resistance and Escape (SERE), Basic Noncommissioned Officer, Equal Opportunity Representatives, Air Assault, Airborne, and Army Advanced Noncommissioned Officers courses and schools.

Military Awards and Decorations
- Bronze Star Medal with "V" device
- Purple Heart
- Air Medal with "V" device, 2 oak leaf clusters
- Army Commendation Medal
- Joint Service Achievement Medal
- Valorous Unit Award
- Army Superior Unit Award
- Good Conduct Medal
- National Defense Service Medal
- Armed Forces Expeditionary Medal
- Global War on Terrorism Expeditionary Medal
- Global War on Terrorism Service Medal
- Korean Defense Service Medal
- Humanitarian Service Medal
- Overseas Service Ribbon

Burial and Memorials

Following a funeral service on July 7, 2005, at the First Baptist Church in Clarksville, Tennessee, Master Sergeant Ponder was laid to rest with full military honors at the nearby Greenwood Cemetery. Tre is survived by his wife, Leslie, and his daughters, Samantha and Elizabeth.

Michael L. Russell, Sergeant First Class, U.S. Army

A resident of Rincon, Georgia, he was born on September 28, 1973, in Virginia. Russell joined the Army in October 1991 as a Chinook helicopter repairer. After completing basic training at Fort Jackson, South Carolina, his first duty station was Barbers Point, Hawaii, where he remained until April 1995.

In May 1996 he departed to the 158th Aviation Regiment located at Fort Carson, Colorado. In August 1996 he was assigned to the 160th Special Operations Aviation Regiment, in which he served as a flight engineer with the 3rd Battalion at Hunter Army Airfield, Georgia.

His military education included the Primary Leadership Development, Survival, Evasion, Resistance and Escape (SERE), and Basic Noncommissioned Officers courses.

Military Awards and Decorations

- Bronze Star Medal with "V" device, 1 oak leaf cluster
- Purple Heart
- Air Medal with "V" device, 1 oak leaf cluster
- Air Medal, oak leaf cluster
- Army Commendation Medal
- Army Achievement Medal
- Good Conduct Medal
- National Defense Service Medal
- Armed Forces Expeditionary Medal
- Afghanistan Campaign Medal
- Iraq Campaign Medal
- Global War on Terrorism Expeditionary Medal
- Global War on Terrorism Service Medal
- Overseas Service Ribbon
- Army Superior Unit Award
- Senior Army Crew Member Badge
- Meritorious Service Medal
- Master Army Crew Member Badge
- Combat Action Badge

Burial and Memorials

Sergeant First Class Michael Russell is survived by his wife, Annette, of Savannah, Georgia, and two daughters, Lauren and Megan. He was buried with full military honors in Stafford, Virginia.

Marcus V. Muralles, Sergeant First Class, U.S. Army

Marcus V. Muralles was born October 5, 1971, in Louisiana, and was raised in Shelbyville, Indiana. He joined the Army in December 1988 as an infantryman. After completing Basic Combat Training and Advanced Individual Training, he was assigned to 3rd Battalion, 75th Ranger Regiment, Fort Benning, Georgia. After completing his initial enlistment obligation, he was assigned to the inactive ready reserve in 1993.

In August 1998 he returned to active duty and graduated One Station Unit Training at Fort Benning in the summer of 1998. His first duty station was Company B, 3rd Battalion, 75th Ranger Regiment as a medical administrator, platoon medic, and company senior medic. In August 2003, Muralles was assigned to 3rd Battalion, 160th Special Operations Aviation Regiment as an aerial flight medic.

His military education and training included the Emergency Medical Technician, Basic Airborne, and Ranger schools, as well as the Primary Leadership Development, Jumpmaster, Special Operations Medic, Basic Noncommissioned Officer, and Advanced Noncommissioned Officer Development courses.

Military Awards and Decorations
- Bronze Star Medal with "V" device
- Purple Heart
- Air Medal with "V" device
- Meritorious Service Medal, 1 oak leaf cluster
- Air Medal with "V" device
- Army Commendation Medal
- Army Achievement Medal
- Good Conduct Medal
- National Defense Service Medal
- Armed Forces Expeditionary Medal
- Humanitarian Service Medal
- Iraq Campaign Medal
- Afghanistan Campaign Medal
- Global War on Terrorism Expeditionary Medal
- Global War on Terrorism Service Medal
- Expert Infantry Badge

- Combat Medical Badge
- Expert Field Medical Badge
- Aviation Badge
- Master Parachutist Badge (2 combat jumps)
- Ranger Tab
- Combat Action Badge

Burial and Memorials

Sergeant First Class Marcus Muralles was laid to rest in Arlington National Cemetery. He is survived by his wife, Diana, and their two children, Anna and Dominic.

Shamus O. Goare, Staff Sergeant, U.S. Army

Shamus O. Goare was born May 28, 1976, in Danville, located in the upper northeastern corner of Knox County in northwestern Ohio. After graduating from Danville High School, he joined the Army in 1994 as a Huey helicopter repairer at the age of seventeen. He got his mother to sign his enlistment papers by convincing her that the forms were for something different. Attracted to the military life in general, he chose the Army because he liked its uniforms. He attended Basic Combat Training at Fort Jackson, South Carolina, and Advanced Individual Training at Fort Rucker, Alabama.

From December 1994 to October 1996, Goare was assigned to Company I, 158th Aviation Battalion as a utility helicopter repairer at Fort Hood, Texas. In October 1996 he was reassigned as a UH-1 crew chief to 1st USA Support Battalion, Sinai, Egypt. Upon completion of a one-year tour in Egypt, he was assigned as a crew chief to 12th Aviation Brigade at Fort Belvoir, Virginia. From January to May 1999, he attended the Heavy Helicopter Repairer Course at Fort Eustis, Virginia, and upon completion became a Chinook helicopter repairer. In June 1999 he was assigned to Company C, 52nd Aviation Regiment, Camp Humphreys, Korea, where he performed duties as a MH-47 mechanic until May 2000.

In June 2000 Goare was recruited and volunteered for the Night Stalkers and assigned to the 160th Special Operations Aviation Training Company. Upon completion of the Basic Mission Qualification Course (Green Platoon), he was assigned as a flight engineer for Company B, 3rd Battalion, 160th Special Operations Aviation Regiment at Hunter Army Airfield, Georgia. His mother, Judy, says that Shamus agreed to join the Night Stalkers because he liked their maroon berets.

His military education and training included the Primary Leadership Development, SERE, Utility Helicopter Repairer, and Medium Helicopter Repairer courses.

Single, Shamus frequently volunteered for additional overseas deployments to allow men who were married or expecting the birth of a child soon to remain with their families, claiming that they would do the same for him. He had successfully completed two deployments to Iraq and was on his fourth deployment to Afghanistan.

Shamus was the frequent target of bullies while growing up. It wasn't until after his death that those in Danville learned that Shamus personified character, courage, honor, humility, and valor.

Military Awards and Decorations

- Bronze Star Medal with "V" device
- Purple Heart
- Air Medal with "V" device, 1 oak leaf cluster
- Air Medal
- Army Commendation Medal
- Joint Service Achievement Medal
- Army Achievement Medal
- Good Conduct Medal
- National Defense Service Medal
- Armed Forces Expeditionary Medal
- Iraq Campaign Medal
- Humanitarian Service Medal
- Afghanistan Campaign Medal
- Global War on Terrorism Expeditionary Medal
- Multinational Forces and Observers Medal
- Kuwaiti Defense Service Medal
- Meritorious Service Medal
- Army Service Ribbon
- Combat Action Badge
- Senior Army Aviator Badge

Burial and Memorials

Shamus Goare is survived by his parents, Charles and Judith Goare, of Danville, Ohio. His funeral service was held at 11:00 AM on Tuesday, July 12, at the Fischer Funeral Home.

He was laid to his earthly rest with full military honors in St. Luke's Cemetery in Danville. At the funeral, Lieutenant General Philip Kensinger, the commander of the U.S. Army Special Operations Command at Fort Bragg, North Carolina, presented Shamus's parents with the Bronze Star with "V" device, the Purple Heart, and the Afghanistan Campaign Medal.

Kip Allen Jacoby, Sergeant, U.S. Army

Kip was born September 2, 1983, to Stephen and Susan Jacoby of Pompano Beach, Florida. After graduating from Northeast High School in June 2002, he enlisted in the U.S. Army in October that same year. He successfully completed basic training at Fort Jackson, South Carolina, after which he attended and subsequently graduated from Advanced Individual Training at Fort Eustis, Virginia, in May 2003.

In June 2003 he was assigned to the 160th Special Operations Aviation Training Company and completed the Basic Mission Qualification Course. He was subsequently assigned as a helicopter repairman for the 3rd Battalion, 160th SOAR.

In February 2004 he was reassigned within the battalion to Company B as a CH-47D flight engineer. Sergeant Jacoby's military schools included the SERE school, the Basic Mission Qualification Course, and the Heavy Helicopter Repairer Course.

Military Awards and Decorations
- Bronze Star with "V" device (posthumously)
- Purple Heart (posthumously)
- Air Medal with "V" device (posthumously)
- Meritorious Service Medal (posthumously)
- Good Conduct Medal (posthumously)
- Combat Action Badge (posthumously)
- National Defense Service Ribbon
- Army Service Ribbon
- Global War on Terrorism Expeditionary Medal
- Global War on Terrorism Service Medal
- Afghanistan Campaign Medal
- Iraq Campaign Medal
- Army Aviation Crewmember Badge

Burial and Memorials
A memorial service was held for Sergeant Kip Jacoby on July 8, 2005, in his hometown of Pompano Beach, Florida.

CHAPTER SEVENTEEN

No One Left Behind

I pray that our Heavenly Father may assuage the anguish of your bereavement, and leave you only the cherished memory of the loved and lost, and the solemn pride that must be yours to have laid so costly a sacrifice upon the altar of freedom.

—ABRAHAM LINCOLN, letter to Mrs. Lydia Bixby, November 21, 1864,
Abraham Lincoln Online, http://showcase.netins.net/web/
creative/lincoln/speeches/bixby.htm

Having previously completed their JCET missions, Lieutenant Mark Hernandez and his squad had deployed to Baghdad. On June 28 they were informed of the events surrounding Operation Red Wings, and watched the Predator drone feeds of the helo crash site on a wall-mounted screen at the SEAL Team Seven headquarters in downtown Baghdad. All realized that with the RPG hit, the subsequent crash and resulting explosion, and the nature of the terrain, there could be no survivors. By this time all on board had been identified. Hernandez was staggered by the realization that he had just lost four of his SEALs and that another four men from his platoon were still missing.

With the fate of those on the helo known, full attention was directed to the four SEALs still on the mountain. While there had been no contact since Lieutenant Murphy's call for help, all remained optimistic—after all, they were Navy SEALs, and SEALs are never out of the fight.

Lieutenant Seth Dunn, the task unit commander, was a former Army captain. He made use of his Army contacts and received up-to-the-minute information on the continuing and ever expanding search for his SEALs. In addition to the SEALs in the second helo, nearly three hundred Marines and Army Rangers were involved in the search, but they had found nothing.

After a few days of watching the Predator feeds, and being in frequent communication with the unit's remaining SEALs in Afghanistan, Dunn and Hernandez advocated that they and their squad be "pushed forward" (moved to Afghanistan) to assist in the recovery of their SEALs. They enlisted the help of Commander Michael Clark of SEAL Team Seven. Clark sent detailed e-mails to Naval Support Activity Bahrain and NSW in Coronado recommending that Dunn be permitted to push forward to Afghanistan and assist in the search, stating that doing so would be in the best interests of all involved.

July 3, 2005

Although most of their missions had been completed, Dunn and Hernandez and their squads were dispatched to Fallujah for a snatch-and-grab mission that was completed without a shot being fired. They quickly returned to Baghdad to monitor the search-and-recovery effort. Upon their arrival they were informed that Marcus Luttrell had been recovered alive. At his debriefing, Marcus was able to describe the battle and the wounds he had witnessed the others receive, and also gave a more detailed location of the battlefield. Search efforts for the other three SEALs were narrowed down to that area.

July 4, 2005

Early in the morning of July 4, Commander Clark approached Dunn and Hernandez and asked, "How soon can your guys be packed and ready to head to Afghanistan?" Lieutenant Hernandez immediately ran to notify the remainder of the squad while Lieutenant Dunn coordinated travel arrangements. Within an hour the squad was packed and had arrived at the airfield for immediate deployment to Bagram.

When they arrived at Camp Ouellette, they were informed that the bodies of Michael Murphy and Danny Dietz had been recovered and were on their way back to Bagram. Also found during the search was the body of Lance Corporal Kevin B. Joyce. At about 11:00 PM on June 25, Joyce's Marine unit was returning to its base on a dirt road alongside the dangerous and fast-moving Pech River. The weight of the vehicle caused the edge of the road to collapse and the vehicle to slide into the river. The three Marines inside the vehicle abandoned it, but Joyce was swept away. The other two were rescued or managed to get out of the water.

As the helos that carried the bodies approached, all SOF personnel lined the runway to welcome their brothers home. After the remains were removed, transferred to ambulance truck, and taken to the base mortuary, Dunn and Hernandez were given the grim task of officially identifying the bodies of their fallen comrades.

As Dunn and Hernandez entered the mortuary room, they struggled to keep their emotions in check. It was decided that Hernandez, the platoon commander, would officially identify Murphy and that Dunn, as task unit commander, would identify Dietz.

As the men approached the bodies of their fallen comrades, Hernandez was drawn to the table on the left, where he saw the bright orange FDNY patch on the right shoulder sleeve of the uniform shirt laying over the body of the man he now believed to be Michael Murphy. Although Murphy and Dietz looked completely different from what he remembered, with both having grown heavy beards since their arrival in Afghanistan, Hernandez immediately recognized the Celtic Cross tattoo on the man's right shoulder. He remembered Michael telling him the story of the Celtic Cross on several occasions.

Hernandez became mesmerized while he stared at the cross. Snapping himself back to the present, he scanned down the body and saw the wounds described by Marcus. There was no question. Hernandez identified the remains of his AOIC, Lieutenant Michael P. Murphy. Lieutenant Dunn also positively identified Petty Officer Second Class Danny Dietz to the mortuary staff. After completing the required paperwork, they returned to the B-huts to pack up the dead men's personal belongings and prepare them for return to the families.

Upon finishing their grim task, both Dunn and Hernandez met with other SOF commanders and devised an operational plan to continue their search for Petty Officer Matthew Axelson. Based on the information Marcus had given at his debriefing, they knew that Axe had received a severe head wound; nevertheless, they approached the upcoming mission as a rescue, not a recovery, and developed their plans quickly.

July 5, 2005—Ramp Ceremony

At 6:30 AM on July 5, a large silver C-17 sat on runway D-3 at Bagram Airfield, with the shadow of the Afghan mountains in the distance. With the rear ramp down, the aircraft appeared dark and cavernous. Designed to carry more than a hundred troops, that day its manifest would show, in addition to its two pilots, single loadmaster, and escort, only three passengers. Even at this early hour the sun rose high in the sky and the temperature was already over 80°. Farther down the tarmac sat the two A-10 Thunderbolt jet aircraft that would escort the C-17 out of Afghan airspace.

With the camp's flags at half-staff, three empty green camouflaged open-bed trucks lined up just outside the Bagram mortuary. Over the next several minutes, hundreds of Army Rangers, Night Stalkers, Green Berets, and Delta Force troops joined with Air Force pararescue PJs, Marines from Force Recon, and Navy SEALs to form a single line that ran from the base mortuary down the tarmac nearly one hundred yards to where four lines of additional troops extended back nearly fifty yards from the C-17's open ramp. A single troop with bagpipes took a position about twenty yards behind the double-lined troops. An honor guard consisting of two armed troops flanked two flag bearers, one with a ceremonial gold-fringed American flag and the other the ceremonial gold-fringed dark blue flag of CJTF-76, stood at attention at the end of the double line of troops. Both flags were fully extended in the stiff breeze, the silver special operations forces spear atop of each flag staff glistening in the bright morning sun.

A jeep brought a heavily bearded Marcus, dressed in loose fitting jeans, a blue shirt, and a khaki baseball hat, out to the C-17. Despite his injuries, Marcus had insisted on attending the ceremony. Deliberately, he exited the vehicle and walked slowly to the base of the ramp, where he stood at attention to the degree his injuries and pain would allow.

As the loadmaster stood at the top of the C-17's open ramp, he looked off to his left and saw the first flag-draped Zeigler case,* which contained the remains of Lieutenant Michael P. Murphy, being loaded onto the first truck by six body bearers. After carefully placing the case onto the bed of the truck, they lined both the left and right of the truck. The vehicle moved forward about twenty yards and stopped. The second flag-draped Zeigler case, containing the remains of Petty Officer Second Class Danny Dietz, was loaded onto the next truck. It pulled forward about ten yards and was flanked on both sides by a second group of six body bearers. Finally, the third flag-draped case, which contained the remains of Lance Corporal Kevin B. Joyce, was loaded onto the third truck by a third group of six body bearers, who also took their positions on either side.

After all three of their comrades had been placed on the trucks, the crisp and haunting notes of "Amazing Grace" was heard in the distance. The troops in the single line from the mortuary snapped to attention and saluted as the three fallen soldiers slowly traveled the hundred yards and stopped just in front of the honor guard. As the honor guard marched forward between the double lines of troops, they all snapped to attention. Just behind the honor guard was Commander Kent Paro and Lieutenant Commander Patrick Moden, a Navy chaplain wearing his white stole.

Father Moden walked up the ramp and then down the length of the plane. He turned as the first group of body bearers brought on board the remains of Lieutenant Michael Murphy. They lowered him to the floor of the plane at the feet of Father Moden and then stood at attention. The remains of Petty Officer Danny Dietz and Lance Corporal Kevin Joyce followed in order and were also brought to Father Moden, then placed on the floor. The nine bearers all took one step back. Additional troops then lined both sides of the cargo bay and the ramp, extending back more than fifty yards. On the wall of the plane off to Father Moden's left was a large American flag.

---

* A Ziegler case is a galvanized metal case designed to contain a deceased person in an airtight environment, and is used to transport the remains from one country to another.

After a brief but moving service and closing prayer, Father Moden sprinkled each flag-draped case with holy water and invited those who desired to file past and offer their final respects. Hundreds lined up, and for the next ninety minutes or more SOF personnel passed by each of the three cases in a U-shaped pattern. Some reached down and ran their hands along the flag as they walked, others stopped and paused for a moment of personal reflection, while many knelt with their heads buried in their hands and wept quietly. Those grieving individuals who had the most difficulty were supported by their fellow teammates with a hand on the shoulder, or in some cases arm in arm.

While none of the SOF personnel knew Lance Corporal Joyce, the grieving process for him was the same. Many knelt and mourned alongside his body. They all knew the type of individual he was—a Marine, a fellow warrior. He was just nineteen, the same age as many of their siblings, and in some cases the same age as their oldest children. His service, his sacrifice, and his loss were felt no less and were no less important. At that very moment, his fellow Marines were combing the mountains to find their missing SEAL brother, Matt Axelson.

Besides the emotional release it provided, the ramp ceremony was important to those who remained for three very distinct reasons. First, it allowed the remaining warriors to honor the service of those who had fallen. Second, because the warriors who were present at the ramp ceremony would be unable to attend the fallen men's funeral services, it provided a sense of closure for those who remained behind. Third, for those who remained, the ceremony served as a source of strength. Warriors are inherently part of a cause greater than themselves, and, as such, they find a special strength in each other, the one that makes them so extraordinarily formidable.

CHAPTER EIGHTEEN

In the Presence of Warriors

I am always humbled in the presence of warriors.

—COMMODORE PETE VAN HOOSER, Commander, Naval Special
Warfare Group Two, quoted at Militaryphotos.net,
www.militaryphotos.net/forums.showthread.php?t=71680

July 8, 2005: Naval Amphibious Base, Little Creek, Virginia

On July 8, 2005, a memorial service was held for the dead of SEAL Team Ten. During that ceremony, Admiral Joseph Maguire, the commander of Naval Special Warfare Command, provided the opening remarks. Following Admiral Maguire's comments and the presentation of medals to the members of the deceased warriors' families, Commodore Pete Van Hooser approached the microphone and, after a deliberate pause, began to speak.

I am always humbled in the presence of warriors. We have been in sustained combat for over three years—things have changed.

I find myself speaking in public a lot more than I would like, but I always start by thanking four groups of people. The first are our warriors who have fallen; the second, those who have guaranteed that those who have fallen will not be left behind. Some with their bravery, others with their lives.

I thank those who have selflessly pulled themselves off the line to train the next warriors to go forward—so that they may surpass the prowess of those currently engaged.

And I am thankful for the families that nurture such men.

My remarks will be focused on these families and the men who wear the Trident. We would not be able to do our jobs without the brave men and women of the Army, Air Force, and Marine Corps. Task Unit Afghanistan of Naval Special Warfare Squadron Ten, was comprised of SEAL Team and SEAL Delivery Vehicle Team Two and One, had many U.S. Navy rates other than SEALs that trained and deployed by our side, and we recognize and are grateful for the professional efforts of all. But this time and this place is about the SEALs.

Leonidas, the Spartan King, hand-picked and led a force to go on what all knew to be a one-way mission. He selected 300 men to stand against an invading Persian force of over 2 million. They were ordered to delay the advance of the Persian Army. Selecting the battlefield was easy—the narrow mountain pass at Thermopylae restricted the combat power that the enemy could apply—allowing the superior fighting skills of the 300 Spartans to destroy the will of this Persian Army to fight. These Spartan warriors died fighting to the last man.

The Persian invaders were defeated by the Greek Army in later battles. Democracy and freedom were saved.

Most know this story. But most of us don't know how Leonidas selected the 300 men. Should he take the older seasoned Warriors who have lived a full life? Should he take the young lions that felt they were invincible? Should he take the battle-hardened, backbone-proven warrior elites in their prime? Or should he sacrifice his Olympic champions?

The force he chose reflected every demographic of the Spartan Warrior class. He selected those who would go based on the strength of the women in their lives. After such great loss, if the women faltered in their commitment, Sparta would falter and the rest of Greece would think it useless to stand against the Persian invaders. The democratic flame that started in Greece would be extinguished.

The Spartan women were strong. They did not falter. I would even argue that we live in a democracy that has freedom because of the strength, skill, and courage of these 300 men and the extraordinary will and dedication of the women in their lives.

The women in our lives are the same, I see the pride in their wearing of the Trident—I hear it in their voices when they are asked what is that symbol, and they say my husband, my son, my brother, or my dad is a Navy SEAL—usually they say nothing more.

If I were to say to the families, I feel your pain, that could not be so. I can never know the depth of your relationship or the anguish of your personal loss. What I can say is the truth of what I know. Those who wear the Trident provide only brief glimpses into our world to those on the outside. Even our families see only a limited view of the path we have chosen. We are all different, but on the inside we share many common beliefs and actions. We spend most of our adult lives with other SEALs preparing for battle.

On this occasion I feel compelled to share our innermost thoughts. I want to show you a little more of our world so you can understand the way we see, the way we feel about what happened. There is a bond between those who wear a Trident—that is our greatest strength.

It is unique to this very small community. It is unique in its intensity. It is nurtured by the way we train—the way we bring warriors into the brotherhood. This bond is born in BUD/S. It starts to grow the first time you look into the eyes of your classmate when things have gone beyond what you or he thinks is possible. It grows in the platoon as you work up for deployment, and it grows around the PT circle. It's the moving force behind every action in a firefight. This bond is sacred. This bond is unspoken, unconditional, and unending.

When it comes to fighting we are all the same inside. During the first stages of planning, at the point you know that you are going into the battle, we think about our families. The master chief passing the word to the boys sums it up, "I am going home to my kids and you are going home to yours. Here is our next mission."

We never stop planning—we never stop thinking through every contingency—we want to cover every anticipated enemy action. This is the way we face the risk.

There is a significant difference between inserting on a mission where there may or may not be enemy contact or serious resistance and inserting into a fight where forces are already engaged. On April 11, the men of this task unit—during their initial week in Afghanistan, immediately shifted from a helicopter training scenario directly into the fight as a quick response force to help soldiers and marines in a desperate battle. They made the difference—saving the lives of our fellow servicemen and destroying the enemy.

Last week when these fallen warriors launched on this mission, their SEAL teammates were fighting the enemy—fellow SEALs were in peril—as always in the teams—in this situation there is no hesitation. It is not about tactics—it's about what makes men fight.

As you are going in hot—you can't help it—you must allow one small block of personal time. You think of those at home—the people you left behind. For this brief moment, there is no war.

Our souls have touched a thousand times before this moment. Boundless undefined shadows quietly surging through and waking each other on a moonless star rich night we patiently wait for the dawn. There is no distance. You smile a cool wind that takes away thirst. I will never know hunger. I have never known fear. Unspoken—Unconditional—Unending.

It's the same bond—now your focus returns to your SEAL teammates. Total focus on the approaching fight is all that exists.

In April, when I heard of the Task unit's first contact that very first week in country—when I saw the reports of the enemy causalities they had inflicted—I was happy but not too happy. It's more of a quiet internal recognition that they had executed flawlessly.

Last week when I was told of their deaths and saw what they were trying to accomplish, I was sad—but not too sad. It was more of a quiet and internal recognition that they had gone to the wall, and there was no hesitation. They were warriors—they are SEALs.

We are not callous. We don't have the luxury of expressing our emotions at will. In these times our duty is to press on and finish the fight, for all depends on each man's individual actions.

We answer to a higher moral calling on the path that requires us to take and give life. It is this dedication to ideals greater than self that gives us strength. It is the nurturing of our families that gives us courage. Love is the opposite of fear—it is the bond that is reinforced when we look in the eyes of another SEAL that drives the super human endurance. My teammate is more important than I.

The enemy we face in Afghanistan is as hard and tough as the land they inhabit. They come from a long line of warriors who have prevailed in the face of many armies for centuries. It is their intimate knowledge of every inch of the most rugged terrain on earth that is matched against our skill, cunning, and technology.

They are worthy adversaries and our intelligence confirms that they fear and respect us. They have learned to carefully choose their fights because SEALS will answer the bell every time.

When you see the endless mountains—the severe cliffs—the rivers that gen-
erate power that can be felt while standing on the bank—the night sky filled with
more stars than you have ever seen—when you feel the silence of the night where
no city exists—when the altitude takes your breath away and the cold and heat hits
the extreme ends of the spectrum—you cannot help being captured by the raw
strength of this place.

This is a great loss. These men were some of the future—high impact leaders of
Naval Special Warfare, but I take refuge in the thought that there is no better place a
warrior's spirit can be released than in the Hindu Kush of the Himalayas.

In their last moments, their only thoughts were coming to the aid of SEAL
brothers in deep peril. I can say that anyone wearing a Trident would gladly have
taken the place of these men even with the full knowledge of what was to come.

Some of those on the outside may understand that one man who was recovered
would possibly make the loss acceptable. Only those who wear the Trident know,
if no one had come back, it would have all been worth the cost. These are my men.
They are good men. The SEAL teams—this path is my religion. This loss will not
go unanswered. I am always humbled in the presence of Warriors.

With those words spoken, he returned to his seat. The silence was deafening.
In a few moments of deep introspection and verbal eloquence, he had given the
complete story of the Navy SEALs and the events on June 28, 2005. He had told the
story. He had told it well. The only thing left to do was to be seated. He did.

Three days later, Admiral Maguire found himself at another memorial ceremony, this time at the National Memorial Cemetery of the Pacific in Hawaii—
the Punchbowl.

July 11, 2005: National Memorial Cemetery of the Pacific

Few national cemeteries can compete with the dramatic natural setting of the
National Memorial Cemetery of the Pacific, located in the center of Honolulu.
Also known as Punchbowl, the cemetery lies in the middle of Puowaina Crater,
an extinct volcano. It was officially dedicated on September 2, 1949, on the fourth
anniversary of V-J Day. Of all the national cemeteries, this one has been described
as the most beautiful and the most moving.

Members of the SDVT-1 SEAL community gathered at Punchbowl to honor
the sacrifices of their teammates on June 28, 2005. The welcoming remarks were
offered by Lieutenant Commander Alec Mackenzie, the executive officer of SEAL
Delivery Vehicle Team One. He was followed by Rear Admiral Joseph Maguire.
Afterward, the families of the honored dead or their representatives were presented
shadow boxes.

Ideally, a shadow box serves not only as a reminder of achievements and accomplishments, but also as a summation, a culmination, of a career. An American flag
was placed inside each shadow box to symbolize the country that has benefited

from a lifetime of faithful service. An American flag was flown over the USS *Arizona* memorial on Independence Day to honor those who gave their lives on June 28, 2005, as did so many before them, so that we could be free. The shadow boxes were presented to the families of Operation Red Wings with these words: "On behalf of your fellow teammates, we present you with this shadow box. Within the shadow box lie a sailor's most honored and cherished possessions, including the flag of the United States of America, representing a lifetime of valiant and faithful service."

Eulogies were given for each of the dead, followed by remarks by Commander Todd DeGhetto, the commanding officer of SEAL Delivery Vehicle Team One, and Governor Linda Lingle of Hawaii. Standing with his fellow SEALs from SDVT-1, listening to their words, Lieutenant Andy Haffele was overcome with emotion. The shooting incident several years before had effectively ended his SEAL career just as it began and resulted in an initial intense anger and lingering frustration. Now Haffele realized that the shooting incident had saved his life. He knew that had the shooting not occurred he would have been on Sawtalo Sar instead of Michael—and if not on the mountain, without question he would have been on the downed helicopter.

Governor Lingle's remarks were followed by the haunting two-bell ceremony, then by a moment of silence. The performance of "Amazing Grace," the firing of a twenty-one-gun salute, and the playing of "Echo Taps" preceded the Benediction, given by Chaplain David Stroud, which concluded the solemn ceremony.

CHAPTER NINETEEN

Memorials to a Hero

*But within the willingness to die for family and home, some-
thing inside us longs for someone to die beside. Someone to lock
step with, another man with a heart like our own.*

—MATTHEW AXELSON, U.S. Navy SEAL, handwritten inscription
on back of photograph in private collection of Daniel J. Murphy

I n the summer of 2005, Brookhaven town supervisor Brian X. Foley and
Councilman Timothy Mazzei began efforts to create and name a park at the
Brookhaven town beach at Lake Ronkonkoma in honor of Michael Murphy.
Dan Murphy and Tim are longtime friends from when both served in the Suffolk
County district attorney's office in the 1980s.

Soon after Michael's funeral, Tim approached Dan about doing something
to commemorate Michael's life and achievements, and suggested a small piece
of ground at the intersection of two streets near Lake Ronkonkoma for the placing of a monument. After further consideration, it was decided that the location
was not suitable, because of its inaccessibility. Councilman Mazzei subsequently
approached Dan about plans to create a memorial park at the lake. With Dan's support the project grew, and as the concept became more widely known, local businesses and organizations pledged support with labor, supplies, and donations. The
plans settled upon were ambitious and would require time, expense, and effort. As
word of the project spread, other efforts were launched.

On October 7, 2005, the first annual Patrick Henry Open Golf Outing, sponsored by the Suffolk County Prosecutor's Association, was conducted with the proceeds going to fund the newly created LT. Michael P. Murphy Memorial Scholarship
Foundation.

On October 20, 2005, Representative Timothy Bishop (NY-1), along with
twenty-eight cosponsors, introduced United States House of Representatives
Resolution (HR) 4401, "To designate the facility of the U.S. Postal Service located
at 170 East Main Street in Patchogue, New York, as the 'Lieutenant Michael P.

Murphy Post Office Building.'" Identical legislation was introduced in the Senate by Senator Hillary Rodham Clinton.

Little League Baseball Fields, April 29, 2006

With the Murphy family's blessing, Lance Marquis and his wife, Brenda, neighbors of Maureen Murphy, began efforts to rename the Little League baseball fields where Michael played and his father coached in honor of Michael. Their efforts were successful. On April 29, 2006, hundreds of players, former players, coaches, parents, family members, and friends gathered at the ball fields, which were renamed and dedicated in Michael's honor. The Murphy family was there, with Dan dressed in a blue jersey, Maureen in a white one, and John in a red jersey, each with "LT Murphy 1" on the back.

Lake Ronkonkoma, May 7, 2006

The bipartisan efforts to honor Michael Murphy in the town where he once was a lifeguard were successful. On what would have been Michael's thirtieth birthday, local leaders, the media, family members, friends, and Navy officials gathered at Lake Ronkonkoma to dedicate the Navy SEAL Lt. Michael P. Murphy Memorial Park. One of the speakers was Rear Admiral Joseph Maguire.

In his remarks, he provided the most public accounting of the details of Operation Red Wings to date. He stated that satellite reconnaissance had shown that a group of about eighty Taliban fighters had been coming across the border from Pakistan. Having never seen such a large concentration of fighters in one location, CJTF commanders believed they must be guarding a high-level Taliban or al-Qaeda operative. As a result, Michael's team had been inserted behind the fighters to perform reconnaissance on the large group. This revelation was news to everyone in attendance as well as the Murphy family.

Admiral Maguire also revealed that Michael's "award was being reviewed and upgraded." Given Maguire's disclosure of both the mission details and the upgrading of Michael's award, coupled with a previous news release that the secretary of the navy had already approved the awarding of the Navy Cross to Michael's teammates, the Murphy family assumed that their son would also be receiving the Navy Cross.

Naturally, this created a lot of speculation in various Internet blogs. The conjecture was widespread that while Michael's actions on June 28, 2005, were certainly worthy of the Medal of Honor, his award was being delayed by red tape. The Medal of Honor approval process involved a two-year investigation into the circumstances surrounding the action in question and required supportive testimony from at least two eyewitnesses. The latter was potentially a problem in Michael's case. Marcus Luttrell was certainly qualified to be one eyewitness, but with no other survivors available, could the video images of the firefight taken from the Predator drone be used in their stead?

Additional honors for Michael continued. On May 31, 2006, the Patchogue-Medford High School Father's Club honored Michael as its Person of the Year for 2005.

No further information or activity regarding military honors occurred until the Oval Office Ceremony on July 18, 2006, in which the Navy Cross, the nation's second-highest award for valor, was awarded to Petty Officer Second Class Marcus Luttrell.

The efforts of Representative Bishop and his cosponsors in the House of Representatives, along with those of Hillary Rodham Clinton and Charles Schumer in the Senate, paid off on August 1, 2006, when both houses of Congress passed Public Law 109-256, which would rename the Patchogue Post Office as the Lieutenant Michael P. Murphy Post Office Building.

Navy Memorial, September 16, 2006

Dedicated on October 13, 1987, the 212th birthday of the U.S. Navy, the Navy Memorial honors the men and women of the United States Navy. Located on Pennsylvania Avenue, N.W. (between Seventh and Ninth streets), it features an outdoor plaza, towering masts with signal flags, fountain pools and waterfalls, and the Naval Heritage Center. The plaza, known as the Granite Sea, is a round ceremonial amphitheater paved in granite to form a one-hundred-foot-diameter map of the world. A symbolic statue, *The Lone Sailor*, stands watch near the edge of the plaza.

Presenting the Navy Cross to the families of Matthew Axelson and Danny Dietz was the secretary of the navy, Dr. Donald C. Winter. At the ceremony, James Gordon Meek, the Washington correspondent for the *New York Daily News*, approached Dan. He said, "You know there's a rumor going around here in Washington that Michael is up for the Medal of Honor." This statement caught Dan completely off guard. His only response was "Huh?" Meek continued: "Don't you think it odd that you're here for a Navy Cross ceremony for Dietz and Axelson, Luttrell has already received it, and Michael's not mentioned?" Dan dismissed Meek's speculation and probing, saying, "We've really never thought much about it; we just think that Michael's review process is just taking longer than the others, that's all."

After the conversation with Meek, while Dan returned to Maureen, he began seriously thinking about the reporter's comments, as well as the conversation he had had with the Navy officer who invited them to the event. Several questions came to Dan's mind. If Michael was indeed being considered for the Navy Cross, why hadn't that been mentioned before then, or at least that day? Certainly Rear Admiral Maguire was not mistaken in his remarks on May 7 last year? What if Meek was correct?

After returning to Maureen, he said, "You know, Maureen, all three of Michael's teammates have received the Navy Cross. The Navy Cross is the second-highest award given for valor. Now, either Michael's review is just taking longer or he is up for a higher award. The only award higher than the Navy Cross is the Medal of Honor. Michael may be considered for the Medal of Honor." Maureen scoffed and responded, "Yeah, right." Dan was not so sure. The matter was dropped, but his questions remained.

Continuing to Wait

After returning home, Dan began monitoring the military blogs much more closely and noticed there was increased speculation regarding Michael and the Medal of Honor. Dan was also doing research and due diligence on the medal's requirements and review process. The blogs continued to speculate on the second of the two required eyewitnesses and the distinct possibility that the Navy at the highest levels was considering using the photographic and video images from the circling Predator drone, as well as radio communications.

Dan, like everyone else, could only speculate and wait for the review process to play itself out.

Patchogue Federal Post Office, October 24, 2006

On October 24, Main Street in Patchogue was blocked off, and a huge white tent stood erect before the Post Office Building. A full representation from the U.S. Navy, including Rear Admiral Maguire, Senator Hillary Clinton, and Representative Timothy Bishop joined the Murphy family and hundreds of local officials, relatives, and friends to officially rename the Post Office Building, the oldest federal building on Long Island.

After the ceremony, Representative Bishop took Dan off to the side and confided, "Dan, I was just approached by Admiral Maguire and the Navy asking if Michael was awarded the Medal of Honor, would I be the sponsor. I told him I would be honored." It was then that Dan really began to believe that his oldest son, Michael P. Murphy, was being considered for the Medal of Honor.

January 30, 2007

During the preceding five months, Dan and the rest of the Murphy family had been cooperating with *Newsday* reporter Martin C. Evans on a multipart series entitled

Born to Serve about Michael to be published sometime around May 7, Michael's birthday. Dan received a telephone call from a reporter at the *Washington Post* asking if she could come to Patchogue and interview the family. Dan promised to get back to her on the arrangements.

January 31, 2007

Shortly after arriving at his office at 8:30 AM, Dan received a telephone call from *Newsday* deputy Long Island editor Steve Wick, a longtime friend dating back to when Steve was a crime reporter and Dan was in the Suffolk County district attorney's office. Steve inquired whether there was any news regarding Michael's medal upgrade. When Dan denied knowing anything new, Wick responded, "Oh well, I was just wondering because we are hearing rumors, and would you keep us posted?" Dan assured him that when the family knew, Steve would know.

Wick continued by saying that *Newsday* wanted to do a follow-up story on Michael and have something ready in case it was announced that he would receive the Medal of Honor. During the conversation Dan informed Wick of the previous day's telephone call from the *Washington Post* who wanted to interview the family. Wick, concerned, then asked, "Did they say why?" Dan replied negatively, stating that he thought she just wanted to do a follow-up on the Born to Serve series. Wick replied, "That's very strange." Dan agreed, then added, "We don't know anything. They are there in Washington, maybe they have some contacts and maybe they are hearing something, and that's why they want to come up." Wick ended the conversation by stating that he was going to do some checking and would get back to Dan.

At 4:30 PM Steve Wick again called Dan. He said, "Dan, you know, I've talked with my other editors. The one thing we don't want is to get scooped on our own local story by the Washington newspapers. This phone call from the *Post* has got us all abuzz here. We think we are going to go with our story tomorrow."

Dan cautioned Wick, stating, "You'd better be careful because we all could have egg on our face if you sit here and say something about Michael being under consideration for the Medal of Honor and it doesn't happen." Wick acknowledged the risk and hung up.

February 1, 2007

Newsday ran a cover story about Michael on February 1, with a large picture of him under the headline banner "HERO. Fallen Navy SEAL from LI is up for nation's highest combat honor." Inside was a two-page story. As the source for its story, the paper was able to get Representative Timothy Bishop to admit that Michael Murphy was under consideration for the Medal of Honor.

Later that day Steve Wick called Dan and said, apologetically, "Dan, I hope you understand. We didn't want to get scooped by the Washington papers." Dan acknowledged his understanding and ended the call. Dan's next call was from Representative Bishop, who was also very apologetic. "I hope I didn't say anything that would cause the family a problem," he said. Dan was sympathetic toward Bishop and assured him that there would be no problem.

Several minutes after hanging up with Congressman Bishop, Dan received a call from *New York Daily News* reporter James Gordon Meek. Meek is a seasoned war correspondent and was in Afghanistan at the time of Operation Red Wings. He acknowledged reading the *Newsday* story, stating that "there is a lot of buzz going around. Let's hope that this does not put the kibosh on the medal." Dan inquired as to his meaning, to which Meek replied, "You know, the military people don't like to get ahead of themselves. They are really funny about things like that." Now irritated, Dan replied, "Well, if in fact he is under consideration, what difference does that make? Either Michael did what he did or didn't." Then he hung up.

Additional Memorials and Honors

On May 26, 2007, the Patchogue-Medford High School conducted a Memorial Day ceremony honoring Michael. Performing at the event was the U.S. Navy's elite parachute team, the Leap Frogs.

Kings Park High School established the Lieutenant Michael Patrick Murphy (U.S. Navy) Scholarship Award on June 6, 2007. On June 10, Team Murphy, named in honor of Michael, competed in the Race Across America, a cross-country bicycle event, to raise money for the Naval Special Warfare Foundation.

On June 12 Marcus Luttrell's book *Lone Survivor* was released without any prior knowledge of the Operation Red Wings families. Michael's father received a call from *Newsday*'s Steve Wick asking if Dan knew about the book. Dan acknowledged having just learned of the book's release and was on his way to purchase a copy.

In late August Dan received a telephone call from the Navy extending an invitation to both of Michael's parents to attend an upcoming ceremony at the Navy Memorial in Washington, D.C., at which the Navy Cross would be awarded posthumously to both Matt Axelson and Danny Dietz. Concerned about Maureen's emotions, Dan questioned the invitation and Michael's status. The Navy officer replied, "Don't worry, you'll get a sense of what's going on when you get down there." Dan agreed, for the family, to attend.

CHAPTER TWENTY

Of Service and Sacrifice

Guys like Murph don't die as old men. They die as heroes.

—LIEUTENANT JAMES QUATTROMANI, U.S. Navy (ret.),
quoted in "Born to Serve: The Michael Murphy Story," *Newsday*,
www.newday.com/.../ny/murphy/seal-sg.0.6675676.storygallery

While at his law office on Friday, August 19, 2007, Dan received a telephone call from Vice Admiral Joseph Maguire. Maguire had been promoted and assumed the duties of deputy director for strategic operational planning at the National Counterterrorism Center on June 28, 2007. After an exchange of pleasantries, Maguire said, "I'm not trying to steal anybody's thunder here, but I want to let you to know that Michael's Medal of Honor recommendation is on the President's desk and has been signed by him." He added that the family would be receiving official notification from the White House at a later date. After several more minutes of catching up, Dan thanked Admiral Maguire for the information and promised to keep it confidential within the family until they were officially notified. Elated, Dan telephoned Maureen to inform her of the news.

A week later, sitting in the sunroom at his home enjoying a leisurely afternoon cup of coffee, Dan casually sorted through the week's correspondence. It was Saturday, August 25, a rare weekend break from the breakneck pace of his hectic law career. As a devoted husband and father, he balanced the ever-increasing number of personal appearance requests on Michael's behalf, sitting on corporate boards, and serving our nation's veterans as the national judge advocate of the Military Order of the Purple Heart.

While his wife, Karen, and her daughter, Kristen, were out shopping, Dan took in the bright late August sun through the enormous full-length windows. The welcome calm and silence was broken only by the occasional passing automobile in this upper-middle-class subdivision outside of Wading River. The ringing telephone startled Dan, who, with a sigh, reached for the cordless receiver and answered. The caller identified himself as Colonel John Martin, chief of military affairs at the

White House. Martin said, "President Bush asked me to call and inform you that he has signed your son's recommendation for the Medal of Honor." Dan was asked to keep the information within the family until the White House made an official announcement. Dan thanked Colonel Martin, and agreed to keep the information confidential.

After he finished speaking with Martin, Dan telephoned Maureen to tell her that the Medal of Honor was official and to keep the information within the family until the official White House announcement was made. His next call was to Steve Gilmore, a retired Navy captain, who served as the executive assistant of Naval Special Warfare. He told Gilmore about the news and inquired as to when the official announcement would be made. Gilmore advised him that it would "probably take about two weeks" to coordinate schedules and itineraries between the White House and the Navy.

To begin the Medal of Honor process, Steve Gilmore arrived on Long Island from NSW in San Diego on Tuesday, September 5, and met with both Dan and Maureen at the Suffolk County courthouse in Riverhead. The purpose of the meeting was to get better acquainted with the Murphys and to provide them with a general overview of the entire Medal of Honor process. Gilmore informed the Murphys that the White House ceremony was scheduled for October 22 and inquired as to what else they would like to do while in Washington. After a few minutes of discussion, a general itinerary was worked out. Prior to his departure, Gilmore informed them that he, along with the new NSW commander, Rear Admiral Joseph D. Kernan, and his aide would be returning to meet with them on the twentieth.

Catching a red-eye flight from San Diego, Admiral Kernan, Gilmore, and Kernan's aide, Commander Bryan Williams, arrived at the Long Island MacArthur Airport midmorning on Tuesday, September 20. They were met by Dan and Maureen. The Murphys took the group to see the Navy SEAL Lt. Michael P. Murphy Memorial Park at Lake Ronkonkoma and described the plans for an upcoming addition of the Serenity Plaza.

No one had eaten, so Dan and Maureen treated everyone to brunch at a local favorite restaurant near the park. After brunch, they went to the post office named after Michael, where postal officials gave them a tour of the facility and detailed their plans for the permanent memorial.

Following the post office tour, everyone enjoyed several hours of talking and looking at mementos of Michael at Dan's home. Then Steve Gilmore gave them a briefing of the detailed itinerary, which included the ceremony date of October 22. Dan and Maureen also provided a list of things they wanted to do while in Washington. On their way back to the airport, they stopped at the small memorial park at the Navy Industrial Aircraft Facility not far from Dan's home.

In mid-September, Dan received a telephone call from Martin Evans at *Newsday*, who asked, "Dan, have you heard anything yet?" Dan always made it his practice to never lie to the press. In keeping with that practice, Dan responded, "Martin, I do not lie. All I can tell you is I can't tell you anything." Evans responded, "Oh, I understand, and I certainly don't want to put you on the spot, but let me ask you a hypothetical question. If I were to go on vacation, when should I not go?" Dan laughed and said, "I believe a poor time to go on vacation would be October 22."

The meetings continued on Sunday, October 9, with the arrival of Lieutenant Commander Tamsen Reese, deputy public affairs officer for the Department of the Navy. At her meeting with Dan and Maureen, also held at the Suffolk County courthouse in Riverhead, she told them she would assist in coordinating the upcoming round of media interviews and appearances in conjunction with the White House announcement and the Medal of Honor ceremony. The first press conference would be on the date of the official announcement in two days' time.

The official White House announcement was made on Tuesday, October 11, 2007, followed immediately by another announcement by the Department of the Navy. The Navy's Public Affairs Office having made all the arrangements, the Murphys were escorted into a conference room in the Marriott Courtyard East Side, in Manhattan. All of the major broadcast and print media were represented. After about an hour of taking and answering question, the news conference was closed by Lieutenant Commander Reese, and the Murphy family returned home.

Quick Travel Preparations

The East Room of the White House seated 250 guests. The Navy claimed 150 seats, while the remaining 100 were given to the Murphy family and split equally between Dan and Maureen. Needing to dole out tickets carefully among the members of their large extended family and friends, Maureen and Dan sat down and developed their list. Maureen's 50 tickets were quickly allocated to her relatives and Heather. Dan had a smaller family and needed to allocate only about a dozen to relatives.

Dan contacted Owen O'Callaghan and invited the six members of the O'Callaghan family to attend the ceremonies. He also informed Owen that he would like to invite three representatives of the New York City Fire Department, specifically from the fire station whose patch Michael wore. Firefighter Nate Evans, Captain Eugene Kananowicz, and Lieutenant George Brennan were selected. Dan also provided tickets to Patchogue mayor Paul Ponteri, Brookhaven town supervisor Brian X.Foley, Councilman Tim Mazzei, and eight members of the Military Order of the Purple Heart, as well as members of the local bar, court services, law enforcement, postal officials, and retired military. To obtain access to the White

House, complete names, addresses, and Social Security numbers were provided to the Navy for the necessary security background checks.

FDNY to Washington, D.C.

More than fifty members of the FDNY voiced strong interest in attending the White House ceremonies. Unfortunately, with the limited tickets, this simply would not be possible. Undeterred, the firefighters were determined to make the trip and attend the public ceremonies honoring Michael's Medal of Honor that were scheduled to be held at the Pentagon's Hall of Heroes and the Navy Memorial, as well as visit Arlington National Cemetery with the family. A charter bus was obtained through someone's personal contact. Arrangements were also made for the firefighters to visit the wounded at Walter Reed Medical Center and distribute FDNY hats and T-shirts, which became an annual event.

Another Round of Media Interviews

With the aid of Lieutenant Commander Reese, the Murphys, joined by Marcus Luttrell, conducted another round of news conferences on October 15 and 16, this time at the Marriott Marquis on New York's Eighth Avenue in Times Square. In addition, the Murphys appeared on *FOX & Friends*, where they were interviewed by Brian Kilmeade, and NBC's *The Today Show* with Matt Lauer. Numerous other print and broadcast media interviews were conducted.

Washington, D.C.—October 21, 2007

The Murphy and Jones families left Long Island on an early morning flight from the Long Island MacArthur Airport to the Baltimore/Washington International Thurgood Marshall Airport. They arrived just after 10:00 AM and were met by Steve Gilmore. They were taken to the Marriott Hotel in a bus arranged for by the Navy.

After taking a few minutes to freshen up after the flight, Dan, Maureen, and John met with Steve Gilmore and Tamsen Reese in a conference room and were provided detailed briefing books that included a complete itinerary as well as biographies on all the individuals they would meet. After lunch, they all loaded into the bus for the trip to Arlington National Cemetery with a law enforcement escort.

Arlington National Cemetery—October 21, 2007

Escorted by two members of a Navy honor guard and Steve Gilmore, Dan, Maureen, and John Murphy were given a tour of America's premier national cemetery. Arlington National Cemetery, located in Arlington, Virginia, was established during the Civil War on the grounds of Arlington House, which was the former estate of the family of Robert E. Lee's wife, Mary Anna Custis Lee, a descendant of Martha Washington. Located near the Pentagon, it is directly across the Potomac River from Washington, D.C. More than 290,000 of this nation's heroes from the American Revolution to the wars in Iraq and Afghanistan are buried in its 624 acres. With more than twenty funerals per day and fifty-four hundred per year, it is the nation's second-largest national cemetery, behind Calverton National Cemetery, which has more than thirty funerals per day and more than seven thousand per year. The Murphy family tour of Arlington was conducted at their request so that they could pay their respects to the men who had served with Michael.

Wreath-laying Ceremony for Michael's Teammates

With the assistance of a Navy escort, the Murphy family, along with the family of Lieutenant Michael McGreevy, laid a wreath at the graves of Lieutenant Michael McGreevy, Petty Officer Second Class Jeffrey Lucas, and Petty Officer Second Class Jeffrey Taylor, then visited the graves of Chief Warrant Officer 4 Chris Scherkenbach and Sergeant First Class Marcus Muralles, all buried in Section 60. The closeness of the Navy SEAL community made this event quite emotional.

Tomb of the Unknowns

At some point during the visit to Arlington, soldiers of the Army's 3rd U.S. Infantry, traditionally known as "The Old Guard," on duty there became aware of the Murphy family's tour of the cemetery. The Old Guard is most widely known as the ever-vigilant sentinels of the Tomb of the Unknowns. Army officials approached Dan and Maureen and requested that they participate in a wreath-laying ceremony at the Tomb of the Unknowns. Honored and humbled by the request, the family agreed and were escorted to the Memorial Amphitheater, just above the Tomb of the Unknowns, by the Navy and Army honor guard units. They could see a large wreath resting on a tripod stand located on the far-left side of the Tomb of the Unknowns, where a lone sentinel maintained his post.

Descending the marble stairs with military precision, the Sergeant of the Guard made an announcement: "The ceremony you are about to witness is an Army wreath-laying ceremony to be conducted by Dan and Maureen Murphy in honor of their son, Navy Lieutenant Michael P. Murphy, who was killed in action in Afghanistan on June 28, 2005, and will be awarded this nation's highest award for valor, the Medal of Honor, by President George W. Bush tomorrow afternoon in a White House ceremony. It is requested that everyone remain silent and standing during the ceremony. All military personnel in uniform will render the hand salute, and it is appropriate for all others to place your right hand over your heart upon the command of 'Present arms.' Thank you."

Turning toward the Tomb, the sergeant saluted and made a military left turn and walked to the end of the plaza to retrieve the large wreath on a white tripod stand, while Dan and Maureen were escorted down the marble steps by both an Army and Navy honor guard. With perfect timing, the sergeant made the turn and faced the Murphys at the exact moment they arrived. Dan and Maureen placed their hands on the wreath as the sergeant backed up just in front of the Tomb of the Unknowns.

As the wreath was set into position, the order to present arms was given. The Murphys placed their right hands over their hearts as a single Army bugler echoed the somber notes of "Taps," which released the raw emotions they had experienced two years earlier at Calverton National Cemetery when they buried their son, the newest recipient of the Medal of Honor. At the conclusion, they were escorted back to the Memorial Amphitheater and given a tour of the Old Guard's quarters.

Later that evening they attended a social gathering at Sines, a local Irish pub. Also there were members of the Navy leadership, their families, Michael's teammates, who had arrived from Hawaii to attend the ceremony, and Marcus Luttrell.

The Capitol Building—October 22, 2007

With nearly fifty friends and family involved in the visit to the Capitol Building, getting there from their hotel required a lot of coordination. The task was left to Steve Gilmore, who was working closely with Navy officials. Three buses were utilized, and the visitors were divided into three groups, designated red, white, and blue. The blue group was made up of the immediate family, including Dan, Karen, Kristen, Maureen, John, Cathy, Colleen, Kelly, and Maureen's parents, along with Steve and Kathy Gilmore and Marcus Luttrell. They received a private guided tour of the Capitol and met with Senator Charles Schumer and Representative Timothy Bishop of New York. The other two groups also received a guided tour of the Capitol, but as a single group. At around noon, the three buses loaded for the return trip to the hotel. After a quick lunch and an opportunity to freshen up, they loaded back aboard the buses for the trip to the White House.

The White House—October 22, 2007

Having provided both the Navy and the Secret Service with names, addresses, Social Security numbers, and other security-related information, access to the White House was much easier and quicker than both Dan and Maureen had expected. After entering the White House, the Navy aide to President Bush greeted everyone and escorted them to the Blue Room, where refreshments had been provided. The Blue Room served as a gathering place before and after the Medal of Honor ceremony.

Dan, Maureen, Maureen's parents, Steve and Kathy Gilmore, and Marcus Luttrell were then escorted to the Oval Office. After arriving at the outer office, Dan and Maureen were escorted into the Oval Office for a brief private meeting with President Bush.

As they entered the president greeted them at the door, extended his hand, and said, "Dan and Maureen, welcome to the White House. It is an honor to meet the parents of an American hero." After exchanging pleasantries, the president made a few comments about Michael's service to the country. Dan and Maureen presented President Bush with a gold-engraved dog tag with Michael's birthday, the date of his Medal of Honor ceremony, and a portrait holograph on the reverse side. The president loosened his necktie and unbuttoned his light blue shirt and placed the dog tags around his neck, then rebuttoned his shirt and straightened his tie. He looked at the Murphys and said, "Dan, Maureen, despite how the press may play this, the loss of each and every one of my men affects me deeply. Sending America's best and brightest into harm's way and then having to sign letters to the parents of those brave men who have given their all for their country is the hardest thing I have ever had to do." After a few more intimate moments, the members of the Murphy party who had waited in the outer office were escorted into the Oval Office. Upon seeing Luttrell, President Bush extended his hand and said, "Marcus, I want to show you something." Going around his desk, he opened the middle drawer. "See, I still have the patch you gave me last year, and it is going in my Presidential Library, as will this dog tag."

The president greeted everyone, shook their hands, and welcomed them to the White House. As he shook Maureen's father's hand, Frank said, with a tear in his eye, "I came to this country on a ship from Ireland many years ago. Who would have thought that an Irish immigrant would ever have the honor of meeting the President of the United States?" President Bush responded, "This country is made up of great people just like you. Immigrants have added so much to this country and have given us heroes like your grandson. Sir, this country owes you and your family a debt of gratitude that can never be paid. No sir, it is my honor to meet you."

After about thirty minutes, the visitors were escorted to the East Room and prepared for the formal ceremony. Along with the three representatives of the New York fire department, members of SEAL Delivery Vehicle Team One, and Captain Andrew Bisset, Michael's Navy mentor, the Murphy party joined the other guests in the East Room of the White House. The Murphy family was escorted to seats in the front row just to the left of the platform. At exactly 2:24 PM President George Bush was introduced and walked down the center aisle to the platform, turned, thanked everyone for coming, and invited all to be seated. After his opening remarks, the president invited Dan and Maureen to join him. As Dan and Maureen stepped onto the stage, the President moved beside Maureen, now in the center. When the military aide began reading the Medal of Honor citation, President Bush reached over and took Maureen's hand and gave it a gentle squeeze. When Maureen looked up at him with her tear-filled eyes, he smiled.

After the presentation and following the extended applause, President Bush broke with protocol and invited both Dan and Maureen to walk with him as he exited the East Room. Once out into the red-carpeted Cross Hall, White House photographers snapped dozens of both posed and impromptu pictures. After several minutes, President Bush gave both Dan and Maureen a hug and told them that he would be unable to attend the reception in the Blue Room, but instructed them to have a good time and said that the White House staff would see to their needs. With that, the president walked back down the hallway, shadowed by Secret Service agents. As he reached the end of the hall, he turned and looked back, waved, and then disappeared down the hallway.

Reception

Dan and Maureen joined the other guests in the Blue Room for an elegant reception that went for the next two hours. Dozens of photographs were taken with the Navy admirals in attendance, including Mike Mullen, Gary Roughead, Joseph Maguire and Joseph Kernan, as well as Navy Secretary Winter and Deputy Secretary of Defense Gordon England. At the conclusion of the reception, the guests were escorted out of the White House to reboard their buses for the return trip to the hotel.

Dinner with Admiral Roughead

For Dan, Maureen, and her parents, the arrival back at the hotel provided but a brief opportunity to relax and freshen up, as they were the expected dinner guests of Admiral and Mrs. Gary Roughead at their home in the Washington Navy Yard. Admiral Roughead had just been confirmed as the Navy's thirty-first chief of naval operations on September 29, 2007. Both Admiral and Mrs. Roughead greeted the family on the front porch as they arrived. The Murphys signed the register as the first guests of the new CNO and his family. After a relaxing evening, Dan, Maureen, and her parents returned to their hotel for a welcome night's rest.

The Pentagon's Hall of Heroes—October 23, 2007

Arriving at the Pentagon just after 8:30 AM, the three buses carrying the Murphy family and their friends were again divided up into their red, white, and blue groups. The blue group remained the same—Dan and Maureen, John, Maureen's parents, Karen, Kristen, Cathy, Colleen, Kelly, the Gilmores, and Marcus Luttrell. Navy personnel provided them with a detailed briefing of the morning's agenda and an escorted tour of the Pentagon, the largest single office building in the world. Located in the Pentagon is an entire section dedicated to the elite warriors whose service and sacrifice placed them in a league of their own. Known as the Hall of Heroes, it enshrines the extraordinary feats of ordinary men that have inspired many generations. Following their tour, the blue group met privately with Deputy Secretary of Defense Gordon England, Secretary of the Navy Winter, and Admiral Roughead. This was the first of two emotional events planned for the day. The second would be the evening Medal of Honor Flag ceremony at the Navy Memorial.

Induction to the Hall of Heroes

On October 23, 2007, at 11:00 AM, Lieutenant Michael P. Murphy took his place among the honored elite. Following the presentation of the American flag by a Navy color guard, Rear Admiral Gary Burt, the Navy's chief chaplain, opened the ceremony with the invocation, followed by Petty Officer First Class Michael Bolinki's powerful rendition of the national anthem.

The first speaker, Admiral Gary Roughead, who has more than thirty years of active duty experience, serves as the principal naval adviser to the president, the secretary of defense, and the secretary of the navy. A man of imposing presence, he is the highest-ranking officer in the U.S. Navy and a member of the Joint Chiefs of Staff. Although an accomplished speaker, he admittedly was somewhat uncomfortable speaking at such solemn and highly emotional commemorations such as that marking the tragic loss of Lieutenant Michael Murphy, one of the Navy's best and brightest, and this nation's most selfless and courageous.

Following his introduction by Secretary Winter, Deputy Secretary of Defense Gordon England walked to the podium. Prior to being tapped for his position, he served two terms as the secretary of the navy, becoming the first service branch secretary to be reappointed to the position. A white-haired gentleman with a soft voice, he spoke at length from notes but made no prepared remarks about Michael's character, service, and sacrifice, which resulted in his receiving the Medal of Honor.

Medal of Honor Flag Ceremony, Navy Memorial

As the family requested, the Medal of Honor Flag was presented to them at the Navy Memorial. At 6:00 PM, following the invocation by Commander Robert Coyle, James McEachin, Dan's longtime friend and fellow MOPH member, was introduced. McEachin, a decorated Korean War veteran, became a Hollywood actor, an author, and a noted public speaker, as well as a staunch advocate for the plight of our veterans. He presented his award-winning tribute to America's veterans. Concluding the ceremonies, Dan spoke for the Murphy family, and after presenting gifts from the family to Marcus Luttrell, Admiral Roughead, and Steve Gilmore, he invited everyone in attendance to the reception that followed

Medal of Honor Flag

The Medal of Honor Flag, a light-colored flag with white stars adapted from the Medal of Honor ribbon, commemorates the sacrifices and blood shed to defend our freedoms and gives emphasis to the Medal of Honor being the highest award for valor by an individual serving in the Armed Forces of the United States. On October 17, 2006, a public law gave the secretary of defense the authority to award the Medal of Honor Flag to deceased Medal of Honor recipients.

United States Naval Academy, Annapolis, Maryland— October 24, 2007

Included on the Murphy family's list of things they wanted to do was a trip to the Naval Academy to pay their respects at the grave of Lieutenant Commander Erik Kristensen. The morning following the Medal of Honor Flag ceremony, the family traveled to Annapolis, where they were met by Edward and Suzanne Kristensen, the parents of Lieutenant Commander Kristensen. Admiral Kristensen, a former superintendent at the Academy, gave them an extended tour of the campus, including the famous chapel, site of their own son's funeral service. The tour ended in the Academy's cemetery at the grave of Erik Kristensen. Following the emotional tour, the Murphy family caught a late afternoon flight back to Long Island.

On Thursday, October 31, 2008, the Kristensens traveled by train to New York City and joined the Murphy family and the author for a daylong tour of the various places named in honor of Michael Murphy. A particularly emotional moment occurred when the Kristensens visited and prayed at Michael's grave in Calverton National Cemetery.

CHAPTER TWENTY-ONE

Growing Legacy

The greatest use of life is to spend it for something that will out-last it.

—WILLIAM JAMES, quoted at iwise.com,
www.iwise.com/hYdUg (accessed May 21, 2008)

A Time of Tribute and Ceremony

The legacy of Lieutenant Michael P. Murphy began to develop almost immediately after his death. First came the creation of a memorial scholarship fund by his family, followed by the memorials described in the preceding chapters.

On October 4, 2007, the 233rd anniversary of the founding of the U.S. Navy, the New York City Police Department, in conjunction with the New York Navy League, sponsored a dinner at which Michael posthumously received the USO's 2007 George Van Cleave Military Leadership Award. At his college alma mater, Penn State University honored Michael during halftime of the Ohio State–Penn State football game on October 27, 2007. As his family was led onto the field, they were met with a standing ovation from the capacity crowd of 107,000.

On November 4, 2007, during halftime of the New York Jets' Military Appreciation Day game against the Washington Redskins, Michael was honored for his service and sacrifice. The Town of Brookhaven issued a proclamation on November 8, 2007, that recognized Michael's Medal of Honor service. On November 24, the New York Islanders hockey team conferred its Hometown Hero Award on Michael. At Long Island's Calverton National Cemetery, the original military headstone at Michael's gravesite was formally replaced with the Medal of Honor headstone and its distinctive gold lettering on November 27. On December 6 the United Service Organizations (USO) named Michael Murphy Sailor of the Year.

Motivate America, a company providing solutions in the disciplines of business and personal development, presented Michael Murphy with its 2007 Person of the Year award at its annual awards banquet in Manhattan on January 2, 2008.

On March 17, 2009, the 247th St. Patrick's Day Parade honored Michael Murphy and all of America's armed forces. On July 7 Admiral Gary Roughead, chief of naval operations, dedicated the new Lt. Michael P. Murphy Combat Training Pool at Naval Station Newport, Rhode Island.

On April 10, 2008, former White House press secretary Tony Snow and Lieutenant Michael P. Murphy were honored at the Media Research Center's 2008 Gala, held in Washington, D.C. There, T. Boone Pickens donated $1 million in Michael's name to the Congressional Medal of Honor Society. Two days later the Patchogue-Medford High School dedicated its Wall of Honor, depicting the career of Michael Murphy.

The Penn State Alumni Association conducted a tribute to Michael Murphy on May 2, 2008, during which he was posthumously awarded the Distinguished Alumni Award. The Serenity Plaza at the Navy SEAL Lt. Michael P. Murphy Memorial Park in Lake Ronkonkoma was dedicated on May 7, 2008, by the Town of Brookhaven, and a memorial was dedicated by the Military Order of the Purple Heart. At the May 7 dedication ceremony, Secretary of the Navy Donald C. Winter announced that the Navy's newest *Arleigh Burke*–class guided missile destroyer would be named the USS *Michael Murphy*. During his remarks, Secretary Winter declared, "Every Sailor who crosses the bow, every Sailor who hears the officer of the deck announce the arrival of the commanding officer, and every Sailor who enters a foreign land representing our great nation will do so as an honored member of the USS *Michael Murphy*."

The LT Michael P. Murphy Navy SEAL Sailor's Cross Memorial, dedicated at the American Legion Post 269 in Patchogue on May 26, 2008, is a solid bronze "cross" constructed from a rifle, fins, a mask, and helmet draped with the Medal of Honor. The San Diego–based organization First American Military honored Michael during Operation Red Wing Tribute, held on board the USS *Midway* in San Diego Harbor on June 28–29.

On September 21, 2008, the board of directors of the New Island Hospital in Bethpage, New York, dedicated the Navy LT Michael P. Murphy Emergency Department, and also hosted the very first annual LT Michael P. Murphy Memorial Benefit 5K Run/Walk for emergency medical equipment.

Roger Froehlich, a staunch military advocate, organized the biannual LT (SEAL) Michael P. Murphy Medal of Honor Memorial Golf Tribute on October 2, 2008, at the Mt. Kisco Country Club in Westchester County, New York, with all proceeds going to the LT. Michael P. Murphy, USN, Memorial Scholarship Foundation, the Navy SEAL Warrior Fund, and the Naval Special Warfare Foundation.

At the Special Operations Command at MacDill Air Force Base in Tampa, Florida, Lieutenant Murphy's name was entered into the Special Operations Command Wall of Heroes and his photograph raised on the Medal of Honor

Corridor on November 17, 2008. On November 20, 2008, conservative Christian singer Patti Clark Barnett released "There," a tribute song to Michael.

The Navy SEAL Lt. Michael P. Murphy Memorial Conference Room was dedicated at the Penn State University Department of Political Science on April 23, 2009.

The Power of a Legacy

Despite all the fanfare and notoriety that accompanied all of the preceding events, the one that clearly demonstrated the true power of Michael's legacy occurred on November 1, 2008, at Calverton National Cemetery. Nannette Furio, the cemetery's supervisory program manager, described the chance encounter.

> While in front of the administration building waiting for an incoming funeral, I noticed a woman walking into the cemetery and it was obvious she had used public transportation, getting off the bus at the front gate. Dressed in khaki pants, dark sweater and sneakers, her blond hair was pulled back in a pony tail which swayed out from above the adjustment strap in the back of her baseball cap. She carried a purse and flowers wrapped in white floral paper in one hand and a shopping bag in the other with a faux fur leopard coat draped over the bag.
>
> With no burial sections within a reasonable distance from the front gate, especially for someone bogged down with bags, I radioed for one of our employees to drive her to the gravesite she wished to visit. I then went over and introduced myself as a cemetery employee, telling her that I had someone coming to pick her up. She was extremely grateful, an attractive woman in her early 50's, she spoke with a thick Polish accent.
>
> I asked her what section she was visiting and she said that she was going to Section 67 to visit Michael Murphy. I asked her if she knew the Murphy's and she said no, but had learned about Michael's death in the newspaper. She was gifted a copy of Lone Survivor, was captivated by the story and since reading the book has visited Michael's grave several times. She told me that she lives in East Hampton and must take two busses in order to get to the cemetery. The funeral procession I was waiting for had arrived and I instructed her to just stay there and someone would be along shortly to pick her up.
>
> Several hours later, I was going to head home but decided to visit Michael's grave to see what type of flowers she had left. As I approached Section 67, I noticed her speaking to a gentleman visiting a nearby grave. I parked the car so we could talk. We both walked over to Michael's grave and saw she had left him three magnificent red roses with fern and baby's breath. She explained to me that today is All Saints Day and the Polish tradition is to visit the grave of a loved one. Both of her parents are deceased and interred in Poland and was compelled to again visit Michael. As a young girl, her father would tell her stories about the Warsaw invasion and how they would always move from one neighborhood to another in order to keep ahead of the Germans. When she read, Lone Survivor, the experience Michael and his men had that fateful day took her back to the stories once told by her father.

Aware that Michael had been awarded the Medal of Honor, she strongly believes our brave men and women who fight for our freedom should never be forgotten. I then escorted her to the grave of each of the men interred in Section 67 and gave her a brief story of each who had died in Operation Enduring Freedom.

Ewa [pronounced Eva] Banas is an accomplished but undiscovered artist. She showed me some photographs of her work and her paintings are absolutely beautiful. She then told me about a picture she painted of roses in a vase and the vase had a heart which appeared to be broken down the center because of the shadows she had painted on the canvas. Ewa wanted to give this painting to Marcus Luttrell because she remembered reading in his book that his heart would break when he had to talk to the Murphys. She completed this painting on June 28, 2006, one year after Michael's death.

Dan, having been notified of the meeting by Nannette, contacted Ewa, and he and Maureen had the pleasure of meeting her for dinner. She had brought along her well-worn, heavily highlighted and marked copy of *Lone Survivor*. Dan offered to send the book to Marcus for his autograph. Although somewhat apprehensive about parting with her only copy, she consented. A couple of weeks later, Dan returned to her the now-autographed copy of the book, which she considers one of her most treasured possessions.

Michael Murphy Memorial Trophy

As a lasting memory of Lieutenant Michael Murphy from the SEAL Recruiting District Assistance Council (RDAC), the Michael Murphy Memorial Trophy is awarded each year at the annual SEAL RDAC Christmas party to the SEAL officer candidate with the top scores achieved in the SEAL Physical Screening Test (PST) competition. Ironically, the first recipient was Midshipman Matt Shipman from the Penn State Naval ROTC program. Dan and Maureen Murphy personally award the trophy each year.

The Nature of a Legacy

A legacy can be defined as something that is handed down from an ancestor or a predecessor from the past. What attracts people from around the globe to the story of Michael P. Murphy? Some would claim that it was his selfless sacrifice on the field of battle; others might say it was his love of freedom and his willingness to die for it. I would argue that it is far more fundamental. While his selfless sacrifice on the field of battle is a matter of record and his love of freedom self-evident, these are but manifestations of the nobility of his character. It is his nobility of character that draws people from all walks of life, from all ages and creeds and nationalities, to his story.

In the short four-plus years of Michael P. Murphy's military career, he traveled the world in defense of America and that for which our nation stands. Although physically taken from our midst, Michael P. Murphy, in a much larger sense, continues to traverse the world instilling, and in some cases igniting, the flame of freedom.

He had spoken of his plans after he concluded his military service. Building on what he had learned, and cognizant of the ever-growing threat of terrorism, he had voiced a strong desire to join the FBI as a counterterrorism specialist. However, that was not to be. Michael P. Murphy believed that while a single man cannot do everything, he could do something. It is this belief that one man can make a difference that serves as an inspiration for us all.

Postscript

June 28, 2005, was the deadliest day for American special operations forces since World War II. On July 8, 2005, at a memorial service for the eighteen known dead from Operation Red Wings, Captain Pete Van Hooser declared that their deaths would not go unanswered. What he knew, but could not say, was that Operation Red Wings was only part of the overall plan to rid the Korangal Valley of Taliban and al-Qaeda forces.

Captain Von Hooser's words proved prophetic. Like the American bald eagle circling and stalking its prey, on August 11, 2005, U.S. and Afghan forces launched a devastatingly successful strike against the Taliban and al-Qaeda forces in response to the killing of nineteen of America's best, in what was called Operation Whalers. Coalition forces moved into position at one end of the valley and constructed a forward operating base (FOB) in a nearby cornfield. During the next forty-eight hours, Marines from 2nd Battalion, 3rd Marine Regiment, Marine Corps Base Hawaii trekked into the rugged terrain while numerous A-10 warplanes circled overhead. Over the next eleven days, the Marines endured twenty-nine separate Taliban and al-Qaeda counterattacks in their effort to wrest the valley from Shah's control. During the operation, the Mountain Tigers were tamed and Shah himself was severely wounded. He managed to crawl his way back across the mountains into the safety of Pakistan's North-West Frontier, known as Sarhad, the smallest of Pakistan's four provinces.

Requiring only an occasional flap of its wings, the American eagle circled, knowing it was not a question of if its prey would appear, but only a question of when. The eagle circled and waited. On Tuesday, April 15, 2008, the prey reappeared. Afghan security forces opened fire on Mullah Ahmad Shah and those traveling with him after he failed to stop at a police checkpoint near the Afghan border. Shah and his men were killed as they were attempting to smuggle a kidnapped Afghan day laborer back to an al-Qaeda hideout on the Afghan side of the border.

While Mullah Ahmad Shah and his Mountain Tigers no longer prey on the Afghan people and U.S. forces, the memory of Lieutenant Michael P. Murphy, U.S. Navy SEAL, remains permanently immortalized in the Pentagon's Hall of Heroes.

Michael P. Murphy was not perfect. He certainly made his share of mistakes— in one case, a mistake that cost a SEAL teammate his career. An extraordinary man, Michael P. Murphy was instilled with the seeds of greatness derived from his ethnic background, family legacy, community, and a faith learned in the arms of a loving mother and at the knee of a wise father. Consistent with his faith, he possessed an inner belief of always putting others ahead of self. He also possessed the innate sense of leadership and determination that allowed him to overcome obstacles that would stop those less motivated or determined.

Marcus Luttrell, Michael's SEAL teammate and the lone survivor of Operation Red Wings, gave the following tribute to his friend: "If they built a statue of him as big as the Empire State Building, it would not be big enough for me."

Lieutenant Michael P. Murphy's character, compassion, determination, and leadership resulted in his receiving this nation's Medal of Honor on earth and a place of honor serving in the Army of the Lord in the world eternal. His earthly legacy continues to grow. *Newsday*'s Legacy.com Web page for him continues to average two to three new posts per week from around the globe nearly four years after his death.

While political and military leaders change, our trust and commitment toward those who volunteer to wear this nation's uniform must never change. All who put themselves into harm's way in defense of freedom, as well as the families who endure their absence, deserve our unwavering gratitude and support. While we all cannot be Michael P. Murphy, we all can be patriots.

May God continue to comfort those of us who grieve, bless and watch over those who defend freedom, and continue to bless the United States of America.

Epilogue

asps broke the silence as the small group touring the legendary Bath Iron Works shipbuilding facility entered the cavernous Ultra Hall. Above them, towering nearly four stories high, was the name of their son, brother, grandson, and friend. "Michael Murphy" was emblazoned on the massive, 800-ton hull of what would soon become a U.S. Navy guided-missile destroyer.

The family knew, of course, that the name would be there. Aware of the project from its inception, they were present at the shipbuilding facility on June 18, 2010, for the keel-authentication ceremony for the ship named to forever memorialize the sacrifice of their son. The sheer astonishment and emotional impact of seeing his name across the hull of the ship, however, was something none of his family members had anticipated.

Michael's parents, Dan and Maureen Murphy, and his brother John embraced. Maureen's sister Eileen, Michael's godmother, joined the embrace; their sobs broke the silence. Scott Kay, the guided-missile destroyer project manager for Bath Iron Works and the tour guide for the day, took that moment to compose himself as the family embraced. Although he had conducted many tours for the families of ships' namesakes, the task never became any easier or less emotional for him.

Construction on the $170 million guided-missile destroyer *Michael Murphy* (DDG-112) began on September 7, 2007. During the dedication ceremony on May 7, 2008, Secretary of the Navy Donald C. Winter declared, "Michael Murphy's name, which will be forever synonymous with astonishing courage under fire, will now be associated with one of the U.S. Navy's most technologically advanced, most powerful, and most capable warships."

The keel-authentication ceremony on June 18 was the first of what will be several emotional ceremonies in bringing the ship to life. During the ceremony the workers at Bath helped Dan and Maureen weld their initials in a steel plate that will become part of the ship. The initials of all nineteen of those killed in Operation

Red Wings also will be welded into the keel plate as a lasting tribute to their service and sacrifice.

The anticipated christening is currently set for May 7, 2011, on what would have been Murphy's thirty-fifth birthday. The commissioning is tentatively scheduled for June 28, 2012, in New York Harbor. The USS *Michael Murphy* will be the seventh destroyer and the fortieth Navy ship named to commemorate a Medal of Honor recipient. Although its fleet assignment has yet to be determined, the destroyer and its 23 officers and 250 enlisted personnel likely will be home ported in Pearl Harbor, Hawaii, home of Murphy's unit, SEAL Delivery Vehicle Team-1.

Naval Special Warfare
Community Support Groups

There are several organizations and agencies that provide valuable, thought-ful, and helpful assistance to the families of U.S. Navy SEALS and other American military personnel who have been seriously wounded or killed in action or training.

LT. Michael P. Murphy, USN, Memorial Scholarship Foundation

The foundation was formed by Michael Murphy's parents, Daniel and Maureen, and his brother, John, in August 2005. It was given New York Department of Education approval on August 3, 2005, and incorporated in New York on August 11, 2005, as a 501(c)(3) nonprofit corporation with the expressed written purpose of providing academic scholarships. The Internal Revenue Service (IRS) granted the foundation tax-exempt status on May 4, 2006 (EID # 16-1730124).

The original board of directors consisted of Daniel J. Murphy, Maureen T. Murphy, and John D. Murphy. Since that time, three additional directors have been added: Mike's best friend, Owen O'Callaghan, a New York City firefighter, and his cousins Catherine Jones and Kristen Bishop.

The foundation provides four scholarships. Two are given through the Patchogue-Medford High School, one through the Suffolk Federal Credit Union and the Long Island Credit Union League to a Suffolk County resident, and one through the Military Order of the Purple Heart in Washington, D.C., to a combat-wounded veteran or the child of a Purple Heart recipient. Other organizations that support the foundation include the Suffolk County Prosecutor's Association, through its annual golf outing; the Long Island Council of Credit Unions; and the Chicago Title Insurance Company. Many other individuals and organizations honor Michael with their donations as well. The foundation in turn also actively supports the Navy SEAL Warrior Fund and the Naval Special Warfare Foundation.

To assist in its work and to perpetuate the growing legacy of Lieutenant Michael P. Murphy and his selfless dedication to public service, a portion of the proceeds from the sale of this work and any derivatives will be donated to the foundation to further expand its charitable work.

In addition, the foundation lends Michael's name to numerous fund-raising events in support of the Navy SEAL Warrior Fund, the Naval Special Warfare Foundation, and the Special Operations Warrior Foundation.

All donations receive a written acknowledgment and may be sent to:

LT. Michael P. Murphy, USN, Memorial Scholarship Foundation
c/o William F. Andes Jr., Esq.
224 Griffing Avenue
Riverhead, NY 11901

Navy SEAL Warrior Fund

Governed by a board of directors, the Navy SEAL Warrior Fund is also a 501(c)(3) nonprofit organization (tax ID # 20-2827819; Combined Federal Campaign/CFC # 11454) established to raise funds in support of families of U.S. Navy SEALs who have died while serving our country, or who are presently serving in harm's way in trouble spots around the world. The organization, comprised of volunteers from around the country, has no paid employees. All funds raised, after expenses, are used to improve the education, health, and wellness of spouses and children of deceased and active-duty SEALs. The Navy SEAL Warrior Fund is also the largest fund-raising organization for the Naval Special Warfare Foundation.

Contributions may be made to:

Navy SEAL Warrior Fund
162 West 56th, Suite 405
New York, NY 19919

Naval Special Warfare Foundation (NSWF)

To provide educational and motivational support, promote health and welfare programs for the Naval Special Warfare community, and perpetuate the history and heritage of the U.S. naval commandos, the NSWF was incorporated in 2000 as a National Non-Profit Charitable Corporation (tax ID # 31-1728910; CFC # 11454). The NSWF provides multiple scholarship opportunities to dependent children and spouses of active-duty SEALs or SWCC (Special Warfare Combatant-craft Crewmen) and other active-duty military personnel currently serving in NSW commands.

The NSWF also provides computers to the surviving children of Naval Special Warfare personnel killed in training or combat. The program helps ensure that the children are provided one of the basic resources they will need to help them excel in their education. The NSWF also provides numerous health and welfare programs for the Naval Special Warfare community. The NSWF provides airfare so that family members may be present at their loved one's memorial service and pays for hotel rooms for the family. It organizes a food delivery service for bereaved families that provides them with baskets of necessities often overlooked during stressful times. Additionally, NSWF also provides free financial counseling to widows.

If you would like to make a contribution, the Naval Special Warfare Foundation Web site (www.nswfoundation.org/donate.htm) has a downloadable donation form. Donations may also be made over the phone by calling 1-757-363-7490 or by mail to:

Naval Special Warfare Foundation
P.O. Box 5965
Virginia Beach, VA 23471

SOURCES

I t is clearly evident that the level of detail contained in this book came from eye-witnesses directly involved in Operation Red Wings, the rescue effort, and the recovery of the fallen. In some cases pseudonyms were used to protect both them and their families. While their true identities may have been disguised, they know who they are.

Representatives of Naval Special Warfare and the Army's 160th Special Operations Aviation Regiment (SOAR) reviewed the manuscript to ensure accuracy. Many individual members of these organizations sacrificed precious moments of their free time from hazardous duty around the globe to assist with this effort.

Tape recordings of interviews by the author and his discussions with various individuals, written and electronic communications, and other miscellaneous unpublished documents used as source material in the preparation of this book are in the possession of the author.

Alvarez, Heath. Personal Web site. www.heathalvarez.com (accessed January 3–19, 2009).

Axelson, Cordell. Discussion with author, July 28–29, 2008.

Axelson, Donna. Discussion with author, July 28–29, 2008.

Bisset, Andrew. Interview by author, June 6, 2008.

———. Electronic communications with author, May 9, 2008–October 30, 2009.

Bogenshutz, Maureen. E-mail communication to author, March 5, 2009.

Bonelli, Garry J. Discussion with author, July 28–29, 2008.

Bradley, Myron [pseud.]. Interview by author, October 22, 2008.

———. E-mail communications with author, July 5–6, September 3–12, 2008.

Commander, Navy Region, Mid-Atlantic. *Casualty Assistance Calls Officer Guide.* N.p: Bureau of Naval Personnel, n.d. Commander, Navy Region, Mid-Atlantic. www. cnrma.navy.mil.

Couch, Dick. *The Finishing School: Earning the Navy SEAL Trident.* New York: Crown, 2004.

———. *The Warrior Elite: The Forging of SEAL Class 228.* New York: Three Rivers Press, 2003.

Coyle, Robert. Electronic communications with author, June 6–8, 2008.

DeGhetto, Todd. Interview by author, March 16, 2009.

Dietz, Maria. Discussion with author, July 28–29, 2008.

Easter, Chad [pseud.]. Interview by author, October 16, 2008.

Emmerich, James. Discussion with author, October 30, 2008.

Evans, Nathan. Discussion with author, November 1, 2008.

———. E-mail communications with author, November 6, 2008, January 5, 2009.

Furio, Nannette. Discussion with author, October 31, 2008.

———. E-mail communications with author. November 3, 25, 2008.

Geisen, Gregory. E-mail communications with author, June 4, 2008–September 30, 2009.

Goare, Judy. E-mail communications with author, December 5–7, 2008.

Goodnature, Lori. Discussions with author, July 28–29, 2008.

Haffele, Andrew. E-mail communication to author, January 31, 2009.

———. Interview by author, January 30, 2009.

Healy, Natalie. Discussion with author, July 28–29, 2008.

———. E-mail communication to author, July 28, 2008.

Hernandez, Mark [pseud.]. Discussion with author, July 28–29, 2008.

———. E-mail communications with author, October 5–7, 2008.

———. Interview by author, October 5, 2008.

Kernan, Joseph D. Discussions with author, May 6–7, July 28–29, 2008.

Kristensen, Edward. Discussion with author, October 30, 2008.

Kristensen, Suzanne. Discussion with author, October 30, 2008.

Lasky, Larry. Discussion with author, July 28–29, 2008.

———. E-mail communications with author, July 7–15, 2008.

Luttrell, Marcus. *Lone Survivor: The Eyewitness Account of Operation Redwing and the Lost Heroes of SEAL Team Ten.* New York: Little, Brown, 2007.

Martin, Michael. Discussion with author, May 7, 2008.

———. E-mail communication to author, September 4, 2008.

———. Interview by author, May 20, 2008.

McCain, John. *Why Courage Matters: The Way to a Braver Life.* New York: Random House, 2004.

McCombie, Ryan. Discussion with author, October 28, 2008.

———. E-mail communications with author, November 3–6, 2008.

McElhone, Eddie. Discussion with author, October 30, 2008.

McKenna, Sharon. E-mail communication to author, September 27, 2008.

Murphy, Daniel. Discussions with author, May 2008–December 2009.

———. E-mail communications with author, May 5, 2008–October 30, 2009.

———. Interviews by author, May 20, 2008, January 4, February 19, April 13, 2009.

Murphy, John. E-mail communication to author, October 3, 2008.

———. Interview by author, April 10, 2009.

Murphy, Karen. Discussions with author, October 26–November 2, 2008.

Murphy, Maureen. E-mail communications with author, May 5, 2008–October 15, 2009.

———. Interviews by author, May 28, 2008, January 14, February 11, 2009.

Naval Education and Training Command. www.netc.navy.mil (accessed January 3–19, 2009).

Naval Special Warfare Command. www.navsoc.navy.mil (accessed December 5–18, 2008).

Navy Recruiting Command. www.navyocs.com. (accessed January 3–19, 2009).

Navy SEALs. www.seal.navy.mil/seal (accessed December 5–18, 2008).

O'Callaghan, Jimmie. Discussion with author, November 1, 2008.

O'Callaghan, Kerri. Discussion with author, November 1, 2008.

O'Callaghan, Owen. Discussion with author, November 1, 2008

O'Callaghan, Sean. Discussion with author, November 1, 2008.

Paro, Kent. Discussion with author, October 26, 2008.

———. E-mail communications with author, November 2008–April 2009.

———. Interview by author, November 10, 2008.

Pexton, Patrick. "Trying to Tame a New Breed of Cats." *Navy Times* (May 30, 1994).

Ponder, Leslie. E-mail communication to author, August 27, 2009.

Pressfield, Steven. *Gates of Fire*. New York: Doubleday, 1998.

Public Law 109-256. To designate the facility of the United States Postal Service located at 170 East Main Street in Patchogue, New York, as the "Lieutenant Michael P. Murphy Post Office Building." 109th Cong. August 1, 2006. *Congressional Record* 152 (2006).

Queen, G. *Navy Military Funerals*. N.p.: Bureau of Naval Personnel, 1999. Commander, Navy Region, Mid-Atlantic. www.cnrma.navy.mil.

Reich, Jill. E-mail communications with author, August 26–September 8, 2008.

———. Interview by author, September 4, 2009.

Reserve Officer's Association. "The Meaning of a Flag-Draped Coffin." Reserve Officer's Association. www.roa.org (accessed January 13, 2009).

Risotto, Elizabeth. Discussion with author, July 29, 2008.

———. E-mail communications with author, July 3–5, 2008.

Sauers, Ben [pseud.]. E-mail communication to author, October 9, 2008.

———. Interview by author, October 9, 2008, January 23, 2009.

Scherkenbach, Michelle. E-mail communications with author, September 19–October 1, 2008.

Schoenberg, Richard. *The Only Easy Day Was Yesterday: An Inside Look at the Training of Navy SEALs*. Annapolis, Md.: Naval Institute Press, 2006.

Sheeler, Jim. *Final Salute: The Story of Unfinished Lives*. New York: Penguin, 2008.

Stegman, Robert. Text of eulogy for Lieutenant Michael P. Murphy. Private collection.

Widenhofer, Jeffrey. Interview by author, August 27, 2008.

INDEX

Gary Williams is the training officer at the Warren Correctional Institution for the Ohio Department of Rehabilitation and Correction in Lebanon, Ohio, and a member of the faculty at Sinclair Community College in Dayton. He began his corrections career in 1985 at the Marion Correctional Institution and transferred to the Corrections Training Academy in Orient, Ohio, in 1995, where he served as a training officer until 2002. While at the Corrections Training Academy, he developed the midlevel leadership program that received recognition in the American Correctional Association publication *Best Practices.* He transferred to the Warren Correctional Institution in 2002 and published his first book, *Siege in Lucasville: The 11-Day Saga of Hostage Larry Dotson,* in 2003 and *Siege in Lucasville: An Insider's Account and Critical Review of Ohio's Worst Prison Riot* in 2006; the latter was rereleased in 2009.

The oldest of five children, Williams was reared with a near-reverent respect for those who wear our nation's uniform. His father is a decorated Korean War combat veteran. Williams holds a Bachelor's degree in human resource management and leadership from Franklin University in Columbus and a Master's degree in public administration from the University of Dayton. He has six children and lives in West Chester, Ohio, with his wife, Tracy.

The Naval Institute Press is the book-publishing arm of the U.S. Naval Institute, a private, nonprofit, membership society for sea service professionals and others who share an interest in naval and maritime affairs. Established in 1873 at the U.S. Naval Academy in Annapolis, Maryland, where its offices remain today, the Naval Institute has members worldwide.

Members of the Naval Institute support the education programs of the society and receive the influential monthly magazine *Proceedings* or the colorful bimonthly magazine *Naval History* and discounts on fine nautical prints and on ship and aircraft photos. They also have access to the transcripts of the Institute's Oral History Program and get discounted admission to any of the Institute-sponsored seminars offered around the country.

The Naval Institute's book-publishing program, begun in 1898 with basic guides to naval practices, has broadened its scope to include books of more general interest. Now the Naval Institute Press publishes about seventy titles each year, ranging from how-to books on boating and navigation to battle histories, biographies, ship and aircraft guides, and novels. Institute members receive significant discounts on the Press's more than eight hundred books in print.

Full-time students are eligible for special half-price membership rates. Life memberships are also available.

For a free catalog describing Naval Institute Press books currently available, and for further information about joining the U.S. Naval Institute, please write to:

Member Services
U.S. Naval Institute
291 Wood Road
Annapolis, MD 21402-5034
Telephone: (800) 233-8764
Fax: (410) 571-1703
Web address: www.usni.org